Rumspringa

A NEW ENGLAND BILLIONAIRES BOOK

By Odessa Alba

A NEW ENGLAND BILLIONAIRES BOOK

For Dave

You are the swell that lifts me, the wind pushing me in the right direction, the thrill in my heart as I rise, and the voice that reminds me to claw my way back up every time I fall.

& for Mary Byler

You are one of the toughest individuals on the planet.

Rumspringa

Definition: The English term for a period of Amish adolescence in which boys and girls are bestowed a wider array of personal freedoms and allowed to form romantic relationships.

This period is typically followed by either the young person's choice of baptism and agreement to adhere to the Ordnung and church or by a ban (also called a *bann*) from the Amish community.

The word Rumspringa translates to *"running around"* in Pennsylvania Dutch.

In plain communities, this time is also often referred to as *"going with the young folks."*

Other Works by Odessa Alba

The Billionaire's Assistant

The Ugly Sweater Party (with Aurora Alba)

Content Warning:

This novel contains profanity, sexually graphic descriptions, and mentions of (inferred) sexual assault. Please be advised if these are triggers for you.

Note: This book is not intended to *purposefully* inflame lovers of the more typical *closed-door* or *sweet, fade-to-black* Amish romances. Rumspringa is meant to be a sexual coming-of-age tale and contains the most accurate fictional portrayal of Amish culture that I can offer after several months of diligent research.

"I shall be dumped where the weed decays
and the rest is rust and stardust."

— Vladimir Nabokov, *Lolita*

1

Velda

"*Liebchen*, stop. You're going to get your dress dirty," *Mamm* grumbles. She licks a thumb and wipes a smudge of powdery loam off of my cheek with it. The cresting morning sun lights her frowning face with its apricot glow. "How on *earth* did you manage to get so filthy?"

"I got up early to help *Fater* harvest celery for the tables," I mumble. *Mamm* rubs harder, and I yank my face away.

Mamm stares at me for a long moment as if she's peering straight into my unbaptized soul. Finally, she speaks, this time to my eldest sister. "Rebecca, go to *Dawdi Haus* and fetch *Mammi* and *Grossdaddi*."

Rebecca nods obediently and takes off down the path to one of several modest structures on our property. My sister's infant son, Amos, clings to her hip, and her three-year-old son waddles up the brick path in the wake of her sky-blue bridesmaid's dress.

Mamm looks me in the eye, stern and unyielding, and shakes her head. She smooths her simple teal dress and black apron and adjusts her

1

matching cape so that it's straight across her torso. She glances at me with an unblinking stare that turns my blood to ice. "This is Saloma's day. It'll be your time soon enough, Velda."

"Yes, *Mamm*." I nod and adjust my *kapp*, tucking a renegade tuft of wheat-blonde hair back up inside it.

"Fetch Menno. It's almost time to leave." She swings her head back toward the front door, and I take off without another word.

The smell of fresh herbs and stuffing fills the air as I step inside and take a left into our dining room. *Fater* is seated, elbows on the table, temples in his hands. There are envelopes and papers sprawled out in front of him, some stamped with bold words.

Notice of foreclosure. Past Due. Lien. Failure. Repossession.

I don't know what they all mean, but from the expression etched in his features, and the recent dwindling of our food portions, things are not good.

"*Fater*, *Mamm* says it is time to go," I say, almost inaudible. I catch a whiff of roast slow-cooking as the smell oozes in from the kitchen where my *bruders*, Atlee, Levi, and Abram stand clustered together, speaking quietly in their formal attire. Atlee, the eldest, straightens Abram's suspenders.

My *Fater's* nose twitches, and I hear him sniffle. Concern and worry are wearing deep, permanent grooves into his face, like troughs

2

through a cornfield. It is no secret that he has the weight of the world on his shoulders.

Uneasy lies the head that wears the crown. I read that in a Shakespeare book once. It feels fitting in this moment.

We are losing the farm, one that we have owned since I was only four. We don't seem to be making enough from the farmer's market in town to afford the property taxes and farm supplies.

I feel the heaviness in the air from *Fater's* despair. I feel our family's financial ruin like a wet rag over my face.

For all of the freedoms that men like *Fater* are granted in this community, I still cannot fathom the weight of having to make decisions that will affect several generations, all on one piece of land. I wish there was something that I could do to help him.

"Yes, I'm coming," he mutters and tidies the papers into one pile. He lifts himself, and I don't know who groans louder: him or the chair.

Fater follows me out into the fresh morning air, and I know as soon as it is in his lungs, the summer air will do him some good.

Atlee's wife, Sarah, stands silently in the corner of the porch, staring out at the barn where we will all feast together in celebration later and then shifting to the red-veined patch of beets to the west. The look on her face has become increasingly sad the past year or so. Grave lines of despair have become permanent fixtures on her despondent face. I gravitate toward her, anxious to

3

escape the chaotic bustle of the rest of the extended family as they prepare for the wedding. I soak up the silence alongside her.

Sarah forces a smile at me. "This is a big day for Stephen and Saloma."

"It is." I nod, though I am not sure it was worth her breath to state such an obvious thing. I suppose she is just making polite conversation.

"I remember when Atlee and I were wed. You were just a *maedel* then, barely old enough to work the fields."

It feels like that day was only last year, but Sarah is right. I was only eight then, just about halfway through my schooling. Sarah was a lovely bride.

I place a hand on her back and rub her cape in an attempt to comfort her. "Are you alright?"

Tears fill her eyes, hazel ones reflecting the intensifying glow of dawn. "It is just..." she presses three fingertips to her chapped lips. "I am afraid another year will be gone soon, and still I..."

I know what she means to say, though she can't get the words out. It has been rumored around Berks County that Sarah is barren, unable to bring life into this world, unable to serve her main purpose to her husband. She is no doubt afraid that Atlee feels her responsible for the fact that he is nearly thirty and has no children.

I want to tell her that there is more to life than this. I want to tell her that some women outside of Berks County have lived fulfilling lives without children. Some have careers that they love. Some travel. Some have sex just for fun.

But if I told her these secrets that I'm privy to, I would have to explain where I *got* this information. And if Sarah -- *or anyone else in my family* -- knew about the three books I acquired in town, the ones hidden beneath my mattress with dog-eared pages... my family would no doubt view me as a promiscuous heathen, a wayward member of their flock, straying from *Gott.*

"Anna, Isiah, Stephen... come here this instant." Abram corrals all four of his young children like they're unruly fowl, scattered like ducklings along the path.

Sarah watches them through a well of tears and smiles weakly through the pain, looking haggard for a woman of only twenty-nine.

As soon as *Mamm* sees Rebecca heading back across the field with my grandparents, she claps her hands together. The sound rises over the chatter of the twenty-five relatives milling around in the sparse patch of grass in front of the porch.

Our heads all snap toward her. When *Mamm* speaks, we all listen.

"Alright, let us go. We mustn't be late!"

2

Ansel

"One-thirty-three over ninety-one. That's hypertensive, Ansel," James says, peeling the cuff off of my arm. The loud tear of Velcro rips through my expansive open-concept first floor.

"How?! Jesus Christ, James. I'm thirty-one years old."

The Nigerian cocks an eyebrow at me and leans back. His starched white coat rustles through the silence. "What did your dad die of again?"

I sit in silence for a moment, flexing my jaw and feeling my pulse thud in my neck.

"And how old was he?" He folds his arms over his cobalt-blue stethoscope.

The questions make me agitated. I am desperate to change the subject.

"This cannot be the same. My Dad had a paunch and smoked a pack a day. That was a totally different scenario."

"Sometimes these things can be heavily influenced by genetics."

"Okay, so... what? You're tellin' me I need to... what... work out more? I surf and swim damn near seven days a week, James."

6

James stares at me, his coffee-colored irises boring into my soul. He reminds me of Lenny Kravitz, but with James's taste in music, I doubt he'd know who Lenny was if I made the comparison.

"Look at me." I lift my *TwinFin* shirt to expose a six-pack most men only ever dream of having. I dip a finger into the waistband of my board shorts and tug downward, exposing the deep-cut chiseled grooves between muscle groupings that lead like downward arrows to my groin. "Two percent body fat, doc."

"That may be so, but your blood pressure is sky-high, and this is while you're relaxed. If you get angry or over-exert yourself, this is like a ticking time bomb. We need to get this number down. Like *yesterday*."

"What the *fuck*?" I feel myself getting angry despite what he just said.

"When I see it this bad, it's typically because your diet is full of sodium, or you're not getting enough sleep, or you're stressed."

I scoff. "Shit, probably all of the above. You know I've been sleeping for shit for years."

It's true. I haven't slept a full eight hours in about seven years, not since I was living with my ex. I always used to sleep so much better when I was lying next to a warm body. But hell, I'd rather have shitty sleep for the rest of my life than a girlfriend who cheats.

Good riddance.

"Are you stressed?"

"Yeah. Of course, I'm fuckin' stressed, James. You ever tried owning a one-point-two billion-dollar company? It's anarchy. Every time I turn around, I've got shareholders breathin' down my neck trying to roadblock creativity in literally *any* direction. I juggle the press, oversee the ads, and all the shit that goes along with our sponsorships for the surf competitions. We've got a charity now, too, underway. And then, we've got the clothing company, the bread-and-butter, and with that, we gotta combat every other fuckin' surf company's fluctuating prices," I pause, barely giving myself enough time to breathe, "We just launched the new kids' grommet line, and that's not doing great. In a couple of months, I have to pitch all of the designs for our new ladies line, which some of my board members are already starting to buck me on."

"That's a lot." His tone doesn't match his words. His eyes don't offer me any pity. "Sounds like you need an assistant."

"I have an assistant. He's great. Without him, I'd probably be in a white, padded room with a hug-me jacket on."

"How's your diet?"

There is a moment of silence. I know this is the one avoidable culprit where he's got me dead-to-rights.

"I'm always working or on the road. I eat what I can when I can."

"Lotta fast food?"

8

"I mean," I feel my blood pressure rise at the question. *For Christ's sake, I'm doing the best that I can.*

"I'm going to take your silence as a 'yes.'" James leans back on the distressed bar stool, one with supports made of polished driftwood.

"You need to reduce some stress, get some sleep, and start cutting back on all that salty stuff. Stay *away* from fast food. Some of those combo meals have enough sodium for three or four days at the suggested daily value. When you did the blood panel, your thyroid looked fine. You weren't anemic. Your blood sugar was normal. But your sodium was through the roof. Too much for too long really does a number on the heart."

"I'm on the road all the time, James. I can't always eat organic home-cooked shit all the time."

"I know it's hard, Ansel, but you got *fuck-you* money," he waves his ebony hands around to point out my house as an example, "and that excuse... it's a cop-out. For the cost of this driftwood stool, you could probably hire someone to cook for you for a week."

"That stool cost thirty thousand," I mumble cooly.

James not-so-subtly slides off of it and stands. "Okayyyyy, so you could probably hire someone to cook for you for a *year*, then. Ansel, we're talking about your *health*. You get *one* body. If you really want something, you'll find a way. You need to take this seriously. You need *sleep*, you need to *de-stress*, and you need *better quality food*.

9

You keep going at this rate, piling all this on with *your* family history, and you'll end up just like your Father if you aren't careful."

The words hit me like a Mack truck.

I will never forget the day my father died.

I'm gonna go take a shower.

Those were the last words he ever uttered on this earth.

I will never forget the sound of my mother's scream, oozing down the stairs like a burbling, poisonous oil, slickly coating everything in utter blackness and pain in a moment that changed everything.

I sit in silence for a moment, soaking up James's words, letting them stoke the already-kindled rage inside of me. These kinds of restrictions are unfair. This will never work. He's asking me to try to juggle even more on top of everything.

The pressure makes me want to scream.

I run an empire that brings in over a billion dollars annually. You don't get that without making sacrifices. And, yes, sometimes those sacrifices are health.

"Tomorrow, I'm flying down to Reading to meet with the *TwinFin* board designers about the new mock-ups. What the hell am I supposed to eat while I'm there? Am I supposed to hire a fucking chef so I can fly him down on the jet with me to make me fuckin' sandwiches or something?"

"Well, I wouldn't recommend sandwiches. There's a *lot* of sodium packed into deli meats and certain types of bread."

I growl. I want to punch something. "Ugh! Okay, smoothies then?"

"That's an option, yes."

"I can't live off juice and shit, James!"

"No one said anything about living off *smoothies.* You could make food before the trip and bring it with you. That's what *I* typically do. Even high-end restaurants cover everything in butter or salt. If you watch the dressing, you could pack salads—"

"I'm not a *rabbit*, James. I *surf.* I burn a *lot* of calories. I can't just put that all back on with fucking collard greens and *kale.* I need *protein.* I need carbs."

"Look, Ansel, you're an adult. Whether you choose to acknowledge what I'm saying or not is your decision." He tosses his stethoscope and blood pressure cuff into his bag and closes it. "There are lots of resources on the internet for recipes and things. My advice: adhere to a low-sodium diet for a while. Shoot for half the recommended daily value. It's roughly twenty-three hundred milligrams a day. I want you to shoot for *eleven* hundred. Try a bunch of the salt-free seasonings. Cut out all the sodium-laden stuff. You know, like pickles, salsa, fries, beef sticks, chips, deli meats, bloody Marys... *all* that. Let's see if we can get your numbers back to something manageable."

I nod and glance through the sliding glass door at the placid waters beyond. It's high tide and glittering in the sun.

"Oh, and trade that Rolex or whatever in for a smartwatch for a little while."

That makes me laugh. A Rolex is like a plastic child's watch compared to the one on my wrist.

"Make a note of your heart rate. If it starts getting high, sit and do some deep breathing. Yoga is good, too."

I groan, low and frustrated. "Can't I just take a *pill* or something? For God's sake, I take home sixty-six-mil-a-year. I should be able to get my hands on a pill or something that'll fix it."

"Oh, I am absolutely going to prescribe you some medication. That's not even a question. It'll help, but that won't solve everything, Ansel. Get the *sleep*, ditch the *stress*, and cut the sodium. You have a lot of years ahead of you on the water if you can do right by your body."

James might as well be asking for the world. Salt, it pisses me off, but it's doable. *Sleep?* Yeah right. I haven't slept right in years. Back then, I used to be able to sleep ten, twelve hours a night. Nowadays, I'm lucky if I get four.

And cutting the stress?

Yeah, let me just swap lives with someone right now because that's about the only way to do that.

James places his hand on my shoulder, and I stare at it, drowning in my anger.

"I implore you to take this seriously. I'll call the meds into your pharmacy, but in the meantime, make the changes, and you'll ride those waves until you're old enough to break a hip on your longboard. Trust me on this, Ansel."

Trying my best to let go of the anger I feel coursing through my veins, I force a chuckle.

"Those are for beginners, James. I ride guns and fishboards. If I'm ever back to riding a longboard, just put two between my eyes and cremate my ass."

3

Velda

The service was standard. So traditional that I could nearly mouth along with the bishop and ministers as they read aloud from the Bible. My mind drifted off somewhere in the middle, and I fantasized about one of the books beneath my bed, one where, in the end, the woman getting married wore a long, flowing white gown adorned with beads and a lace veil. The man she said 'I do' to donned a black suit and a bow tie. They stood out from the crowd, and the bride was revered.

But here in Berks County, things are different. We all must adhere to our prescribed dress code and blend together so that we don't stand out as prideful, vain individuals. We look alike and work together. We aren't afforded chances to be flashy.

Even on a day like this, where Saloma looks almost the same as every other woman in this barn.

Everyone in my family seems to hold this way of life sacred. To uphold the same instilled values since their ancestor's persecution, no matter the personal cost.

But what if they're wrong?

What if it is *not* a bad thing to stand out? Or to be noticed. Admired.

…Desired.

What it must be like to feel desired. *Craved. Envied.*

I can't even imagine.

And I can't openly admit that I envy the fictional women in these books, ones made up entirely of inked letters printed on thin-sliced dead trees.

I would surely be punished by *Mamm* and *Fater* just for knowing that I *have* such filthy smut in my possession. I read them with intrigue nonetheless. At least as much as I can understand with my education, which ended in eighth grade.

"I saw you daydreaming during the service," a voice says lowly into my ear as my eyes scan the bustling reception in the barn. Without even seeing her, I know it is my sister, Lavina. Growing up in the same room together, I would know my sibling's voice anywhere.

On the other side of me, another voice speaks. Male this time. My *bruder*, Atlee.

"You are lucky the bishop did not see you with your head up in the clouds like that."

I feel my cheeks grow pink, and I cover them with my hands. "Did everyone see it?"

"No. Levi was struggling to keep his eyes open, and Abram was too busy playing with his beard. You'd think he would be used to having it by now." Lavina cracks a smile and smooths the apron of her bridesmaid dress.

We watch our young nephews, Amos and John, walking hand-in-hand in their tiny suspenders and pants as they make their way toward an opening on the bench by their *Fater*. He is seated before the banquet, itching the strap of hair along his chin that every man in our community grows once they are wed.

More of our family trickle into the barn and extend fellowship to one another before claiming their seats at the long table.

I don't care where I sit. No point in claiming a spot early on. No matter what, the people around me will pry about who I plan to marry once I am done running around.

Our pool of eligible men is small here. I already know the men that they will all try to force on me, as I've grown up around them all of my life. I don't have the heart to tell them that I would rather be celibate than bear children for any of them.

"*Mamm* and *Datt* are going to start asking you about when you are to be baptized, Velda." The voice comes from Atlee's bearded mouth.

"I know." I can feel my shoulders slump.

"What will you tell them?" Now, it's Rebecca who has me in the hot seat.

"I will tell them that I am not ready yet." I am stoic, displaying all of the defiance that I can without getting chastised for it. "I have not yet seen all I want to see. I have not even been more than a few miles past Reading yet."

16

"So?!" There is a hint of frustration in Atlee's voice now. "There is nothing out there worth exploring. *Trust* me. When I was running around, I took a train from the station past the market and rode it straight across the country for days. I was convinced that there was something out there that I needed to see, needed to do. I took it all the way to California, Velda. Do you know what I found?"

I shake my head, staring up into his stern eyes with sincerity.

"Sinners. Vain women and slovenly men. People who sit around all day and walk around with half of their bodies hanging out of their clothes for all the world to see. There is nothing redeemable out there, Velda. You must believe me on this."

But I don't.

I can't.

Not the last part.

I wonder what other states look like. I wonder if the air smells different, or if the ground feels strange, or if the sky looks any different there than it does here on our farm.

"How much longer do you plan to be running around?" One of my aunts asks, as if on cue. She stares me dead in the eyes as she breaks her bread roll apart and dips it in the juice from her roast.

Before I can speak, *Fater* speaks *for* me.

"Velda's is nearly done running with the young folk." There is no trace of a smile on his bearded face. It feels like it has been years since I have seen him smile. "Isn't that *right*?"

I don't speak. I refuse to let him rush me into my baptism.

It is true. Many others are ready to settle down by seventeen, but I feel like I have barely seen *anything* yet. How am I to know for certain that this is the life I want to lead unless I go beyond Berks County?

"She's already got a perfectly suitable young man with intentions toward marrying her." My *Fater* chews a stick of celery and grinds it in his cheek like a rabbit.

I feel like I want to be sick at his admission. But I can't argue with him. Not aloud. Only with my eyes.

I have no intention of ending this day with a beating.

The suitor is Amos Miller. My parents have been pushing for him as a potential mate since I was twelve. They love Amos' parents, who are admittedly nice. I have no idea how the apple was able to fall so far from the tree. I can't stand Amos, nor could anyone else at the schoolhouse growing up. He has a darkness to him, and he is a bully at heart, one with cold eyes. My most vivid memories of him are when he used to catch toads down by the pond and pull the creatures limb from limb for his own morbid amusement.

Amos is a blight, casting his sick little disease on everything he touches. A spotted lantern fly, sucking the life out of anything thriving, impossible to repel.

Of course, my parents never learned about his vile, amphibious pastime. They never had to sit next to him in class and hear the flatulence he always found humorous or saw the violent fits he would throw after school in the woods when he didn't get his way.

"The Miller's boy, Amos, will make a fine addition to the family," *Fater* says before downing half of his cup of water in one chug. He dusts the front of his pastel shirt. "He helped with the work bee this spring. The boy seems capable. Very bright."

Bright?

Bright?!

I've had pet grasshoppers brighter than Amos Miller. The kid couldn't tell you where Texas was on a U.S. map if he was looking right at it!

Inside, I am screaming for *Fater* to wake up and realize I wouldn't be caught dead with Amos Miller, much less bearing any toad-murdering grandchildren.

"May I be excused?" My voice is meeker than I'd like it to be with as loud as my brain is shouting. The thought of eating any food after thinking about the Miller boy makes me feel green.

Fater's nod is almost imperceptible, and like a frightened sparrow, I leave the table in a dust cloud and flee the barn in search of fresh air.

4

Ansel

My Rivian glides down the curved Narragansett road home, peppered with massive boulders and short tangles of indigenous flora patched across sandy outcroppings. Run-down dive bars and rinky-dink ice cream shops dot the narrow roadway in between signs that say things like, *'Don't Litter. Keep Our Rhodes Clean.'*

I smile as I pass one of several pastel surf shops. One of my new *TwinFin* heated wetsuits is displayed on a mannequin in the large front window with prominence next to our new seasonal line of boards, emblazoned with the conspicuous *TwinFin* logo. The suit is the same color as the thicket of blooming tangerine beach roses where the cracked parking lot meets the beach behind it.

The color choice was in no way an accident. Every shade in the *TwinFin* line has been inspired by something I've become enamored by in my lifelong beach adventures.

As I cruise down the coast, I eye the water. The surf is sloppy today, left-breaking waves churning into bubbling white froth long before they reach shore. Almost no one is on a board, save for a few kooks and junkyard dogs with poor form wiping out with regularity, where there is normally a long row of neoprene-clad locals.

These surf conditions remind me of the day my Dad gave me my first lesson. I busted my ass multiple times and swallowed what felt like a quarter of my body weight in saltwater, but the memory of him pushing my board as the waves swelled still makes me smile.

Most of the people I know who've lost someone miss them the most on birthdays or holidays, days when that person would've participated in some sort of celebration.

Not me.

I miss my father the most on the days when the bubbling saltwater can't quite form a proper crest.

Don't get me wrong. I miss my mother, too, especially on days when I catch a whiff of rising bread, like the kind she used to make us every Saturday night with dinner.

Though the days of breaking bread with my mother and surfing with my father are long gone, the odor of seaweed and salt in the air today reminds me that the people we love leave their true mark on this world through the memories of those who live on.

Despite my inheritance being the seed money for the ever-expanding *TwinFin* empire, I'd give every single penny of the obscene fortune I've made with it back just to have another year with them.

A *month*…

Hell, what I wouldn't give to have just a fucking *hour* on this beach with my father.

A four-foot rock wall, one common to southern Rhode Island, lines the street home, weaving a snake-like path through looming maples and spindly dogwoods all the way to the edge of my property.

I turn in and creep down the paved drive. Sun dapples me through the monumental willows that line the perimeter. I park and retrieve a canvas tote full of sewing notions and a bag of raw vegetables from my trunk and head inside.

The house isn't enormous, but for only five million, I feel like it's an absolute steal for where it's located. The lot is only a little over an acre in total, but it butts right up against the Block Island Sound, which I love. I feel like, with the purchase of it, I own part of the vastness of the ocean. I can hear the dueling sounds of my in-ground pool and its cascading waterfall fighting against the roar of the tumultuous tide.

I make my way up the blue stone patio, fumble with my keys, and then finally get in and drop my bags on the marble island. I peer out at the rocky shoreline and vivid pink sunset, one the same shade of salmon that inspired an entire line of *TwinFin* summer wear last year.

I toss my keys on the counter, and the noise rattles around the open-concept main floor, saturated with color from the sky's myriad of hues.

It's peaceful here. Tranquil and quiet.

But it is also cold and empty.

After the ex and I split, I decided on a fresh start and bought this little plot of oceanfront property, a home that fourteen-year-old surfer-me would have gotten a hard-on just *looking* at. In the years since I've lived here, I haven't done much with the place, minus a few canvas prints I purchased after attending the neighbor girl's gallery showing a few years back, including a few of me macking the drop on the waves outside as the shutter clicked from her yard.

The point is a Realtor could show the place tomorrow. It just looks… *staged*. Bare. A mirror reflecting back the melancholic boredom.

But my God… *that view*. It's all I ever really cared about.

I glance at my watch and groan at how late it already is. I still have to pack for my trip, respond to my emails, and organize my notes and sketches so I can give the designers some ideas for the new line of fishboards I'm urging the others at *TwinFin* to release in time for Christmas.

My eyes fall to the tuna steak, Caesar salad fixins, and a handwritten list of 'heart-healthy' foods James left on the counter. My stomach gurgles. I haven't had anything to eat beyond a banana after my morning swim and the handful of pretzels I ate just before the doc threw a big goddamned *wrench* in the system with his high blood pressure bullshit.

I debate whether it is worth the trouble to cook tonight and make a mental note to hire a fucking chef when I get back from Pennsylvania.

I simply don't have time for this shit.

5

Velda

"Get off the road," a man brays like an angry mule through the open window of his vehicle. He swerves across the double-yellow line into the wrong lane, honks long and loud, and speeds past us at a dangerous speed.

Rebecca shakes her head and ties off her long golden braid in the front seat.

My sister, Lavina, seems unfazed by the aggressive display. She straightens her back in a more regal pose and tightens her hold on the reins of Chappy, the draft horse drawing our black buggy down the straightaway. Our standardbred trots unperturbed toward Reading's Amish Farmer's Market, where my sisters and I all work several days a week selling vegetables from our farm to the Englisher to try to keep the farm afloat. Most of the people who come into our market are tourists hoping to gawk at the Amish locals and swear the food is fresher there than anywhere else.

And it *may be.*

I wouldn't know.

I have rarely eaten outside of the food our community grows. Although, I must admit that the smells wafting from the diner near our strip mall make my mouth water sometimes. I have always wanted to try it, but I haven't been able to work up the courage.

The buggy has the distinct smell of a fresh tomato vine, powerful and earthy. Every breath fills my senses, and I feel giddy and nervous as the plaza comes into sight. Not because we are almost at work but because of the red letters of the word 'CINEMA' above the awning at the other end of the plaza.

I finish my crown braid and pull my *kapp* out of my burlap satchel. Beneath the white fabric sits my Englisher clothes: a pair of jean shorts and a white T-shirt. My parents know I own them, but I hide them like a dirty little secret nevertheless. They are often the cause for argument if *Mamm* happens to be in a sour mood. It is not uncommon for boys to dress like the Englisher, drive, drink coffee, and smoke cigarettes whilst *they* are running around. But most *girls* do not. We are *allowed* to, of course, but there is a certain unspoken shame we are almost socially programmed to feel when we partake of these same things.

It does not feel fair sometimes. Or just.

Having my set of Englisher clothes next to me makes my stomach flutter and twist. I stuff them to the bottom of the bag, eager to keep them hidden from my sisters. I haven't told them about my plan for tonight yet. I know they will not be happy. Lavina is often curt with me when I ask her to drive the buggy home without me. She doesn't like me walking the three miles home in the dark. She would be even more upset if she knew that sometimes I get rides part of the way back from travelers passing in that direction to save time.

But ever since I saw the poster for *Set it Free* framed on the side of the movie theater a week ago, I knew I had to see it. I knew the moment I saw the image that it was based on one of my favorite books, one of the novels under my mattress that I have snuck away to read in the hayloft at least six times.

It is such a beautiful love story. *If you love something, set it free...* The thought of Tim and Sarah's tearful reunion at the end sits in my throat like a swallowed stone as a torrent of emotion ebbs through me.

If it comes back...

I'm so nervous. It will be the first movie I have ever seen. *Mamm* and *Fater* are not fond of them. They always say it is a waste of good money to go watch people pretend. But I'd like to see that for *myself*.

The buggy turns into the parking lot of the plaza, and Lavina parks it carefully around the rear of the building. We start pulling fresh baskets of produce out of the back. Tomatoes, sweet potatoes, beets, eggplant, garlic, onions... It feels nonstop as our trio shuffles everything inside.

I eye one of the workers of the cinema as he stands beside the open door to his part of the building, sucking down a cigarette. I have seen him before, back when they had a ticket window outside. He always waved to me, and I always thought he reminded me of a fish in a tank.

I bounce on the balls of my feet as if I have to go to the bathroom. "I will be right back."

"Where are you going?" Rebecca growls, frustrated with me already before our day together has even begun. Sometimes, I think I irritate my family just by existing.

I dart across the hot asphalt over to the man without giving her an answer. He looks me up and down as I approach.

"Can I help you?" he asks. A spiral of smoke leaks out from between his chapped lips.

"Yes, sir. I would like to see *Set it Free* tonight after work. What time is it showing?"

He snickers, grinding a thumb into his temple while the flaming roll of paper sits, loosely pinched between his index and middle finger, alarmingly close to his short hair. "Seven forty-five and ten fifteen, I think."

Seven forty-five. That could work! We close up shop at six!

"Thank you." I start to bolt away and stop in my tracks. I spin on the low heels of my black, strapped shoes and grimace. "Oh, and sir... how much do tickets cost?"

The man chuckles, no doubt laughing at my attire and ignorance. Finally, he sucks another deep drag and says, "Twelve and change for an evening showing like that. Ten bucks for a matinee."

He senses my confusion and clarifies. "Matinees are showings earlier in the day."

"Oh, okay."

"So, yeah, 'bout twelve." His eyes study me as he takes another drag.

"Velda!" Rebecca sounds annoyed.

"Twelve dollars? Okay." I smile at the man. But inside, I'm dying.

Where in the world am I going to get twelve dollars?!

I start to walk away and he speaks again. "It leaves theaters tomorrow when the new movies come, so if you wanna see that one, tonight's the last night."

Oh no!

If that happens... *that's it*. I will never be able to see it.

Books are *one* thing. I can hide away to read those.

But a *movie*...

"Thank you, sir." I nod politely and start back toward my sisters, who are glaring at me with a look of disappointment.

"What are you doing? We have *work* to do." Rebecca sounds more like a parent than a sister at this moment. Though she is only twenty-three, she has had a fair amount of practice at mothering with her own two boys.

"For that little stunt, you will work the register," Lavina says, jamming a basket of unshucked corn into my arms.

"But," I am interrupted with a sharp flash of Rebecca's eye. Her expression tells me to shut up, and if I am going to that cinema tonight, I need to be invisible for the rest of the day.

***

"Wow, this place is so cute!" A middle-aged woman with bright orange hair slaps a butternut squash, three ears of corn, a twine-wrapped bundle of asparagus, and five bell peppers on the counter. She looks at Lavina as I start to tally everything up on paper and place it in a bag for her.

"Aww, bless yer lil' heart." She smiles at me as I bag the last vegetable. Her Southern twang is so peculiar.

"I like your cute little outfits." The friendly woman points to my sister's mint green dress and black apron.

Lavina forces a tight smile. She hates the Englishers. It always amazes me that she allows my parents to make her work here instead of helping with the children, cooking, and laundry. She has a visible disdain for people outside our community.

I feel the opposite.

I want to sit them down and ask a million questions about the world outside of Berks County. We learned about so many things in school, but I feel like what I know has only

30

scratched the surface of what lies beyond this place.

"Why do y'all wear the little bonnet thingies?" The woman points to her own head.

Instead of answering the question, I ask my own. "Ma'am, where are you from?" My voice comes out dreamy as if I am speaking from some make-believe world. I am already slightly enamored by her. I could listen to her strange accent all day.

"Macon, Georgia." The woman smiles and offers up several folded bills mindlessly as her eyes drift to Rebecca.

As I make change for her, Rebecca informs her about the significance of our prayer coverings, caressing the loose strings of her *kapp* as she talks. She knows that the locals come here for this very thing.

It isn't the groceries.

It's to get a firsthand glimpse at a real-life Amish person.

It is a booming industry, these farm stands, the handcrafted furniture, the electric fireplaces, the colorful hand-sewn quilts, the faceless dolls. We are taught to wave at the Englisher from our buggies and treat them with a level of meek kindness to preserve our pacifistic image of rural tranquility to the outside world.

The more they think we are adorable and quaint, the fresher they think our pies and apple butter are, the more at home they are made to feel, the more they spend.

As I count out the cash to make her change, the thought occurs to me that I know how I might be able to make enough for the cost of the movie tonight. I know that it is a sin, that *Gott* would not be pleased at all, but I also know that soon I will be pressured into a baptism that will wash my soul clean of all past transgressions, and I will be born anew, that all will be forgiven.

My hand trembles, shaking one of the dollar bills from the change I've made her like a leaf on a pear tree. While no one is looking, I slide it into a small compartment beneath the counter, a three-inch crevice that holds nothing but spare paper and more pens. I also have a tattered romance paperback shoved in the very back of it, hidden for days when I am left here to work alone.

I know it is wrong to take the money. I do.

But I feel like a piece of my heart will break if I do not get to see this movie tonight.

I swallow hard, feeling a sheen of sweat rise to the surface of my skin. I pray that *Gott* knows that in my heart, I am an otherwise good person, save for this sinful act done in desperation.

I offer the woman the wad of incorrect change with a smile, and she finishes whatever she is talking about with Rebecca. She stuffs the cash in her tight blue jean pants without counting it, snatches up her purse, and shouts, "Y'all have a good'n!" as she walks out the front door.

I breathe a huge sigh of relief, knowing that she did not even look at the change I gave her.

One dollar down…

Gott... I am so sorry for what I am about to do.

...Times eleven.

6

Ansel

I park my rental car at the hotel, and I can't check in fast enough. I want to drop off my shit at the room and get this goddamn meeting over with. The flight was short, but it was long enough for the desperate flight attendant to eye me like a piece of meat, making off-hand comments about being single and wanting to settle down.

She was pretty enough. Somewhere around thirty-nine, I'd guess. She had a great body with thighs like a marathon runner and eyes that said she would rip me apart if given the chance, but that hunger to be a 'kept woman' seeped through her pores like sweat. She was prowling for a sugar daddy. I could see it in her eyes, hear it in her tone. It's the same look I've gotten with regularity since *TwinFin* hit the New York Stock Exchange.

The check-in process goes smoothly, and I make my way up to the penthouse suite, which in this small-ass town is only on the fourth floor. I fling my curtains back. The view is less than stellar. The hotel is right on a thoroughfare bustling with cars and…

Is that a fucking horse-drawn carriage riding down the highway?

Oh shit. I forgot this is like... Amish country. *Wild*.

The building is sandwiched between a steakhouse, a *Waffle Hut*, a shopping mall, and a dinky strip mall full of little shops. There's a little Asian nail salon with sun-faded Nigel prints in the window, an insurance company, a little Amish farmer's market, someplace called *Husks*, whatever that is, and a movie theater.

Jesus, how long has it been since I saw a movie at a theater?

The mall is dying, like most malls across America. There is a change in coloring on the tan wall where you can see the old outline of the word Macy's, like a ghost haunting the paint. Next to it, there's a tiny book store whose sign should say "Reading Reads," but the 'G' has shorted out, and it reads in my head like it would from the mouth of someone from Knoxville.

Beyond the strip mall is an industrial building. According to my driver, that's where my board designers are preparing for our meeting in...

I look at my watch.

Fuck.

It's one forty-seven already. Damn. I thought I'd have time for a shower before I headed over there, but I don't.

I dig out my toiletries bag, spritz on some cologne, re-up my deodorant, and check myself in the mirror. My shoulder-length waves are out of fuckin' control in this muggy summer heat. My bird of paradise patterned *TwinFin* shirt hangs over forest green board shorts and a pair of our deluxe cushioned men's sandals. I probably stand out like a sore fucking thumb here in bum-fuck Pennsylvania, looking every bit the New England surfer that I am, but I honestly don't give two shits.

I grab my sketches and key card and leave the mild comfort of this air-conditioned room. My empty stomach rumbles louder than the elevator, and I make a point to grab some food after the meeting.

7

Ansel

"This isn't what we *talked* about," I growl. Hunger and anger churn in my stomach, duking it out inside me. Everything in me wants to yoke this little prick, Trent, up by the front of his stained polo and shake the absolute dumbfuck out of him.

How the fuck does the doctor expect me to lower my blood pressure when I'm dealing with half-wit fucks like *this* asshole? I can feel it rising in me. I feel the tremble rise from my chest to my arms and settle in my clenched fists. Fists I'd pay to pound into Trent's beady-eyed weasel face without any legal or media-related repercussions.

"Why the fuck did I fly all the way down here if you didn't have the fucking prototypes ready?"

"I-I'm sorry," he stutters with a weak shrug from shoulders I want to shake violently. "They'll be done next week." He motions behind him to several half-finished boards. "We're backlogged. Tim just moved to Wyoming to be with his Dad, who got Parkinson's. Erin got a higher-paying job down in Tampa. We're down—"

"I don't want any fucking excuses." I suck in as much air as I can gobble up through my flared nostrils, and dig my hands into my hips like shovels into hard soil. My eyes dart around the warehouse. It's clear to me now that I need to start shopping around for a new company to manufacture the new boards. I really thought these guys were a good fit, but the way this place looks now, it's gone to hell since Lawrence paid them a visit in January and emailed me photos of the place.

Despite the fact that there is nothing more to be said or done here, I still feel my heartbeat quicken, pounding blood hard through the temples where I'm going to start getting wisps of gray dealing with imbeciles like Trent.

This is the time where, if I were back in Narragansett, I would hit up one of my old booty calls and enjoy a round of angry fucking hair-wrenching sex to let off some steam.

But I can't do *that* either.

***

On my walk back to the hotel, my stomach groans like a sci-fi creature. Skipping dinner last night and breakfast this morning was a mistake. And it probably made me fucking hangrier than I needed to be with ass-face Trent.

I stop in my tracks and look around.

Up the side road a stretch, I see the shiny red lettering for a chain chophouse I love. The image of a spicy bloody Mary, along with a rare prime rib, makes my mouth water.

The only other place I see that has food is the little farmer's market in the squat plaza on the way back to the hotel. The painted signs on the window tout vegetables, fruits, soups, and salads made fresh daily.

That's it.

I don't see any other food around the hotel. Just a bookstore, a few defunct clothing stores, the theater, and the salon.

Hmmmm. The siren's call of *au jus* and rare beef are nearly moving my feet for me, but just like a siren, I wonder if that urge is stepping me closer to my doom.

I'm gonna go take a shower...

I know what James said about the sodium. Hell, the *au jus* alone is probably my halved allotment of salt for the day. Not counting the rest of the meal or a spicy bloody Mary. Hell, the damned *olives in the drink* are probably my total daily value.

...Or I could do my ticker a solid and check out this little Amish bodega, or *whatever it is*.

I take a few steps closer to the little market in the strip mall and peer inside the windows. Behind raised shelves full of fresh-looking produce, I see a woman wearing the traditional Amish... I don't know... *garb*. Her eyes meet mine through the glass. She offers a polite wave. I return it.

Beside her, at a neighboring counter, I see two other women. One stirring a pot of something steamy, the other layering chopped vegetables for

something that looks like a pie filled with
tomatoes.

My stomach pleads loudly for food.

I'm gonna go take a shower…

The memory of my father's last words makes
my decision for me, and I take a step inside.

8

Velda

The bell over the door tinkles quietly. I finish my cup of water and smile like I always do for the customers. It isn't until the door closes behind him, shielding out some of the afternoon sun, that I get a real glimpse of one of the most interesting-looking men I have ever seen in my life.

"Hello," Rebecca says, greeting him with the melody of a cheerful robin. She has practiced so much that her enthusiasm toward the Englisher sounds real. She ladles hot broccoli soup out of the steaming vat in front of her into disposable lidded bowls that will go in the 'Fresh Foods To-Go' refrigerator behind her once they cool enough.

Her taking the initiative to greet him buys me another two seconds to get a better glimpse of this utterly handsome stranger. We get all kinds of people coming into this farmer's market, but I've never seen someone quite like him.

Tanned skin peeks out of the open collar of his shirt, complimenting his shoulder-length waves of hair, which are all the shades of a stained plank of teak. His stormy, teal eyes pierce. A tattoo claws its way up over his sun-kissed collar bones, behind a tangle of pendants on braided cords, and creeps up the sides of his neck, nearly touching the smooth silver loops in each earlobe.

But the presence of facial hair on his rugged face is like a cold winter Nor'easter ripping through me. My eyes dart away, ashamed for looking at a married man with desire, even if only for a moment.

"Hey," the man says. But instead of saying it back to Rebecca, he says it... to *me*.

The single syllable rattles me, and I feel myself cowering shyly. Lavina sees the language of my body and the blush across my cheeks. She frowns like she can read my mind and all of the thoughts swimming in it. It is rare that I find a man attractive, but when I do, my body always finds a way to betray me.

"Is there anything we can help you with?" Rebecca speaks again as she wipes down her utensil and places the lid back on the steaming pot.

The man's perfect lips turn up into a smile at the corners. "That's a lovely accent."

I watch as he brushes the pad of his thumb across his bottom lip, full and inviting.

"Is it... *German*?"

"Close." Rebecca's head bobs a little as she caps the containers in front of her. "Pennsylvania Dutch."

"Ahh."

"You are not from around here," Lavina says from the corner as she shines tomatoes with a rag.

But she knows already that almost no one who stops in this market is from around here.

"No. Rhode Island." The stranger shakes his head, and that mane of hair sways in time with it. His eyes graze the vegetables. "I saw the sign and the steam and figured I should do something healthy for lunch."

"Well, you have come to the right place." Rebecca smiles. "Velda, why don't you hand this nice man a basket and help him find what he needs."

I feel fire rip across my cheeks, and I know they are as red as the Roma in Lavina's palms now. My shoulders tighten as I make my way out from behind the counter.

I hand him a handbasket and speak, but my voice barely comes out, nearly a whisper still caught in my throat. "Wh-what kinds of things do you like?"

His eyes bore into me for a long moment, and I feel the coals in my cheeks stoke red hot again. I brush the apron against my thighs nervously.

"Velda," he says. My name sounds like softened caramel coming from his lips, sweet and smooth. "My doctor recently told me I need to," his wide, tanned hands stuff into the pockets of his shorts, pulling his shirt open an inch wider to reveal more of his tattoo. I see petals and stems. I have never actually seen a tattoo this close before, only from afar. My parents warned me about how the Englishers desecrate their bodies with them, but this hardly looks like desecration. If anything, it is so detailed that it feels like the opposite.

"He told me I need to start incorporating more of this stuff into my diet." He produces a paper from the depths of his pocket, shaking me loose from this trance I seem to be stuck in.

"Y-yes. Blueberries." I mindlessly wander over to the glass case and slide open the door. I feel the air from the ice below cool my shaky hand as I pull out a bin of fresh berries. I wish I could plunge my face down into the cubes right now to soothe my burning cheeks.

I place them softly in his basket and look down at his list again. I pretend to read it, but how can I read anything when he smells like a perfect blend of blood orange and cedarwood? All of the men that I know smell of sweat and dirt. And then there's the Miller boy, who always seems to reek of manure from tending to the stables...

I gather more things from his list: a container of locally grown nuts, two kiwis, and an orange. "This says broccoli."

He snickers. "That it does."

I blush again, realizing how simple I sounded making the statement. "No, I simply meant Rebecca has hot broccoli soup if you want. It's delicious."

"It's Velda's recipe," Rebecca adds. "She actually slices up nasturtium leaves and puts them in with it. Gives it a little bit of a peppery flavor."

"It is full of vitamins," I choke out quietly.

His smile is warm, and his stomach rumbles audibly. He chuckles at the noise and points to his abdomen. "Well, it seems he has spoken. I'll have a bowl of that. To go, please."

The moment he smiles at me, I feel my nerves tingle, and I realize he is a little like I imagined Rand in my head, the main character in my favorite book, *Set it Free*.

Rebecca readies his container, and I total his produce on the notepad next to the cash box.

"Your total is $22.86," I say.

The man lugs a leather wallet out of his pocket and plucks out a black credit card, handing it to me, scissored between two fingers.

"I'm so sorry. We only take cash or check," I mutter apologetically.

"Really?" He looks at all three of us, one at a time, baffled, as if we can't be serious. A moment later, he puts the card back and shuffles through the bills. I catch a glimpse inside its opening and try not to let my eyes bulge when I see how much money is stuffed inside. He could buy nearly all the produce in this store with it, I imagine.

The handsome stranger hands me thirty dollars, and I hand him back his change, shorted a dollar to put toward the film. He promptly stuffs all of the cash in my empty drink cup on the counter. My whole body stiffens. I think... he thought it was a tip cup.

My heart leaps with joy, slamming against the walls of my chest. If my sisters didn't see it, I will surely have enough money for a ticket tonight.

I place a paper bag down, obscuring the generous donation from my sisters, and place his food inside.

I nudge the bag across the counter to him with a smile. "Thank you, sir."

"Thank *you*, Velda." He smiles at me again, and I feel lightheaded. My eyes don't blink. Neither do his. What is surely two seconds feels like an intoxicating *lifetime*.

Finally, he turns and waves at my kin, hoisting the bag up by its rumpled top. "Ladies. Have a good one."

In a flash, he is gone, making his way across the sizzling asphalt and disappearing out of my view.

My hands tremble as I slide the cash out of the cup and stuff it into the cubby beneath the counter with the other two singles.

"My my," Lavina clicks her tongue and shakes her head. "I have never seen you so quiet since the day *Muder* birthed you." She walks the tomatoes out onto the produce stand in the middle of the store and starts back to tackle the eggplants.

"Usually, you have much more to say," Rebecca chimes in. "It *almost* looked like you were smitten with an Englisher." Her agitated tone says, 'You had better *not* be.'

I shake my head and play with my *kapp* strings, hanging loosely across my shoulders.

"Not at all," I lie.

9

Ansel

The broccoli soup hit the spot, and I have since annihilated the container of blueberries, too. I slide open the door to my narrow balcony and lean against the rail. The sun is lowering over the lush greenery beyond the highway. Traffic is moving slow and steady, like coagulated blood through an IV.

I see another horse-drawn buggy clomp inside the faded lines of the asphalt as modern cars whiz by. Weak, battery-powered headlights cast a soft glow of light in front of the animal, illuminating the road just enough to navigate.

Seeing the buggy makes me think of those girls at the farmer's market today. What a weird fucking life that must be. No cars. No electricity. Hell, that poor girl at the counter didn't even have a POS system or a card reader. Just a notepad and a cash box.

I can't remember the time I had to rely on my own brain to do math like that. Sure, I do measurements and equations all the time for my board line and apparel, but I use a calculator for all of that. Why wouldn't I? It's right there on my phone.

Hell, the Amish don't even have *phones*.

Or *do* they? I don't know fuck-all about the Amish, frankly.

I *do* know that buggy's driver sure as hell isn't using *Waze* to make his way to his destination.

A gentle breeze wafts past, bringing with it the faint smell of buttered popcorn. I peer down at the illuminated CINEMA sign, white bulbs flaring in front of fire-engine-red plastic. I see people walking in, a couple strolling hand-in-hand, followed by a frustrated father skittering after two small kids dressed in minion-yellow shirts. A bored older man talks on a cell phone against a movie poster with a *just-kill-me-already* look on his face, presumably to his miserable wife of many years.

Jesus, when was the last time I went to the movies? I can't even remember. Fuck, Ben Affleck was probably still tappin' J-Lo at the time.

The smell of that popcorn is making my mouth water.

Emails are done. I'm happy with my new sketches. I have some time to kill. I wonder what's playing.

As if on autopilot, I change into pants, throw on a hoodie, stuff my billfold and key card in my pocket, and head out the door.

10

Velda

"Lavina, don't worry about me. I promise I will be safe." My voice is stronger now, firmer.

"It is too far," Lavina growls, wiping a wayward strand from her braid away from her dull, blue eyes and tucking it back under her *kapp*.

"It is only two-and-a-half miles. I have walked it before."

"When?!" This is news to Rebecca, and she seems angry about it.

"Last month. I stayed behind for... something."

...That something was a book club meeting at the library down the street where I listened to two older Englisher women bicker about the ending of the newest Colleen Hoover book. I hadn't read it then, but the women allowed me to sit in, and one gifted me her copy when the evening was over.

Not that it matters *now*, but I do agree about the ending...

I stuff my under-dress, overdress, and apron into my burlap bag and tug a pair of blue jeans shorts up my pale thighs. I got them at the thrift store near the train station, and I have successfully hidden them from *Mamm* and *Fater* for a year now.

I love the way they hug my body. They are so different from the weighty burden of the long dresses.

I pull the white T-shirt over my torso and look at my reflection in the glass cooler. I can see the peaks and color difference where my nipples press against the fabric, and a wave of shame ebbs through me. I pull my *kapp* off of my hair and position it over my breasts. I wish that I owned a brassiere. It is the next thing I plan to buy from the thrift shop when I can earn some more money. I have read about them in some of my paperbacks.

For now, I will have to make do.

I reach under the counter, grab the rumpled wad of squirreled-away cash, and stuff it in the front pocket of my shorts.

"What will I tell *Muder*? Hmm?" Lavina presses her fists into her hips, scowling at my attire, upset about what I am wearing.

"The *truth*." My voice is harder now, even a little defiant. "Tell her that I am running around. This is exactly what this time is for."

There is a double standard for girls in our community. The boys are allowed, no... *expected*, to run amok and get their wildness out of their system. They smoke and drive and even sometimes have sex.

We girls are still expected to be meek and chaste, abstaining from all temptations and continuing to act and dress respectably.

How am I to know that this is the life that I truly want if I am not able to explore anything else?

It is only an illusion of freedom. A cage made of crystal-clear glass instead of iron bars...

But a *cage* nonetheless.

I make my way over to the counter near Rebecca and lean over, the look in my eyes honest and pleading. "Please, trust me. I will be fine. Do not worry."

Rebecca frowns, and Lavina glances up and down the length of my body with judgment and disgust.

But it is not *my* fault that she did not take full advantage of her running around time like I intend to.

"Do not spend time entertaining men. Do you hear me?" Rebecca says with a sigh. She and Saloma have been distrustful of men since I was young. It has been rumored that it is because of people like Levi...

I nod, having zero intention of being around any men. I just have to see this movie. I won't ever have the chance to see it again.

I hug Rebecca, nod at Lavina, and hustle out the door. The moment my shoes hit the sidewalk, I take off like a rabbit toward the movie theater. My heart is racing with excitement. I don't know what to expect, but I am buzzing with energy.

51

The lobby is beautiful, thick with the scent of buttered popcorn. The walls are red, and the floors are an even darker shade of the same. Gold flourishes adorn the molding and carpet. It is nothing like I imagined. It is grandiose and luxurious.

"Excuse me, sir. How do I buy a ticket?" I sound like a giddy child as I approach a seated man in a uniform near a podium.

The old man inside looks at me as if I am mad as a hatter. I look at the off-kilter name tag pinned to his chest. It says 'Gary.'

"Which film?" Gary glances down at the machine in his hand. It is like nothing I have ever seen before.

I am so nervous I nearly choke on the first syllable. "*Set it Free*, please."

"I.D." He holds out his leathery hand. His fingers are long and outstretched, full of wrinkles.

My stomach does a flip, and I start to stammer. "I... I don't have an I.D."

After a moment of silence, his voice cuts through the air. "Sorry, but that movie's rated R."

"What does that mean?" *I am so confused.*

"It means... *it's... rated... R*," he repeats. He looks at me as if to ascertain whether I am slow or not. His short, graying hair stands out against the red velveteen wallpaper behind him.

"Please forgive me. I don't know what Rated R means. I-I-I don't have an I.D. They are against my religion."

He laughs to himself. "You Amish people..."

I cast my gaze toward the door. Maybe it is not too late to catch my sisters in the buggy and get a ride home.

Suddenly, my eyes lock with *his* in an instant.

The stranger from earlier with the wild hair and permanent ink.

The man whose smile made my blood feel like it was going to freeze in my veins.

I look back at Gary, and I hear the door close behind the stranger. I hear the patter of his bizarre-looking shoes against the carpet as he approaches.

"I'm sorry, hun. If you don't have an I.D., I can't let you into that one. Rated R means it is for adults."

"But I *am* an adult," I utter quietly in protest.

For Heaven's sake, I've been graduated from school for years now!

"You're eighteen?" He looks at me through the sides of his eyes like he doesn't believe me.

"Yes," I say with a nod, having just turned a few weeks ago.

"Sweetheart, if you're lying and I don't see an I.D. or a guardian, I'll get in trouble. And you don't want old Gary to get in trouble, now do you?"

Suddenly, I feel a firm hand slide onto each of my shoulders, clasping me gently from behind. "Hey, babe. Sorry, I'm late," the voice says with a gentle sigh. His voice is smooth in my ear, and I feel my entire body tingle like I have a mild full-body sunburn.

I can see Gary's eyes re-processing the situation, seeing things very differently now that the man behind me is talking to him.

"What're we seein' tonight?" The man behind me tucks a hunk of blonde hair that has fallen out of my crown braid behind my ear.

I feel like my knees are melting butter. Like my body could ooze down onto the floor. My heart pounds in my ears, and I don't have the nerve to look back at him.

Frozen, I stutter, "*Set it Free.*"

"Two for *Set it Free*, please," he says.

"Sure." Gary nods, tense, and types a few things into the device before swinging it around to me. There are tiny squares all over the screen. "Select your seats, please."

I don't know what he is showing me or how to do what he is asking. I feel like an opossum, rigid and scared, frozen and ready to drool.

"*May I?*" The man's warm voice coos in my ear. I feel his nose brush my earlobe, and, against my will, I feel my nipples harden beneath the fabric of my shirt. I cross my arms to shield them and nod.

I feel the press of his pendant necklaces against the back of my shoulder and the brush of his wavy hair against my neck. A tattooed arm juts out from behind me, and its finger presses two squares in the center of the screen. They change colors miraculously.

I don't know what is happening.

"Total's $22.76."

I start to dig in my shorts, but before I can pull out any cash, I see his hand offer Gary the same black credit card he tried to offer me earlier at the store. Gary slides the card into the device he's holding, pushes a button, and paper spews out of the end of it. He tears the paper into neat pieces, puts two in a box beside him, and hands the other two pieces to me.

"You're in theater fourteen, which is on the left. Enjoy the show."

"Thank you," the man behind me says. I feel his hand slide into one of mine, and before I know it, he is leading me toward a register with glass-encased popcorn behind it.

I want to thank him, but my body cannot find the strength to even look at him.

I hear his voice in my ear again. "Sorry, saw you were having a little trouble back there."

Without a word, I turn and hug him. His body is hard, firm in a way I had not expected, like hugging the hind leg of Chappy.

I am trembling with emotions and, frankly, fear, overwhelmed by everything around me, feeling out of place and wracked with nervous energy.

"*Thank you,*" I whisper into his chest. My nose is touching bare, tattooed skin where his shirt isn't buttoned all the way. I breathe in deeply, getting a lungful of his delightful scent, unlike any combination I have ever smelled before.

I pull away quickly as if his skin is a hot skillet. "I am... so sorry, sir."

He chuckles. "You don't have to call me sir."

I finally look at his face, eyes filled with tears of joy. "I don't actually know your name."

He leans in and smiles with only half of his mouth, looking like mischief incarnate. "Ansel."

"That is… a great name."

I want to smack myself in the face for how stupid I sound right now.

"And you're… let me see if I remember… *Vvvvvelda*?" He drags my name out.

"Yes!" A tear threatens to fall from my eye. I don't even know how to tell this man how far from the norm this experience already is for me, how overwhelming just getting *in* is.

He pulls me by the hand into the queue and looks back at Gary. "Nosy Ned over there is still eyeballing us, so I'll walk you to your theater before I split." He points up to a board with prices, and it moves, morphing and changing into a different image with even more prices. "But first… *popcorn*."

It is at that moment that I remember that the food here really does smell so good.

"Which movie are *you* going to see?" I ask, unable to take my eyes off of the moving screen until the line moves forward a little.

He shrugs, and I see the tattoo up the side of his neck morph with the changing angles of his body. "Dunno. I wanted some popcorn more'n anything. Had a couple of hours to kill. There's a Michael Bay movie, I think."

He looks up at the red scrolling letters above the woman at the register. They look like other movie names. And times.

"What is a *Michael Bay* movie?"

He smiles at me. "It's an action flick."

"What is a flick?"

"It's another word for movie." He stares at me like a puzzle with no key, trying to decipher the true image.

We step up to the woman at the register, and he leans in on his forearm. "Hi, yes, a medium popcorn," he says, turning to me. "Hey. *You* want a popcorn?"

I don't answer. I am too nervous to reply.

He turns back to the woman. "And... a medium soda."

Ansel whips toward me again.

"Do you want a soda?"

Finally, I force myself to speak. "I've... never had one before. I don't know if I can afford it." I pull out the rumpled bills from my pocket and offer them up in my trembling hands.

He stares at me in stunned silence and blinks hard twice before speaking to the lady again. "Make that two medium sodas, please."

"What kind?" The woman looks bored and chews something like our family's Holstein, Harvey, back on the farm when he's got a mouthful of cud.

"I'll take a diet. She'll have..."

He looks at me and motions to the array of options on the back of a metal machine. I study them as if I am going to be tested.

"Is this one good?" I point to a square image with a lemon and lime on it.

"Yep, that one's good." He nods, and it's strange. I don't feel any judgment coming from him when I ask these questions. Not like Gary at the door...

Ansel points to the drink I've chosen, and the woman fills two cups with the thundering sound of ice followed by loud clicks and bubbling sprays. She caps the cups and slides them across the counter.

Ansel nods to the wad of cash in my hand. "Keep that. Your money is no good here."

I slowly stuff the bills in my pocket and watch the woman pump liquid onto a bucket full of exploded yellow kernels. Ansel puts a straw in each cup and hands mine to me. I take a timid sip, and the sweet, fizzy liquid hits my tongue and stuns me. My eyes go wide. I am pleasantly surprised.

He chuckles at my reaction. "Want to try mine before I take a drink? Just so you can say you tried both?"

I nod, and he aims his straw at me, pinched between two fingers. My lips graze them as I take a sip.

My eyes bulge again. The taste is totally different, but the amount of fizz is the same. I moan a little with satisfaction.

"It's good to try new things." Ansel smiles when he says it. He pulls some napkins out of a metal dispenser and hands a few to me.

Once he has his popcorn, I follow him down the patterned hallway to a door with the number fourteen next to it.

"Well, Velda, this is your stop."

"You're... leaving?" I can't stand how frightened and childish I must sound right now.

"Well... yeah." He leans a shoulder against the wall.

"I'm... scared," I finally say.

He stares at me for a moment, confused. "Why? This is a chick-flick, right?"

"I've never..." I look into his eyes, silently pleading for him to join me. I don't even know how to find the seat he picked for me.

"Have you... *never* seen a movie before?"

Ashamed, I shake my head and fidget with the rolled edge of the jean fabric on my thighs.

He fights the grin creeping up his tanned skin amid the trimmed hair of his face. He looks at me with those eyes, and for a second, I feel like I can't breathe.

He thinks, and the few moments of silence feel like weeks. Finally, he lifts away from the gray wall and pulls the door open, motioning for me to go inside with his drink. "Ladies first."

I feel a wave of relief wash over me as he follows me inside, and I realize that I do not have to navigate the theater alone.

II

Ansel

Watching Velda soak in every frame of this film is *far* more interesting than watching the movie itself. I can't believe she's never seen a *movie* before. I can't even remember the first one I ever saw. Watching the screen glitter across her eyes, I realize I may have taken them for granted my whole life.

Light flickers off her pale skin, illuminating the pure excitement in her features as she watches something larger than life.

She's unique, that's for sure.

I feel my smart watch buzz on my wrist. I look down, but I already know why it's vibrating. It alerts me that my heart rate is abnormally high... once again. I feel my pulse pound through my wrist against the plastic armrest, close enough to Velda to feel her heat radiate from her body.

During a scene with a car accident, the loud screeches and shattering glass scare her. She clutches my hand reflexively, nearly spilling the few remaining kernels of my popcorn. Since her first bite, she's been insatiable. She's eaten the lion's share of it, and I find myself once again anxious to put some real food in my belly so that I'm not up all night with a gurgling stomach again.

The credits roll, and I look at her for the millionth time. A gamut of emotions flashes across her face, and tears stream down her cheeks.

"You okay?" I ask, wanting to rub her arm or something but preferring not to so that I don't come off as creepy.

She nods, frowning, and bursts into a heavy sob as the dimmed lights brighten and the end credits continue to roll.

"It's just... so beautiful."

I laugh. I don't mean to, but it's not what I expected her to say. I'm unsure if she's referring to the cinematography, the storyline, or the fact that she just saw Ewan McGregor's handsome mug forty-feet-tall.

Hell, even as a hetero guy, I see the appeal.

I pull the tissue from her drink holder and place it in her hand. She promptly blows her nose in it and looks over at me. A smile glides across her makeup-free flesh, and though her eyes are ringed red, she looks kind of fucking adorable.

I sit in awkward silence as she composes herself, dabbing her face and clearing her throat. "Thank you."

"For what?" I lean toward her, resting my forearms on my knees.

"That man at the front door wasn't going to let me in without an I.D. and... I almost did not get to see this."

I wave it off. "Pffft. No sweat. Happy to oblige."

"I am sorry you didn't get to see the movie you wanted to see."

I saw something cooler.

I saw someone watch their first *movie.*

"Oh please, it's *Michael Bay*. There's a one-thousand percent chance I would not have had any better a time. I honestly just was craving popcorn."

She starts to cry again, shoulders shuddering. "Oh no! And I ate most of it!"

I laugh as she covers her eyes and sobs. "It's okay. Honestly, I didn't need the butter or salt anyway. You saved me from myself. My *heart* thanks you."

She sniffles and wipes her eyes. "I have twelve dollars. Can I make it up to you?"

I laugh again and fight the urge to grin. This girl is killing me. It's freeing, though, this realization that she has no clue who I am, never having seen my two-page spread in Forbes or my face on T.V. for international surf competitions.

She has no idea I could comfortably buy this entire theater and not lose a wink of sleep at night.

"Keep your twelve dollars."

"I don't know how to thank you."

I check my phone. It's only nine-thirty.

"Tell you what. Are you in a hurry?"

She thinks for a moment and then shakes her head. I am suddenly aware that she is not wearing a watch. She surely doesn't have a phone either.

How the fuck do Amish people ever know what time it is?

"There's a *Waffle Hut* down the block. Sign said it was open 24 hours. Wanna grab a bite?"

She looks at me, and I can tell the saying isn't registering. I rephrase the question.

"Would you like to join me for some food?"

She hesitates.

"My treat."

Her voice is solemn. "My sisters have warned me not to spend time with English men."

I stand and bend my arm for her to take. "Well, today, you're in luck." I smile. "I'm German."

12

Velda

"More soda, hun?" our waitress asks.

If I had to guess, I'd say she has at least seven grown children. She has the wide hips of a fertile mother, though I can tell she is not Amish from the way that she is dressed. Her name tag says Bethany.

"Yes, please." I push my glass toward her.

Ansel snickers and shakes his head. "You're gonna have to pee like nine times tonight."

Bethany takes my cup with a smile and heads back between some swinging metal doors. I watch intently as the cooks crack eggs on a metal countertop. They are both men, which is bizarre to see. I've never seen a man cook.

I smell beef sizzling, and the scent of warm potatoes fills the air. The diner is loud even though it only has a few people in it. It seems like everything makes noise here. The cooktops, the staff, the customers, and the door. Even the lights above us buzz in large glass tubes.

I hear a telephone ring and watch a woman in an apron answer it casually, as if she uses one every day of her life. I am in awe of her. She acts so casual, as if she is not being connected in real-time to someone somewhere else in the world, as if she is not experiencing a miracle.

"So, what did you think of the movie?" Ansel's voice is cool through the chaos. His fingers make a salt shaker twirl around like a sock on a clothesline in the wind. He looks at it longingly, like he wants to shake it right onto his tongue.

"I think the movie was one of the most amazing things I have ever seen."

I do. The lights. The colors. The sheer size. The way it all blended together to tell a story...

"I was a little confused," I continue, "because it was different than the book."

"Oh, there's a book?" Ansel's brow rises a little.

"Yes." I want to tell him more, but I am still hesitant to talk about my contraband. Fearful someone will overhear me and word will get back to *Mamm*.

Bethany sets another lemon-lime soda in front of me, and I suck half of it down in one large draw.

She shakes her head. "I'm gonna bring you another while you work on that."

"Thank you," I chirp with the skinny tube against my bottom lip.

Bethany retreats behind the metal doors again.

"Yeah, movies rarely live up to the books," Ansel says.

"I liked it. I just wasn't expecting it to be so... different."

"I liked the theme. You know, if you love something, set it free."

I nod, still in love with the taste of the bubbly beverage before me.

"It was decent casting. Had some great cameos." Ansel continues and looks around as if he can will his food to arrive faster with his mind.

"What is *casting*?"

His eyes settle on his napkin. He fiddles with the smudged silverware on it. "Casting is... the actors picked and paid to be in the movies."

"Then, yes," I agree, "It was very, very decent casting."

He smirks. Maybe I said something foolish, but I don't know what.

"So what do you do for fun around here? You know, when you aren't working at the store?"

I squeeze my clasped hands between my thighs and lean my sternum hard against the edge of the table.

"I shouldn't say." I try to hide my smile. I shouldn't be laughing about my disobedience.

"Oh, well, now I'm *doubly* intrigued. You *must* go on. I insist."

"I," I hesitate, as if saying the words aloud will seal my fate as more of a sinner than I am, "*I like to read.*" I say it quietly as if it is a secret between myself and the Englisher.

He gasps loudly and covers his mouth, and the noise startles me. "Oh! How scandalous!"

Then, he leans forward and asks quietly, "*Why did you whisper it?*"

My voice is barely audible now over the clang of metal and the bustle of the kitchen staff. "Because... I read books I am not supposed to have."

"Oh my," he mocks, "you little *rebel*. How delightfully naughty of you."

"Not books in our Amish library." I pause for a moment, paranoid that someone is listening in. "*Other* books."

"I don't know what that means." His smile is warm, and I forget what I am saying for a moment.

"Well, one day at work, I had an argument with one of my sisters, Hannah. I decided to walk home instead of take the buggy."

"How far away do you live?"

"Only three miles or so."

He titters. "*Jeeeeesus H.* Three miles. *Christ.*"

I have never heard the name spoken in such a casual manner. For a moment, it reminds me of things my *Mamm* has said about the Englishers trying to corrupt the Amish. After a moment, I decide to keep telling him the story.

"It's not that far."

"...If you're a *horse*, maybe." He sits back. "I'm sorry. Continue. Please. This is already *wildly* fascinating."

I point out the window at the long stretch of highway. "Down that road a little ways, there is a bookstore. That evening, they were putting things away after a book sale, and there were these things called paperback—"

"I'm aware of what a paperback is." He smiles again, and I realize he isn't poking fun; he's being playful. "I'm sorry. Go on. I want to hear the rest of the story."

He slides his fingers from one side of his closed lips to another. I don't know what it means, but I continue.

"Well," I murmur, "this lady was bringing them back inside off the tables before the rain storm came. She saw me looking at one. I told her it sounded interesting, and she just… gave it to me. And then… she gave me the other two books in the series. She said they were in rough shape because one was missing a cover, and the other was really yellow from being in the sun a lot."

"Well, that was nice of her."

"Yes. It was!" I smile, remembering that day with clarity. "By the time I got home, they were damp from the rain in my bag. But I put them outside my window on the roof the next morning, and the sun dried them out. I was so happy."

"Do you still have them?"

"Oh yes! I have read all three books at least five times. They are hidden under my mattress, so *Mamm* won't find them."

"Why?" Ansel smiles, but there is a hint of pity in his expression.

"Because," I don't know how to answer that. I don't understand why they aren't allowed when I really think about it. Instead of finishing my sentence, I shrug.

"Alright, I got here… another soda, one mushroom Swiss with fries, aaaaand one grilled chicken wrap with a side salad, no dressing."

Bethany places a huge burger and fries in front of me and slides another drink next to the nearly empty cup I've been loudly slurping the bottom of with the straw.

She sets the rest in front of Ansel. "Need anything else? Coffee? Water?" She pronounces it 'wor-dor,' making me want to snicker.

"I think… we are good." Ansel smiles up at the older woman. It's genuine and friendly. Bethany double-taps the table and walks off.

"She seems nice." He points his fork in Bethany's direction. Then, he snickers again. "She's keeping you caffeinated as hell."

I look down at my portion size. There is more food on my plate than I usually eat in several days. Our pantry is barren, and many days lately, all I have had to eat is a bowl of Rivel soup.

"What does caffeinated mean," I inquire.

"It means your drink has caffeine in it."

I look at the bubbles popping against the clear plastic cup.

"Caffeine… gives you energy." Ansel finishes the words a split second before he bites into his chicken wrap. He moans, and his blue eyes roll back and flutter. "Oh God, I'm so hungry."

I wrestle my burger into my hands. The cheese is melty, and the mushroom slices start falling off like rain. Juice drips down my wrist. "This isn't like any burger I've ever had before."

"So you *have* had a burger before?"

"Yes, of course." I take a big bite, and the combination of cheese, vegetables, and meat tastes heavenly on my taste buds. After I am finished chewing, I speak again. "I make most of the food for my family and my *Grosdaddi*."

"What's a Gross-daddy?"

"It is *Fater's Fater*."

"Ummm, okay." He thinks for a moment. "So... your grandfather."

I nod. "He lives with us in the *dawdi haus*." I can tell from the look on Ansel's face that he doesn't know what I am saying. "It is a house on the back of our farm."

"Oh, gotcha. I have something like that, too. Where I'm from, we call it a guest house." He wipes dressing from his lips with his napkin. "Or a mother-in-law suite."

"When you say we, you mean you and your wife?" *And kids, I'm assuming.*

He sets his wrap down, licks his lips, and folds his arms across his chest, giving me a glimpse of how far his tattoos travel around his forearms. Through the open top button of his shirt, a little more of his collarbones reveal themselves. I find my eyes drifting down to his corded necklaces and silver pendants and the inked skin beneath them.

"Now, tell me, Velda… why would you assume I'm married?"

I point to his face with a finger glistening from the buttered top bun of my burger.

Still, he seems confused.

"*That.*"

"That *what*?" He shrugs, baffled.

"The hair. On your face."

"I have a goatee. So what? I'm not seeing the correlation."

"Men grow a beard when they get married."

He guffaws, rattling me with the noise.

"Oh wow, you're… you're serious, aren't you?"

I nod, scarfing down some of the renegade mushroom slices coated in gooey Swiss. I am in Heaven. "Yes. Of course."

"Wow, you guys are really somethin' else." He shakes his head and goes back to eating, stabbing lettuce with his fork repeatedly.

"Velda, out here, people have all kinds of facial hair. Mustache, beard, goatee… hell, even a Fu Manchu and mutton chops… none of it means anything. You can have facial hair if you're single, married, gay, asexual… doesn't matter." I stare at him, soaking up this bizarre difference in our cultures. "You see, when we get married, we wear a ring on our fourth finger on our left hand. Allegedly, that is because the veins going through that lead straight to your heart or something sappy like that."

I swallow hard. "I feel… *embarrassed.*"

71

"Don't. It's just funny that you thought that. That's all." He takes another bite of plain lettuce and tries not to show how much he hates it. "Trust me, if I were married, I would not be here right now."

"In my community, men shave their faces when they are single or courting. Once they get married, the women wear different clothes, especially to church, and the men grow beards. That is how they let people know that they are married."

"That is so weird to me," Ansel says before sipping his water.

"I guess it is because, a wedding ring, you can take off to fool someone into thinking you are not married." I slurp down more soda. "A beard you cannot take off and put back on."

"Damn. Good point." He bobs his head toward me. "What about you? Got a boyfriend? Husband?"

"No." I feel shy with my reply. Then, I think about the Miller boy and shiver. Once my time of running around is over, he is essentially my fate. *Fater* will be relentless about it, just like he was with Saloma.

"How old are you?"

The question comes out of nowhere and hits me like a rock thrown from a rooftop.

"Seventeen?"

"Eighteen," I say firmly.

"Wow, must be all of that clean eating you guys all do. You're probably gonna look thirty-five when you're sixty."

"No. I don't think so." Most of the women in Berks County look much older than they are, usually because of how much work it is to rear all of their children and serve their husbands.

Ansel finishes the last of his food and leans back into the torn red leather behind him. He checks his watch, and I lean over to get a glimpse of it. It is so strange. It has words instead of numbers and minute hands.

"Oh Jesus, I thought for sure I'd be in bed right now, flippin' through some trash T.V. reruns in the hotel."

He catches me looking at his watch and lays his hand across the table for me to examine it. "You wanna see it? It's a smartwatch." His eyes study me. "Touch the screen."

I touch the black glass, and it lights up with the time, the date, and colorful symbols for a foot, a moon, and a heart.

"You want it?" He starts to take it off, still fascinated by my reaction.

"No, no, please. I couldn't." I wave it away, uncomfortable.

"You sure?" His eyebrows are high, and he's poised to take off the rubbery-looking band.

"I'm sure. Thank you, though."

"Alright, you guys need any," Bethany trails off as she examines our plates, "Okayyyy, I see you don't need any boxes. How about dessert?"

The woman presses her freckled hand onto the seat behind Ansel.

"Oh no, thank you. I'm… good." He motions to me. "But, go ahead and get you something."

"We have a *great* chocolate cake."

I nod. "Yes, please."

"To go?" Bethany asks him.

Ansel nods and checks his watch. "Yes, please. Early flight."

"Ohhh," she howls. "Where you flyin' to?" Bethany acts like they're old friends.

"Home. Rhode Island."

"Oh Gosh, it's just *beautiful* up there. Flew up to Boston 'bout ten years ago. Got to go down into Rhode Island to see Cape Cod and Newport and all that."

"Yeah, Newport isn't far from where I live, actually. I'm in Narragansett."

"*Lucky,*" she sings it more than she says it. "I went and took a tour of *The Elms* while I was there. Never seen a mansion so big in my life. Heck, the front steps of that building are probably the square footage of my whole place. It was wild to see."

I've never known someone that has *flown* before. Much less *two people*. They're talking about it with such nonchalance. Like everyone does it.

Ansel's eyes meet mine. Through the clatter of utensils and Bethany's prattling, I feel like time has stopped and the world is at a standstill. I feel something flutter in my belly, and my pulse quickens like I am digging up sweet potatoes back up the farm. Only I'm not. I'm sitting still. And out of breath.

In my periphery, I see the waitress disappear through the back, but Ansel doesn't blink. I wish I could read minds. I wonder what he is thinking.

"Was that soup I had today really your recipe?" His voice is low and soothing. His hand smooths the napkin in front of him.

I nod, still unable to tear my gaze from his. "Yes, we have broccoli soup all the time, but I added a lot of things into it to give it a different flavor than usual. I do that once in a while when we have enough food to experiment a little."

He thinks for a moment and looks at the table. I feel like I have been dropped from a choke-hold, and now, in my mind, I'm floundering, gasping for air.

"I know this is coming out of left field, but... how would you like to come work for me?"

The question stuns me. It feels like he asked it in a completely different language.

"I beg your pardon," I squeak.

"How would you like to come to work for me? Back in Rhode Island." He leans forward and rests on his crossed forearms. His green silk shirt presses against every curve of his chest, and I feel my stomach tighten and my thighs clench uncomfortably at the sight of it.

"I'm afraid I don't understand. To do what, exactly?"

He smirks. "To be my chef."

"Oh... I—"

"So here's the deal. Recently, my doctor told me that I have high blood pressure. It's not good. He says I need to eat healthier, to lay off salt and butter and trans fats and all that shit, and start doing better by my heart."

"I... I'm not a chef."

"Well, I know you didn't attend any culinary school, but you can *cook*. You know how to make meals with healthy ingredients. That's literally all I need." He leans one hip back and looks over his shoulder at me.

He hands his black credit card up to Bethany, who trades it for a warm smile and a Styrofoam box. He slides the white container toward me as she scuttles off.

"I could start you at eight hundred a week, flat, plus free room and board."

I can't find the strength to make a peep.

"...Plus a *per diem* since you're away from home," he adds. "With the per diem, it would be closer to thirteen hundred a week."

The knot in my stomach tightens into something hard and unforgiving. I don't know what a *per diem* is, and I feel too foolish to ask, but I've never held or even *seen* that kind of money, never in my life. The most I've ever seen taken back home from the market was a little over five hundred.

My brain flashes to so many thoughts of what that money could do for my family, for

Fater, for the farm. We might not even have to *move…*

But how would any of this work?

"It could even be temporary, just to see if you like it. If you don't, I'll get you a flight home whenever you want."

I am not qualified to do this. I don't even know what this 'high blood pressure' he's talking about even is! I've never heard of such an ailment. Maybe it is only something that the Englishers suffer from.

"If you want the gig, I need to know soon. Like, by 6:30."

I am still stunned-silent.

Bethany returns his card with a receipt and a pen.

"Thank you." He smiles, and she retreats. He fills out the top receipt, and I watch as he writes $200 in the spot where it says 'tip.' He sees me watching and smirks.

"*Two hundred dollars,*" I whisper.

He responds with a smirk. "My mom was a waitress. It's hard work pretending you like people. Who knows… maybe that'll make ol' Bethany's night."

He winks, and my gut wrenches again with a mixture of attraction and nerves from his proposal.

"That's a lot of money." I swallow hard.

"Here. So my accountant doesn't ream me…" He pulls out his phone and points it at the second receipt. Then, flips it over and scribbles something on the back.

"Here's my number. Think about the offer. If you want to work for me, call or text me in the next few hours, and we'll make it happen."

He offers me the receipt with his phone number on it.

"I... I don't own a phone."

"Oh shit." He laughs and pops his palm against his forehead. "Duh. I'm an idiot."

"No!" It comes out louder than intended. I clear my throat. "You're not at all."

"How in the hell do you guys get messages to each other? Carrier pigeon?"

I can't tell if he's joking. I stare at the numbers on the slip of paper.

"There is a phone in the workshop where my *bruders* make fireplaces." I've never used it, but I have seen it there on the walk when I brought Atlee food one day.

"Well, okay. Use it. Call me if you want the job, then. If you do, I'll swing by and pick you up on the way to the airport. If not, well..." He sighs. "Never hurts to ask."

I want the job.

I want the adventure.

I want to experience new things! But *Mamm* and *Fater* will never let me go out of Pennsylvania, *especially* with an Englisher, even during my running around time.

My delighted smile morphs into a frown. "*Fater* will never allow me to go."

I feel my heart start to tear in two at the admission, at the thought of never being able to see the world beyond Berks County. It tears at the thought of being essentially tethered for life to Amos Miller, having to bear as many of his unfortunate-looking children as my body will allow.

"You're eighteen. In this country, that means you're an adult. You can make your own decisions."

I pick at the styrofoam container, feeling the world that I am so curious about slip from my grasp.

He holds up his hands and looks down at the receipt. "Look, I won't push. Offer's on the table if you want it."

He means it quite literally. As he rises from the booth, I sit and stare at his number. He offers a hand to help me up, and I take it, stuffing the paper in my shorts pocket before grabbing the satchel containing my dress, apron, and *kapp*. They are rolled in a wrinkly wad, a sky-blue symbol of all I have ever known.

In the parking lot, I turn to him. "Thank you for… *everything* tonight."

He scoffs, "No problem. It isn't often these days I get a dinner-and-movie date with a lovely young woman. It's usually more like Tindr-and-Doordash with a cougar if anything."

He laughs, but I don't know what any of that means, so I just smile.

"It's also not every day I get to watch someone see their very first movie on the big screen, so *that* was a treat. Wait until you see a Nolan movie in IMAX. It'll blow your mind."

I feel heat bloom across my cheeks being this close to him, close enough for him to lean down and kiss me if he wanted to, just like in the books.

"Well, it was nice meeting you, Miss Velda. Thank you for the company." He wipes a wisp of hair from my forehead and tucks it behind my ear, and I feel like my knees might buckle beneath me.

Then, he looks around, puzzled. "You got one of those carriages for the ride home?"

"Oh, the buggy. No. My family only has one."

"Someone coming to pick you up?"

I shake my head. "It's not that far of a walk."

"It's almost eleven o'clock at night. There is no way I'm letting you walk three miles home in the dark."

He starts to walk toward a shiny vehicle and waves for me to follow. "C'mon. Get in."

13

Ansel

"I can't believe you were going to walk in the dark all this way," I mutter, leaning forward so I can try to get a better view of the miles of darkened farmland surrounding the long stretch of dirt road. "You could be eaten by a fuckin' bear or something out here, and no one would know."

Velda's fingers depress the dome light, and her head moves around slowly, eyeing every facet of the rental's leather interior up and down like she's appreciating fine art in a museum.

I glance back and forth between the high-beam bathed stretch of road and her until she notices that I'm looking. The corners of my lips rise. "Havin' fun over there?"

She blushes. *Actually* blushes. Her innocence is actually a bit endearing.

"I'm sorry. I've just never…"

It still floors me that she's never been in a car before.

"You should see my car back home. Puts the interior of this pile to shame."

She smiles brightly, and then she catches a glimpse of a house in the distance. Her smile falls, and she turns the light off and slinks down into her seat.

"This is my house, up here." Velda points up ahead, voice heavy with anxiety. The dim flicker of some kind of flame illuminates the dwelling's front window.

Maybe she's nervous about me giving her a ride, thinking I'm going to be predatory or *quid-pro-quo* about buying her dinner. Or maybe she's afraid of what's behind that glowing single pane of glass. I'm sure parents out here aren't exactly thrilled about their kids being out late without a means of communication.

"This farm looks *huge*. Your family owns all of this?" I start to turn in at the gap in the wooden fence where the road splits off.

"Stop!" Velda shouts, and I depress the brakes so fast that we jolt. A cloud of dirt envelops the headlights slowly. She clasps her hands around my forearm. They linger against the muscle there, and she looks down at them as if she's lost her train of thought for a moment.

"What's wrong? I was just gonna pull in and—"

"No. Please." She cuts me off. "They cannot see me in this vehicle. And I cannot go in there dressed like this. They don't like when we dress like the Englisher."

"Okayyyy," I say quietly, unsure of what she wants me to do about either thing.

"I will just be a moment."

"Okay. Sure."

I don't know what the hell is going on.

I lean back in my seat, idling in the darkness, staring at the nocturnal bugs drawn to the twin beams flitting beyond the windshield.

Velda scurries out, careful to shut the door quietly, presumably so as not to draw the attention of her parents.

As she peels off her T-shirt behind the car, I get an accidental glimpse of her in the rear-view, a sliver of bare breasts and smooth, pale skin bathed in the crimson glow of my taillights. She isn't wearing a bra, which is something I noticed back at the theater when the air conditioning was blasting. Those pink buds beneath the fabric looked hard enough to cut diamonds. And now, in the chilled night air, they look exactly how I imagined them in my mind: small, pebbled, and fucking perfect.

I pry my eyes away, which takes all of my willpower. She's so innocent. So *young. Too* young for me to gawk. She might be eighteen, but it still feels overwhelmingly perverted to be leering like a voyeur at her nakedness when I have, what, *thirteen years* on this girl?

I focus, instead, on the hoof prints up ahead in the loamy soil illuminated in white light until she slinks over to my window. Now, prim and proper in her bonnet thingy and *Little House on the Prairie* costume, she's a completely different person. Like she's dressed for Halloween as *Sarah, Plain and Tall.*

"Thank you, Ansel. I can never forget tonight as long as I live," she says sweetly near my ear.

I could swear there are tears in her eyes as she says it. I see the faintest puff of her breath against the darkness in my periphery.

"Tonight was one of the best nights of my entire life."

Is she... kidding?

It was literally just a sub-par chick-flick and a greasy spoon diner with sticky menus. Nothing special. She's acting like I just took her on a trip to Vegas.

I force myself to look at her. The stray light from my headlights is making her clear blue eyes twinkle.

"It was nothing." I smile, and it seems to put her at ease. "Remember, if you want the job..."

I don't finish my sentence before she holds up the receipt with my number on it, a hint of mischief in her grin as if she's actually considering it.

"*Gut nocht*, Ansel."

"Goodnight." I hand her the to-go box. "Don't forget your dessert." She takes it with gratitude.

As she steps away from the car, I get another look at her in that long dress, one that goes all the way down to her sock-covered ankles and black little Sunday-school shoes. Then, my mind drifts to the memory of her bare body from just moments ago in my mirror. My hands tighten around the steering wheel, legs widening in my seat as I shift in discomfort.

Moments later, she is up the path and waves from her front porch. I flash my headlights, punch the hotel's address back into my phone's GPS, and turn around, careful to avoid the shallow ditch on either side of the road.

As I make my way down the darkened path back to the main stretch of highway, I feel a little relieved that she won't take me up on my offer. Seeing her breasts in my mirror has my brain suddenly racing. I think about what it would be like to feel those perfect little lips of hers leaving a hungry trail down my abdomen, or what it would be like to pull at the seams of that conservative little frock until it tears, exposing skin that's like rich cream. I think about how those peaked little areolas might respond to being lightly brushed by the pads of my thumbs or how those tiny hourglass hips would feel clutched hard in my hands...

It's only an eight-minute drive back to my hotel, but in that time, I already have a problematic erection that will need to settle before I can comfortably walk past the manned front desk.

Fuck.

I debate whether it is worth the loss of sleep to seek out a late-night booty call on one of the hookup apps. But I settle on the more sensible thing: An ice cold shower and a decent night of sleep.

14

Velda

Fater is in his rocking chair, a piece of furniture passed down for several generations. Worry wracks his bearded face. His voice is low and anxiety-inducing.

In Pennsylvania Dutch, he asks, "Where were you?"

"I was in town," I reply, also in his native tongue. I always speak to my *Mamm* and *Fater* this way to show reverence for our heritage and respect for my elders. "I saw a movie."

I know I shouldn't feel ashamed because partaking in such things is allowed while I go with the young folks before we are baptized and commit ourselves fully to the rules of the Ordnung, but many of the Amish, *Fater* included, feel differently when it is a boy. Boys are encouraged to explore and experiment. Girls are expected to behave.

"What is that?" He motions to the box in my hand.

"Chocolate cake." I set it down on the table beside him and fetch him a fork from the kitchen. While I wanted the treat for me, *Fater* has a small obsession with chocolate. With what I am about to ask him, I want him to be in the best mood possible.

Fater shovels a utensil full of cake in his frowning mouth as *Mamm* makes her way down the stairs. She doesn't speak to me. She only stares, angry as a snake, as she takes her seat in the chair beside him near the lamp.

"We waited up for you," *Fater* says in between bites. He offers a forkful to *Mamm*. She doesn't move or blink. It's chilling. *Fater* brings the food back to his own mouth.

"I'm sorry. I didn't mean for you to wait up." I kneel before them and sit on my heels, feeling like I am five years old again after a thrilling evening of *finally* being treated like a real adult. "I was offered a job tonight."

Fater stops chewing, and anger seeps onto his face. "Oh?"

"Yes, *Fater*. It pays a lot of money. I was thinking… if you allow me to take it, I could send the money home to help out."

"Send it home? What do you mean?" *Mamm* finally speaks. Her voice scares me. She has always been the one to be feared of the two of them.

She has never dared to spare the rod.

He who spares the rod hates his son, but he who loves him is diligent to discipline him, she'd chant as she beat our hands or thighs with a switch, always producing fresh ones made from the apple trees out back.

"The job is not in Pennsylvania. I would be a cook—"

Mamm scoffs, and it hurts my feelings, especially because Lavina and I have done the majority of the cooking for the family the last few years so that *Mamm* can have more time to make the quilts she sells at the spring craft fairs.

Mamm looks at my *Fater,* and his eyes cast down to the floor. I know that despite the fact that the men run everything in our community, she has just quietly made the decision for the both of them, even if the words come from his lips.

"No, Velda."

There is never an open discussion with my parents about the things I want or need. Elders are always to be respected, their orders carried out without question.

Still, I can't keep my mouth from saying it…

"*Fater*, please—"

Fater's eyes turn steely and hard, his gaze like a storm brewing on the horizon. Beside him, *Mamm's* unforgiving expression is bathed in the amber glow of the lamp, whose flame jumps to the beat of my breaking heart.

"There will be no more discussion of this. You are a child. You do not know the sin that lies in wait in the English world," *Mamm* growls.

"How *can* I if—"

" — To your room, Velda," *Fater* orders. "There will be no more talk of such nonsense. Your running around is coming to an end, and we expect you to be baptized with the others after the fall harvest this year. Understood?"

I nod, but there is a fire in my soul, one burning bright with anger at this injustice. They want me to run around so that I can be certain that this is the life I want to lead, but they don't actually want to let me see anything beyond what I already have.

This time of freedom is only an illusion.

We once had a pet bird named Noah that we kept near a window. Noah always stared outside longingly. I kept trying to let him out so that he could fly around the whole house. After all, Noah was a bird meant to soar wild and graceful. I thought: *What would it harm to give him some freedom? Some room to fly?*

The first time, I was scolded. After the second attempt, *Mamm* took him to the Englisher vet in Reading and had his wings clipped.

At the time, I thought it was horribly sad. But now, as time has gone on, I think about it as one of the cruelest things I can imagine. To show a creature what freedom and space *look* like, all while trapping them in a small cage.

Refusing to let them see me cry, I kiss my parents on their cheeks and lug my satchel upstairs begrudgingly. I try to burn the image of their faces into my memory.

I don't think I will be seeing them again for a while. As terrified as I am, I refuse to have my wings clipped before I am allowed to taste the joy of flight.

15

Velda

Lying in this bed, I stare out at the stars in the night sky, listening to my younger *bruder*, Levi, snore from his bed four feet away. I imagine what it would feel like to have my own room. This is the closest I have ever gotten now that Saloma has moved in with her new husband.

But there is a lingering fear here now, a tension in the air without the protection of others, of witnesses, after all of the whispers and mutterings I have heard about Levi. About the things that he'd done to Saloma when no one was around to stop him. Things that, when she told *Mamm* of them, Saloma was blamed and told that to not forgive him for his transgressions would be a sin worse than the acts themselves.

Levi has never done these things to me but with Saloma gone now and the way he sometimes looks at me, part of me fears that it may only be a matter of time.

My mind races with thoughts of Amos Miller, pale skin the texture of curdled cheese. I think about how I may be expected to lie still with that face heaving and grunting over me as I perform my wifely duty of bearing him as many children as possible.

I think about Ansel's skin, smooth and lightly bronzed by the sun with permanent tendrils of ink winding along the angles and curves of his body. I think about his lion's mane of waves, unlike anything I have ever seen before, settling just past his broad shoulders.

I think about the way I accidentally clutched his hand in the theater when I was scared and the way he squeezed it to comfort me. I recall the way his forearm felt as hard as mahogany in the vehicle. I remember staring at it because, until that moment, none of tonight felt real. It all seemed like some sort of wondrous dream.

Thoughts of the movie flickering on that giant screen keep me awake, too. The sounds. The bright colors. The emotion I felt watching it, seeing things and places and people, each so completely new to me. I felt like I was in the book.

I remember the scene, too, where the woman slid her hand into her skirt and moaned. I feel my cheeks radiate with heat, even in the darkness, wondering what she was doing that seemed to bring her so much pleasure.

I stare at the walls, imagining what my new room would look like in Rhode Island, modest but different. I imagine his home with a kitchen sink and cold, running water like one of my distant neighbors I once brought food to for *Mamm*, instead of a washerbasin like our house.

I exhale slow and deep, pulse beginning to race. I cannot stay and let this once-in-a-lifetime opportunity pass me by. This is exactly what this time in my life is *for*.

To explore, to learn, to get things out of my system, to find out the grass is not greener outside of Berks County. I want to be certain that settling down and obeying the Ordnung is what I want to do.

Right now, I don't feel compelled to be Amos' wife, to bear Miller babies and carry them in my womb while I work his family's field and tend to his stables.

I creep out of my bed and quietly don my Englisher clothes. I look at our moonlit dresser, one filled mostly with Levi's garments, and I realize there isn't much for me to take. I dig beneath my mattress to the precariously balanced paperbacks hidden among the supports and stuff them into my burlap bag.

With patience and precision, I manage to get the old wooden window up without waking Levi, and I step quietly out onto the roof. Safely getting down off the second story takes an almost absurd amount of time, but I manage to get down quietly, allowing an unruly row of thick bushes to soften my landing.

Once my feet are on the ground, I am gone, bounding like a quarter horse in the direction of the building where my *bruders* work.

The workshop is silent. Despite the blackness of the sky giving way to a denim blue, it is still so dark that I have to feel my way through the building. I need to hurry. Men start their work early, and I don't know how long I have before I am discovered. I make my way around the benches, and my heart leaps when my hands finally feel the cold, cylindrical handle of a battery-powered flashlight. I click it on and look around.

The space is vast and full of wooden planks, sawhorses, and tools. Hack saws hang from nails in the walls. Clamps hold together several pieces of wood on a workbench in the center where an electric fireplace is underway.

My heart thuds as I search, and it feels like it is pounding in my throat by the time I find the black, corded phone hanging from the wall, with a curly cord hanging beneath like a strange animal tail.

My hand trembles violently as I lift the phone. I saw *Mamm* make a call to the Englisher doctor with it once when my sister Hannah was kicked by the neighbor's horse. I think I remember how to do it.

I retrieve the receipt with Ansel's number from the pocket of my shorts, press my finger into the hole for the first number, and spin it. The loud gear-like grind tearing through the silent space makes me feel like I might crawl out of my own skin. I feel that at any moment, I could be discovered, and things would end poorly for me. Not only would I not get to go to Rhode Island, but I would surely be beaten by both *Mamm* and

Fater, neither of which would dare spare the rod for an offense such as this.

A few numbers later, the phone finally rings.

"H-Hello?" The voice on the other end is groggy, but I recognize it instantly and feel a flutter in my belly. Excitement slowly replaces horrified fear.

"I have decided to take you up on your offer."

There is a long silence as it all registers for him. Then, finally, he speaks.

"Great." Though his voice is grumbly, he seems sincerely upbeat. I am baffled by how this device manages to transmit the warm timbre of his voice through thin air in an instant. "What time is it?"

"I have no idea," I say.

And I *don't*. I have no way to know.

I hear him shift and move on the other end of the phone.

"Jesus, it's four-thirty." He chuckles softly.

I want to apologize, to tell him that I'm sorry for waking him prematurely, but I can't manage to get the words out of my mouth. Instead, I click off the flashlight and stand in dark silence, listening to the movement and little grunts on the other end of the line.

"Cool. Let me shower and get dressed. I'll swing by and pick you up in, like, thirty and we can grab a little breakfast or something and head to the airport a little early. Sound good?"

"Yes."

I am overjoyed and tearing up with relief. It all sounds like music to my ears.

16

Ansel

"I'm shocked as hell that you came. I thought for sure you'd turn me down," I say as I place my overnight bag on the thin metal rack.

In truth, part of me actually hoped she would bow out after seeing her nude body in my rear-view mirror. I had to rub one out later just to get any sleep because I couldn't stop thinking about it. I felt like a fucking pervert jacking off to the mental image of an innocent little eighteen-year-old.

Velda beams at me, soaking in her surroundings. To me, this place is just a dumpy little airport, but to an Amish girl who rarely gets off the farm, this shit's probably wild to see for the first time.

"I'm surprised your folks let you come. I'm glad they had a change of heart," I say, although that isn't totally true. A small part of me was relieved that her parents weren't going to allow her to go. Jerking off felt totally harmless at the moment, but now that she's in front of me again, it feels like a violation. She's meek and innocent, and honestly, I feel a little ashamed.

I should've just had my assistant, Thomas, find me a local chef. Someone whose perfect little blush-colored nipples *haven't* been burned into my brain.

Velda nods, smile bleak. A loose tendril of golden hair dislodges from behind her ear and dangles down from her crown braid. I want to push it behind her ear, but after what I did in bed last night, I have no fucking business touching her. I'm not a goddamn creep.

I look down at her satchel. "Is that all you brought?"

"Yes," she says quietly.

She must not be planning to stay long. All I see in that thing is a few raggedy books. No clothes at all. Amish or otherwise. No white bonnet. No *Sarah, Plain and Tall* dress. No hole-ridden socks. No chaste granny panties.

Jesus, Ansel, get your mind off her damn underwear.

"Ladies first," I say, motioning for her to head up the steps into the jet. She makes her way up the stairs, eyeing everything around her with the fascination of a curious infant, and it hits me that this is fucking crazy. It hits me that I didn't think this proposition through in any way. It hits me that she really has no idea what this new adventure has in store for her.

And then it occurs to me... that neither do *I*.

17

Velda

My belly roils with nerves. As much as I want to be sick from leaving home, leaving everything I have ever known, the view from these windows shows me that there is so much more to this world. Here I am, watching clouds brush by the wings with a grace unlike anything I have ever seen before.

I have read about airplanes in books, but riding in one is nothing like I imagined. Writers always talk about crying babies and cramped seats, but this is anything but that. There are no howling young. In fact, there aren't any other people on board other than Ansel, the men up front who greeted us upon entry, and a lovely woman in a short skirt and neck scarf who keeps bringing me cold cans of lemon-lime soda.

"I think the first order of business, once we get back, is to get Thomas to pick up a phone for you. That way, I can text you with my ETA so you can have meals ready, and you text him when you need a ride to the store to pick up groceries." Ansel stops writing his list and taps the back of his pen rapidly against his yellow notepad like the thumping leg of a rabbit.

"E...T...A?"

Ansel smirks and looks at me as if he can't tell whether I am real or not.

"It stands for... estimated time of arrival. Once we land, I'll text Tom to come over to the house and get a shopping list together for stuff you might need: toiletries, clothes..." He eyes my satchel, and I pull it closer, suddenly feeling a little foolish that these books were all that I brought with me.

"Question." He leans back into the leather of his seat. "Do you want to learn how to drive?"

The inquiry steals the air from my lungs. If my family even knew that I *rode* in a car, they would be appalled. Me *driving* one would surely be even *more disappointing* for them. But the thought of trying it has the writhing mass of nerves in my belly squirming with equal parts terror and glee. The thought of being offered that kind of freedom and trust makes me absolutely giddy.

"Me? Drive?" I think for a moment. "Do you really think I could?"

He laughs. "Yes." He shakes his head and smiles down at his paper before looking back up at me. "You can do anything you put your mind to."

After a moment to consider it, I nod more violently than I intended.

"Okay. I'll have Tom get you enrolled in a driver's ed course. But," he pauses for a moment and tilts his head, "I remember what you said about having your picture taken being against your religion. Is that true?"

I nod. "Some Amish believe photos steal your soul, but my *Mamm* always said that we don't allow our picture to be taken because it goes against our humility. Taking photos is an act of vanity."

"Right. You guys put value on community versus individuality," he adds.

I nod, eyes large.

How did he know that?

He shrugs as if I asked it aloud. "I fell down a bit of an information rabbit hole reading about Amish stuff before I went to sleep." He rolls his shoulders back and changes the subject.

"When you learn how to drive, they have to take your photo for your license. Will that be a problem?"

I think for a long moment and then shake my head. I ran away from home last night to explore this world before I get baptized. I figure when that happens, every last one of my sins and transgressions will be washed away, and I will promise to live life going forward as the Ordnung tells me to.

But until I take that vow, I owe it to myself to have a taste of true freedom like the English do.

Despite the fear I feel at the new adventure awaiting me, I also feel an overwhelming sense of gratitude for this man and this opportunity.

18

Ansel

"So this is it," I say as we turn down the entrance past the four-foot wall of flat, stacked rocks that surrounds my property. As my house comes into view, Velda gasps audibly and cups her mouth in her hands.

"You *live* here?" Her comically wide eyes stare up at me from the passenger seat of the Rivian. It is such a hilarious notion to me, bringing an Amish girl to my home in a fully electric car. I'm sure the irony would not be lost on her if she weren't so busy being enthralled by the local flora, most of it foreign to her neck of the woods, I'm sure.

"Yes. I live here. Bought it about five years ago, before the pandemic drove prices through the roof. I paid four, but I think last time I checked Zillow, it was valued at almost six."

"Six?" she asks innocently.

"Mil."

"Mil?" I can tell the abbreviation isn't registering with her.

"Million," I add softly.

"Six... *million*?" Her jaw drops as we make our way down the wavy drive lined with brown mulch that makes the flowering bushes and flowers Jorge planted pop vibrantly.

"I feel foolish. I did not realize you were rich." She is blushing.

I guess that's fair. I guess there really is very little in the way of my appearance that would scream: *I own a billion dollar company.*

Most of my money went into the house and a few of the toys in it. Some has gone to various charities. Some to stocks and C.D.s. And I have a surfboard collection in my large workshop out back that would make most pro surfers quiver.

As Velda soaks in my two-story sprawling property, I punch the garage door button and watch her jolt in surprise at the burst of movement.

Watching her at the restaurant, in the jet, and now... it's like watching a formerly blind person see the world for the first time. It is starting to make me realize how much I take for granted in my day to day. She thinks even the most mundane things are exciting. I forget that there are people out there, like her, who haven't experienced a *fraction* of what this world has to offer.

I plug the car in to charge and grab my bag out of the trunk, handing Velda the hand-stitched satchel of books.

"Tom'll be here shortly. In the meantime, I'll show you to your room and let you get settled in."

Velda smiles, full of gratitude. Unlike any woman I've ever known, she seems genuinely so easy to please.

"Thank you. Should I call you Ansel? Or something more formal now that I am here to work?"

I smile. "Ansel is fine." I don't know why I tell her that, though. Thomas speaks to me formally. Perhaps it is the casual rapport I have already established with her. It just feels like I would be making her some kind of little Cinderella, working for me like a servant and referring to me like that. Since she will be living on the premises, I want her to feel more at home.

Suddenly, I feel the need to indulge more. "My last name is Wolf, too, just so you know it."

God forbid she ever got lost and had to wander around Narragansett, terrified, looking for '*Ansel-Something*.'

"Like the big bad one?" She says it without a smile, but her eyes show a glimmer of excitement as she recalls the children's tale.

"Yeah, like the big bad one." The comment reminds me just how young she is. Sometimes, when she says things like this, I want to just rest my head on my folded arms and stare at her like I would a tank of sea monkeys just to see what she will do next.

"Alexa, turn on the living room lights," I say as we make our way out of the garage and into the lower level of the house.

Velda looks like her brain is about to explode. Whether it be from the way my house just turned on its own lights, to the view of the churning Block Island Sound beyond the long wall of glass, to the spacious open floor plan, to beige walls punctuated by large canvas prints of the neighbor girl's photography. Shots of me coasting and carving through waves, each stark black-and-white reminders that the ocean is tumultuous, something to be respected, feared, and enjoyed equally.

"Alexa, play Jack Johnson."

Music oozes quietly from hidden speakers all around the living space, and Velda spins, shocked by even the most basic technology.

I lean down and speak quietly near her ear. "Say 'Alexa, volume down.'"

She freezes in place. "*Where?*"

"Anywhere. Say it right here. She can hear you."

"A-Alexa?" She swallows hard again. "Volume down, ma'am."

I pull away and snicker as the music lowers. "You don't have to call her ma'am."

"Where is she?"

I head back toward the kitchen, trying to decide how best to explain it to her. "It's not really a she. It's just a device that controls things in your home. It's a service you pay for. Not a real person." I open the fridge and pull out two bottles of Fiji. I return to Velda and hand her one. She takes it and looks at me as if she is not worthy, as if I just gave her a present instead of something to fulfill a basic human need.

"You can ask her questions, too."

105

"Wow." Velda stares into my eyes and doesn't blink for a long moment. Finally, her gaze breaks, and she starts to wander around while Jack sings about bubbly toes.

The moment she approaches the windowed back wall, she gasps.

"Oh!" She shouts the word and looks like she is going to drop to her pale knees. "Is that...?" She points outside, sinewy arm outstretched, biceps surprisingly defined, presumably from farm labor.

"Yeah, that's the Atlantic. Well, *technically*, Block Island Sound."

"May I?" She points to the sliding glass door leading out to the cobbled path around the in-ground pool. It winds around the cascading waterfall and gazebo straight on out to the sandy beach twenty yards beyond the last structure.

"Of *course*." I unlock the door and look at her to ensure that she's watching so she knows how to get in and out on her own.

I motion to the door. She tugs toward her.

"No, it's a slider."

She looks puzzled.

I motion for her to tug it toward me, and she does. She looks shocked when it slides open with ease. Before I can say anything else, she is galloping down the path toward the water, barely noticing any of the other amenities the property has to offer, including the pickleball court, hot tub, fire pit, and sauna.

The raging wind whips her flaxen hair and baggy white T-shirt like a flag. I chose this house for this exact reason. There is a rocky pointbreak out in the water a few yards that makes for *incredible* surf when the wind is howling from a favorable direction. With no other homes in the way, the area often gets hammered by powerful gusts, and the surf gets large and wild. I could honestly give two shits what the house looked like inside on the walk-through with the Realtor. When I saw the peel of the waves beyond the outcropping, I was sold.

But Velda is enamored for a different reason. If she's never been out of Pennsylvania, then she's never seen the ocean.

Until now.

Seeing her take in the view for the first time makes me envious. I have spent so many hours on the water on the world's various coastlines, indulging in a sport I've always been wildly passionate about. I'd give anything to be able to see its vastness and smell the briny air again for the very first time.

I take in the cloudy gray-blue sky and turn to Velda to speak, but the words halt in my mouth. Tears are streaming from her eyes, ones bluer than the water in front of us.

"Awwww, don't cry." Part of me wants to laugh at how cute it is, but instead, I bite my lip and look back out at the water.

"It's just... *so beautiful*. I thought I would never see it." She sobs into her hands.

Her crying intensifies, and I awkwardly put my arm around her shoulders in an act of comfort, hugging her gently to my side. I'm sure this is all overwhelming for her. At this moment, I've changed my mind. I'm relieved that her parents allowed her to experience this, that they allowed her to come.

Her hands wipe her cheeks dry. "Can I," she sniffles, "touch the water?"

I stifle another laugh at how ridiculous it is that she asked permission for such a thing.

"Of course." I motion to it and then look down at her. "Do you know how to swim?"

She shakes her head with a solemn expression. "No, sir."

"Don't call me sir," I say the second it comes out of her mouth. "That feels… weird." I chuckle.

"I'm sorry."

She genuinely means it.

"If you don't know how to swim, I can give you lessons in the pool if you want. That water can chew you up and spit you out on a day like today if you don't know what you're doing, so I wouldn't advise going in past your knees until you know how to swim. But, yeah, knock yourself out."

I can tell that the phrase doesn't register with her at first, but it only takes her a moment to understand that, yes, she can touch the water.

She kicks off her shoes and strips her socks timidly. I take a seat in one of the four slate gray Adarondak chairs bolted to the blue stone patio at the edge of the sand.

I am thoroughly entertained watching her react to the coldness of the water, her mouth forming a tight "O" as she looks back at me. My gaze wanders to her discarded shoes. They look homemade, overly worn, and basic as fuck. They look like they could be the only pair she's had for years. Her dingy socks look hand-stitched with holes in the heels.

As she kicks the foamy waves and squishes the sand in her hands, I pull my iPhone out of my shorts pocket and snap a few photos of her splashing. It dawns on me as they add to my camera roll full of sunsets and surfboards that she might just be the first human I have taken a photo of in...

God...

Maybe a fucking *year*.

I call my assistant.

"Hello, Mr. Wolf." Tom sounds out of breath, picking up after only the first ring.

"How close are you?"

"Turning onto your street right now."

"Good. Come through the back gate and meet us down by the beach. I've got a list of stuff I need you to pick up."

"Us?" he asks and then immediately follows it with, "Absolutely, Mr. Wolf."

The phone clicks. It irritates me how he never says goodbye or indicates that he is done with the call. It feels rude, but I know he doesn't mean to be. For someone just barely old enough to legally drink, he's efficient as hell. He'll go far, and I know I'll be lost without him when the time comes for him to move up in the company.

Moments later, I hear the whoosh of Tom's shoes through the grass behind me. Velda is on the shoreline, picking up every shell that she sees and inspecting it as the water rushes past her ankles.

"May I, sir?" Tom motions to the seat beside me with his tiny notebook, and I nod.

"You want something to drink? Water? Beer?" I point back to the house.

Tom shakes his head almost violently. "No, thank you, sir."

"Okay then, first things first. The longboard guys down in Reading, I fired them."

I can hear Tom's five-hundred-dollar pen scribble diligently.

"I'll get on the phone with Clarence today about it. I know he suggested a few alternatives, and Father Time will practically jizz in his pants knowing I'm finally asking his ancient ass for his opinion on something around here."

Tom doesn't crack the same smile that I do. In fact, he doesn't smile at all. Maybe that was a shitty thing to say. Clarence is, after all, one of my dad's closest friends.

Was.

"Did FedEx deliver the new prints I ordered?"

"Yes, sir. I brought the boxes upstairs, and I did an inventory. All of the bolts were accounted for except the emerald neoprene. That's still on backorder."

I sigh. "Fuck. Okay. Did they say how long it would be?"

"They estimate another six to eight weeks on that one."

"Fuck. Okay, emerald is out for the pitch. Did the swatches for the ladies' designs come in with the rest of it?"

"No, they said those are coming next week."

"Ugh. Jesus, these guys really don't have their shit together, do they?"

Tom shakes his head, but I can tell it is more just to appease me.

"I'll follow up. The receptionist is going to send me a confirmation email with a tracking number once it ships," Tom says.

"Good." I motion with my square bottle to the girl playing in the sand, the one that Tom's eyes have slyly flitted back and forth to a number of times already. "Velda Yoder. My new cook. Hired her in Pennsylvania and brought her back. She's Amish if you can believe that."

"You don't say," Tom responds flatly.

"She's never seen the ocean before." I chuckle lightly and realize Tom isn't as amused as I am. Then, I say, "She's a damn good cook, but she's brand new here, and she came with practically nothing. She's going to need a lot of stuff."

"Lay it on me, sir." Tom pries his eyes off of her again and forces them back down to the notepad balanced on the knees of his black dress slacks. His shined shoes bobble nervously in front of him.

"Get her an iPhone, a decent one, and some clothes. Some basics. I'm gonna see if the neighbor girl can take her on a proper outing one of these days while I'm at work, but until then, she needs some basics. Socks, couple of shirts, pack of razors, shampoo…"

"You want me to get her a couple of work uniforms, too? Chef jackets or polos or something?"

"Oh God no, she's cooking at home. Poor girl's had to have a damned dress code her whole life. A couple of basic tanks and tees will do fine. And grab anything else you think she will need in the next few days until I can get Helena to take her out. She basically has nothing."

"Sure, no problem."

"Take the Amex."

Tom nods.

"Grab her a couple of 'heart healthy' cookbooks, too. In case she needs some ideas."

"Will do."

"Oh, also, I want to start the process of getting her a driver's license," I add. "Get her signed up for a driver's ed course somewhere nearby and find out what she needs to get her learner's permit or whatever. On the off-chance she sticks around a while, I don't want her to have to fucking Uber everywhere. In the meantime, you may need to run her to the store for supplies a couple times a week."

"Not a problem, sir."

"I'll cover your gas, obviously."

He nods, still writing everything down.

"This afternoon, though, take her to the grocers for enough produce for the next couple of days." Then, I quickly add, "But don't let her cook tonight. Not until I show her how to work everything in the kitchen. I don't need her burning the fuckin' place down."

"Understood."

"Get Bao's. The menu is on the shared drive. You know what I like."

"Chicken and broccoli, sir." He says it almost like a soldier repeating something to his drill sergeant.

"Yeah, and then get whatever she wants. If she can't decide, order a variety. Get yourself something, too. Have it delivered at six o'clock. I should be back from the office by then."

"Will do."

I feel bad for always laying so much on the kid, but he makes four times what I made at his age, and I was upfront in his interview about what he signed up for.

"Did I miss anything important yesterday?"

"No, sir." Tom lowers his pen and crosses one knee over the other. He's scrawny and pale with jet-black hair and a hook nose. Reminds me of a shorter version of that weird guy who played *Willard.* All he needs is a big rat on his shoulder.

"There was a small mix-up with some spring suit stock ordered to the Galveston office, but

Alan, Larry, and I got it sorted out and handled right away. Wasn't a problem."

"Great. When's my next meeting?"

"I kept the morning clear for you in case there were any delays with your flight. This afternoon, you have a meeting with Candace Molter at the office. She's the G.M. in Boston who wants to talk about opening a second store up in Rockport. That's at *two* o'clock. And then, at *four*, you have a video conference with Malik down in Destin about the ribbon-cutting ceremony for the new storefront opening there next month. Then, tomorrow, you have a video conference with the board members at eleven and a call with the guys down in New Smyrna about the competition."

I nod and finish my water, dreading the board meeting. Time for them to, *once again*, shoot down all of my new ideas for expansion.

"Great. Thanks for holding down the fort."

I dig in my wallet and pull out my credit card. I hand it to Tom, and he takes it, eyes drifting to Velda's jean-covered ass as she picks up a young, dead horseshoe crab by the tail and examines its stilled underside with the curiosity of a budding marine biologist.

She is filled with a childlike wonder for the water before her, without any awareness of jellyfish stings, shark bites, undertows, or bacterial infections. She doesn't know enough to be at least a little afraid of the ocean yet. Instead, she is simply enjoying the sand between her toes, the varied array of jetsam washed ashore, and the lap of the cold waves against her skin.

19

Ansel

The meeting with Candace went well. I approved her initial request to open another *TwinFin* in another town up the Eastern Seaboard about an hour north of Boston.

She normally would be my 'type' for a casual hookup, a slightly older 'cougar' with natural D-cups. But as she spoke, I noticed her brown eyes were dull and listless. Void of all sense of wonder or excitement. She seemed hardened by the world. By things like cheating ex-husbands, ungrateful children, a sexist workforce, and stretches of food stamps. She looked like she had clawed her way up from the bottom, but she also seemed exhausted.

Nothing like Velda, a young woman discovering basically the entire world for the first time. Ecstatic over the sweet fizz of soda, tearfully overwhelmed by her first motion picture, excitedly prodding a dead crab as she took in the ocean for the first time. There is something about her sense of wonder and purity that I find strangely *exhilarating* to be around. It's like a color-blind person seeing *technicolor* for the first time, no matter the activity. She is dazzled by even the smallest thing.

I lean back in my leather chair and gaze out of the large window of my office in Newport. The entire third story of the commercial building belongs to *TwinFin* and sits next door to an opulent yacht club, and just a stone's-throw away from tourist hot spots like *The Elms* and *The Breakers*.

My view is a sweeping panorama of the glimmering waters of Brenton Cove. The intensifying afternoon sunlight glints off the Lime Rock Lighthouse, and on a day like this, I can see all the way to the tip of Goat Island from this chair.

Newport is stunning, although it is packed with the stodgy caviar-sucking upper echelon of the East Coast.

Many *insisted* that I buy a home in Newport, along with nearly 20 other multi-millionaires, but the call of the breaks where I first learned to surf was too strong. Narragansett is full of nostalgic memories of my parents. With them both gone now, I would go to great lengths to preserve those.

I flip open my laptop and ready myself for the call with the board. I have twenty minutes until they all start joining the chat, and I decide to take that time to pull up the tab of my favorite online merchant.

Free next-day shipping? Yes, please.

I type in the name of the movie I watched with Velda and quickly find the novel version. I scroll down to the carousel of also-bought books and add almost every single one to my cart.

I saw those tattered paperbacks in her bag, the only things she brought with her for a few-month trip. For less than two hundred bucks, I can start her a little library of her own. It'll give her something to do in her downtime. And knowing her and how excited she gets over everything, hell, it'll probably make her year.

I order thirteen of them to come to the house and receive my emailed receipt almost the exact moment I hear the first chirp of someone joining the call.

I lean back, jam my earbuds in, and smile. "Clarence! How are you? Still alive and kickin', I see."

20

Ansel

Velda holds her chopsticks, mimicking my motions with a clumsy tenacity I admire. She is not about to let those things get the best of her, even if she has to skewer the last of her meat and vegetables and eat them like a kabob. I've offered her a fork four times, but she is determined to figure out how to use the foreign utensils on her own.

I push back my plastic container, toss my sticks on the remnants of my food, and watch her as she finishes her meal.

"Good?" I grin as she takes her last bite.

She nods, a massive, happy smile plastered on her face.

"Thought you might like that. C'mon. Let me give you the run-down." I stand and wave for her to follow me to the kitchen.

I show her how to operate the oven, microwave, and coffee maker. I point out a panini press and waffle maker that have never even been removed from the boxes. They've been stuffed in the cupboards for at least two years now, untouched.

I teach her how to use the Alexa, which she still reacts to like a magic trick.

I give her an evening tour of the grounds, showing her how to work the sauna, where to find the pickleball rackets, how to start the gas fire pit, and where spare dry cushions are held for the gazebo.

Every time I turn around, she is staring back at the ocean, waves crashing like a repetitive lullaby. I fully understand its seductive allure and love how entranced she seems by it.

I point at my building full of surf toys, but she already seems a little overwhelmed by everything, so I don't take her in.

"How about I show you up to your room and let you get settled in? I'm sure it's been a long day for you."

"Yes, thank you." Velda nods with a meek smile and follows me through the house and up the stairs, hands clasped together in an obedient, chaste pose that reminds me she's damn near from another world.

"This is your room." I open the door to the largest room on the upper floor. I point to the door next to it. "And you have your own bathroom. Whirlpool tub, shower... the whole nine."

"A shower?" She looks intimidated as she says it. "I have never seen one before. We just have a bath in the cellar."

I smirk. This all feels so surreal. It must to her, too.

"There's a tankless heater, too, so you don't have to worry about running out of hot water. You can stay in as long as you want. Here, let me show you how to operate it."

I illustrate how to turn it on and off and how to adjust the temp. She watches water fall from the square fixture in the ceiling with eyes large and full of wonder.

"It is like rain!"

"Yeah," I laugh, "only *warm*."

"I have never had hot, running water before."

I don't know what to say to that. She lived in Pennsylvania, but the more I find out about where she's from, it might as well be a third-world country.

"Well, I'm sure you're going to experience a *lot* of memorable firsts here," I say, even though she already has, and she hasn't even been here for 24 hours yet.

I turn off the water and show her where to find the guest toiletries before brushing back out into the hallway.

"You basically have the entire second story to yourself. The only reason I even come up here is to use my sewing room." I point to the door down the hall. It's ajar, and she heads toward it, drawn like a moth to a flame.

"You... have a *sewing room?*"

"Yeah, yeah, tease if you must." I clear my throat and subconsciously lower my voice a third of an octave, "When I started my company, I actually used to sew all the prototypes. The ones that were approved by the board then went into mass manufacturing. It wasn't until we started getting the thicker neoprenes for the heated wetsuits that we had to start farming out to people with commercial machines. But I still sew prototypes sometimes. I like giving the board something tangible when I pitch."

I rub my neck, agitating the skin with how hard I'm gripping it.

"I know it's not the most *manly* pastime…" I trail off.

But Velda isn't listening. She is pushing the door open and gaping at everything like she's just stumbled into an absolute wonderland.

She looks back at me. "May I?"

"Sure, knock yourself out."

The phrase puzzles her. She cocks an eyebrow at me.

"I just meant, sure, go on inside."

She does a slow lap around the room, eyeing the custom shelving on the far wall filled with bolts of fabric in various styles, patterns, and textures. Neoprene, spandex, wool, fleece, cotton, and silk line the shelves. She runs her hand along them, stroking the textures, in awe of the variety. She flips through bins of *Butterick* and *Simplicity* patterns, some already cut out and returned to the envelopes neatly folded. She glances at a plastic tote filled with denim needles and a pronged rack full of various color threads.

Her blue eyes finally land on my fabric cutting station and my grandmother's antique sewing table, topped with an old off-white *Bernina*, my mother's machine. I wouldn't dream of an upgrade. Replacing it would be like replacing a piece of *her*.

Plus, they simply don't make them like they used to. And this one handles my weird fabrics like a champ.

"I do a lot of the sewing for my family," she says, "but I have never seen a machine like this."

"The instructions are in the drawer. And there's an app on your phone called *YouTube* where you can watch videos if you get confused."

"An *app*?"

I bobble my head. "Yeah... it means... like, a *program*. It's short for application."

She grins up at me from the seat in front of the machine. "You mean... I can use this?"

"Sure." I shrug. "Have at it. There's extra needles and notions in the cabinet over there."

She looks like she just woke up from a nap, discombobulated and seemingly content with the idea of operating it.

"Well, I'm going to leave you to it. If you need anything, just holler. My room is downstairs, past the kitchen and down the hall."

She still can't tear her eyes from the room.

"Oh, and if you want your first swimming lesson, meet me down by the pool around seven-thirty. I have a ton of bathing suits down in the shed, and towels and all of that. I should just be getting done with dawn patrol around then."

123

"What is dawn patrol?" She finally turns to me.

"It just means... I get up early to surf in the mornings."

"Oh." She smiles, innocent eyes twinkling in the light of the overheads. I lead her down the hall back toward her room. "Shouldn't I be making you breakfast then? Your assistant took me to the store, and we got the ingredients so I could make potato pancakes with applesauce."

"Sounds... good," I lie, trying not to show my true feelings across my face. It actually sounds like a bizarre combination, maybe even a little gross, but I won't knock it until I try it. "You can make it after the lesson while I get showered and ready for work."

"Alright." Her eyes drift toward her king-sized bed. "You must be the richest man in the world."

I laugh. It's cute.

"Hardly. I'm not even one of the top ten richest in the *state*. This house ain't even a third of the cost of Taylor Swift's over in Westerly. And Judge Judy and Jay Leno got me beat, hands down."

She blushes. "I don't know who any of those people are."

I chuckle, shake my head, and make my way toward the stairs. "Goodnight, Velda."

She presses her face against the side of the door with a dreamy smile. "*Gut novid*, Ansel."

21

Velda

I end this evening with a mixture of sadness, elation, and gratitude blending their way through me. I feel sick, knowing *Mamm* and *Fater* are probably worried. I feel guilty leaving the way I did. No note, no goodbye. I plan to write them tomorrow morning to let them know that I am safe but that I have no plans on coming home for a while.

I wonder, when I come home, what will happen to me now that Saloma has moved out of the room? So many nights, she cried herself to sleep in my bed as I held my big sister, waiting for her tears to give way to sweet dreams of impending freedom. Thankfully, now that she is married, she has gotten that. But these last three weeks before she left, I started sleeping with a whittled hunk of wood beneath my pillow, praying to *Gott* that I would never have to use it to protect myself from my own kin.

When she finally spoke of these things, *Mamm* accused Saloma of being improper. I knew that *Mamm* is wrong. Saloma had done nothing but *exist* around my *bruder*. He would disappear into the basement during her weekly bath or chase her into the woods. At some point or another, all of us siblings heard her screams.

Saloma's dress was the proper eight inches from the floor. She never stood on a ladder above him. She never said anything bawdy or unchaste or did anything that our *bruder* to have such urges.

Mamm said she was disappointed in *Saloma* instead of *Levi*.

I can still hear her voice in our room, telling my crying sister that not forgiving her brother for transgressions 'beyond his control' would be a greater sin than anything that Levi had done. It appalled me to see her *blame* my sister instead of protecting her.

I know that it would only be a matter of time before my *bruder* turned to *me,* the only girl left for him to terrorize.

Still, I cannot help but feel worry tense my stomach. *Mamm* and *Fater* are probably worried sick. I fret about whether I have made the right choice to come here, if the decision was too rash, if my pay will actually help save *Fater's* farm, if this adventure will end in tears and tragedy or a better understanding of the world outside of Berks County.

As the water rushes over me like hot rain, I revel in this exciting sensation I have never felt before. In my heart, I feel grateful. Grateful to *Gott* for this chance to leave home.

Grateful for this shower and how truly cleansed it makes me feel, the same way I imagine one feels after a baptism.

I dry off with a luxurious towel, and I realize this bathroom is nearly the size of the bedroom that I shared with several siblings.

And then, for a moment, I feel alone.

I lock the door to my bedroom and test the knob. I lock the windows, too, just in case. I change into the pair of long pajamas that Thomas brought me this afternoon before nestling into bed.

I reach beneath my covers and touch the chopsticks from dinner beneath my pillow. They will have to do for now. Hopefully, I won't have to use them to protect myself. Hopefully, my clothing and behavior haven't sparked something animal in the Englisher downstairs.

Mamm has always preached that the Englishers are not good people, that they have bad intentions, that they forsake *Gott* for their own worldly desires.

But Ansel doesn't strike me as the kind of person she has warned me about. So far, he has been nothing but generous and considerate.

He is handsome, too, and I feel shame for thinking that. It feels wrong to have… *urges*… for him. I've had them since we saw the movie at the cinema last night, and so far, they have only grown. I imagine what it might be like to kiss him, like in the movie.

I know it is impure and immoral to have such thoughts, but no matter how many times in the last twenty-four hours I have prayed to *Gott* about it, the feelings persist.

The buzz of excitement for tomorrow and all of the new adventures that it will bring radiates into the darkness. I drift off to sleep imagining Ansel in the bed behind me, caressing my hair with his tan fingers, wrapping my torso in his art-covered arms until I am tight in his comforting embrace, soothed of all of my fears.

22

Ansel

The glow of the lamp's Edison bulb illuminates my newest handful of sketches for the women's surfwear line. I imagine Velda modeling my long-sleeve hibiscus-print rash guard on the cover of *Wavelengths* magazine. In this vision, she is in the water beyond one of the Ruggles point breaks in Newport, straddling my turquoise pinstriped fishboard, *owning it*, thighs draped over either side with the slight vulgarity of a Maxim model. Her youthful face is bathed in the tangerine glow of the sun, and her ornate crown braid is drenched and dripping saltwater.

I know I'm on the right track with these designs now that I can envision them on a model. Now I just have to convince the fucking ancient ass board of directors not to fight me on this shit. It seems to be the trend lately.

They fought tooth and nail on the kid's *Grommet* line, child-sized wetsuits in bold prints. They battled me on the *Hang Loose* outerwear line of wind and waterproof fleece coats that nearly made *SurfFur* obsolete. They fought me on the *Goofy Foot* water shoes and sandals line *and* on the *Kook* sunglasses.

Look dangerous.

I can still see that two-word slogan above it in the first full-page print ad feature. The excitement for that line *alone* brought *TwinFin* stock up nearly nine whole dollars within two weeks of the launch…

All this, and *still,* the board seems hesitant to trust my instincts. Instincts that have, so far, rarely been wrong.

Why do they insist on making every idea I have an uphill battle? This is *my* goddamned company, after all.

I lean back into the couch cushions and down the last of my chocolate milk stout. I flick through the screens of my phone and glance at the calendar's upcoming dates. My schedule looks like Swiss cheese. Meetings nearly every day until the *Amped* Surf Competition in Florida. Then, another blur of meetings and day trips to find a new manufacturing warehouse to handle the boards, all coming to a head before the bi-yearly board meeting down in Louisiana at the end of the summer to pitch these concepts.

I'm exhausted just thinking about it all. And people wonder why I don't have a fucking personal life…

I gather my papers, toss my empty, shuffle down the hall, and start to strip. It isn't until my pants are around my ankles that I realize that, for the first time since I moved in, I am not the only person in this house. I close my bedroom door for the first time in years and settle into bed, suddenly acutely aware that, for once, I am not alone.

23

Velda

I love the feel of this sand between my toes, gritty and abrasive, like it is scrubbing my past off of me, making room for new growth. The wind is cool, and the sky is more vibrant than one of *Mamm's* quilts, its plum colors fading into magenta and eventually pumpkin-orange as the sun makes its way up.

I cross my legs and sit down near the water's edge, letting the waves lap at my bare toes. I tighten the robe I found in the upstairs bathroom around me like a fur coat.

Gulls squawk, making scream-like sounds that I've never heard a bird make before. A shell scuttles across the sand by me on its own. I didn't know they could move! It feels like the whole ocean is alive in some way.

Far away, beyond some huge rocks jutting out of the moving surface, I see a man wearing all dark gray. He is sitting on top of the water like a bird in a pond. He waves, and even from this far away, I know it is Ansel. I wave back, feeling the cool waves creep up to my calves, bubbling foam tickling me on its way back out.

Moments later, I see Ansel's head whip back and forth. The monstrous wave forming behind him looks like it will swallow him whole, gobbling at him like the mouth of some deep blue beast. He spins onto his stomach and paddles away from it like he is trying to escape its maw with his life, thick arms slicing through the rising water.

I kneel, feeling the panic grow within me as seashells and sand gnash into my skin. If that thing swallows him up... if he is pulled under and can't get air, *what will I do?*

What *can* I do?

I can't swim to save him!

I scream and cover my mouth as he is swept up to the top of the wave. In one quick motion, he's up, standing on the board with one foot in front of him, one behind.

His arms lower as he finds his balance, and he coasts down the face of the wave. The white tip keeps crashing down just behind him. The water nearly encapsulates him like a tube, but he glides serenely along its base, using his feet to aim him toward the shore. He maneuvers every changing curve with a graceful ease.

Once he has navigated carefully through the exposed rocks, his board slows, and I can see his smile now, huge and bright, framed by a mess of dripping brown curls. His exposed legs are flexed hard beneath the line on his thighs where his dark suit ends, showing off every beautiful muscle below.

The board stops abruptly, and he leaps off, regaining his balance quickly once his feet touch sand. Something long and rubber is attached to one of his ankles. He reaches a strong arm down, scoops the surfboard up into his armpit, and walks toward me, beaming like the sun.

"Morning!" he shouts from where the waves turn into burbling ankle-high foam. He walks to shore, bare feet splashing the area around him as sand hungrily gobbles up the fallen drops.

"Good morning," I chirp.

"Sleep okay?"

I don't know how to tell him that it was the best night of sleep I have gotten in years, that I felt secure and safe, alone and with a lock on my door, not having to sleep lightly out of fear of those I share a room with. But if I say that, I might have to explain the situation back at home, and I don't want to do that.

Instead, I nod and smile, tightening the robe around me.

"Ready for a quick swim lesson?"

I nod again and watch him unstrap the thing attached to his ankle with a loud *shiiiink* sound. He winds the rubbery cord into a coil.

"Great." He checks his watch and nods for me to follow him back toward the yard.

"I got about twenty minutes before I need to go shower and get ready for work. That should be enough time to teach you a few of the very basics."

I follow like a duckling and watch as he sets his board down in a rack of wooden pegs near the gazebo and steps into a concrete square with a drain in the center. He twists a handle, and water flows out of a faucet above him.

I am in awe of this.

He even has a shower *outside*!

I watch as he rinses off his rubbery, short-sleeve suit and runs water through his thick hair.

"Is that... a bathing suit?" I ask, pointing to what he is wearing.

"This?" He pulls a piece of it away from his body, and it moves like a second set of skin. "No. It's called a wetsuit. This one is called a spring suit because it has short sleeves and shorts. People wear these for water sports. They're good for insulating and protecting your body. Most have full arms and legs. People typically wear the spring suits like this when the water is warmer."

"I like it." I smile.

"I'll give you one." He chuckles. "Or better yet, we'll make you one. A custom one."

I feel my cheeks blush. I do not feel like I deserve these acts of kindness.

He wrenches an arm up his back and yanks the long string of the zipper down. He peels out of the top of the suit, exposing his bare chest and all of the inked images on it. I try to turn my head, but I have never seen someone with art like that on their skin, and I can't seem to stop staring.

He catches me and flashes a smile that is so handsome that my stomach twists. I feel embarrassed that I've been caught looking, and my eyes dart away.

135

"You might wanna avert your eyes for a sec. I gotta change into my shorts."

I feel my heart beating in my temples, and I suddenly have trouble swallowing. I look away. At the grass, the birds, the willows... anywhere but him.

A moment later, he speaks. "Okay, I'm decent. You can turn around now."

I turn timidly just as he turns the knob to make the water stop. He shakes his head like a dog, flinging the water from his hair in a wild circle around him. All he is wearing is a pair of shorts now. They have some sort of strange, blooming red flower on them, one I don't recognize.

"Come, let's get you a suit, too, real quick."

I follow him across the perfect lawn to a shed about the size of my *Grosdaddi's* home back in Pennsylvania. He types in a long code into a black box against the door, and finally, it clicks. He opens it to reveal a huge space that reminds me of Atlee's fireplace warehouse but filled with surfboards instead.

"Oh," I cover my mouth in awe of the space, of all of the beautiful, shiny boards in it.

Ansel rummages through a large plastic bin full of spandex and pulls out a bikini.

"Here we go."

My face pales at the sight of it. The thought of wearing so little in front of an Englisher I barely know makes me feel ill.

"No, wait here. I have a much better idea." Ansel looks at me like he is having a revelation. He dashes out of the shed and sprints toward the house.

While he is gone, I look around, running my finger along the cherry-red stripe of one board and around the green palm tree design on another. There are more in the center. One, he is in the middle of sanding, while others sit with roughened paint, busted tips, and cracked fins.

I hear his galloping feet moments before I see him round the corner.

"So... it's a... long shot..." He is out of breath. "This is a... mock-up I sewed... for a pitch. I think it might fit you."

As soon as I lay my eyes on it, I adore it. It has long teal sleeves and the outlines of pink flowers on the front of the torso, bisected by a zipper that starts at the neck and goes down to the belly button.

"It's called a rash guard. I figured you might like it. It's got a lot of coverage."

"I love it," I say quietly.

"Okay." He smiles, and I feel weak. He hands me the garment. "I think it's pretty self-explanatory. Zipper goes in the front." He hands it to me and retreats.

"You get changed. I will be out in the pool when you're ready."

"Thank you," I mumble.

He disappears, and I change, feeling more naked than I ever have before in my life, despite no one being here to see me but the boards. The rash guard fits like a glove, and I love how the long sleeves hug my arms.

I timidly make my way to the pool, trying desperately to cover up my bare lower half with my clasped hands.

"Wow! That looks *great* on you!" He beams from the blue depths of the pool.

I step down into the frigid water and hiss at the temperature.

He laughs. "Yeah, it's heated, but it's always a little chilly in the mornings."

"You got right in and didn't even *flinch*!"

"I was just in the Sound. It's *way* colder out there. This feels like a hot tub in comparison."

"And you don't freeze to death?"

"Nope," he shakes his head, and I feel water patter my skin from his brunette curls. "I surf year-round. Winter, too. But I wear a wetsuit with a heater in it during the colder months. I'm crazy, but I'm not *that* crazy."

I try to picture what his spring suit would look like with a kerosene heater stuffed into it, and I laugh. The concept doesn't make sense but he says it with so much confidence that I believe him. There is so much I don't yet understand.

"I wasn't expecting it to be so... *cold*." My teeth chatter.

"Normally, I'd say it's better to just jump in. You'll acclimate faster. But since you don't know how to swim, I think that would be terrible advice."

I make my way into the water. It rushes around my knees, my thighs, and I am relieved once the water finally swallows up the entirety of my lower half. With it below the surface, I feel far less exposed.

Ansel's face is serious. "Alright, so one of the first things you gotta know about the water is that you can't ever panic."

I nod.

"No matter how scary things get, panicking only makes things worse when you're in the water. You've got to try your best to remain calm at all times, okay?"

I nod again, but I can't take my eyes off all of his exposed skin. His entire chest is on display. His abdomen is taut and muscular, and his inked-on art travels from his left arm, up his neck, across his chest, and down around his right side. I see waves with a silhouette of a man in the water that looks like he just did minutes before. The lines of it blend up seamlessly into the bundle of blooming lilies on his chest, shoulder, neck, and arm.

"Alright," he says as he descends further into the crystal clear water and holds a hand out for me, "We will stay in the shallow end until you gain a little more confidence and skill. Today, we will just work on holding your breath and learning to relax and float. Even if you aren't actively swimming, being able to just loosen up your body and be buoyant can be really tranquil and fun, and, who knows, it could save your life."

"I'm nervous." I take a baby step toward him.

"You've got nothing to be nervous about. It's good to have a healthy respect for the water, but don't let that fear rule your life." He wades closer to me and dips down until only his head is above the surface. "You got this. I promise, while you're with me, I won't ever let anything bad happen to you."

There is sincerity in his eyes. I feel like he means it, and at this moment, *I actually feel safe.* The tension in my body lessens a little.

So far, Ansel has done nothing but try to expose me to new things. I remind myself that *this* is truly what this time of my life is for.

I wanted a new adventure.

And I *got* it.

He extends his hand for mine. "Remember, there is *nothing* in this world you aren't capable of with a little practice."

What he's saying seems wildly foreign to me, but he seems to mean it.

Suddenly, I realize how close to him I once again am, just like in the movie theater, just like in the car. He makes me feel strangely at ease, and I just keep feeling myself gravitate toward him.

He seems… genuinely *happy*, even more so since he went surfing. I so rarely have ever seen that kind of joy in a man's face. Though, in fairness, he hasn't been planting corn since dawn or sanding down the wood on a rocking chair. He's probably never raised a barn in his whole life.

Ansel takes a few minutes to teach me how to hold my breath beneath the glassy surface, how to blow bubbles, and how to open my eyes underwater. It stings a little, but when I do it, I've never heard or seen anything quite so serene in my life.

Eventually, he asks if I am comfortable trying to float. I nod excitedly.

He shows me how to do it, placing his hands gently beneath my back and my legs, telling me to relax my body and breathe slow and deep. My ears dip below the surface, and I feel like I am in a womb, safe and quiet. I feel my body unwind and slacken one muscle group at a time, feel his hands slip away, feel myself...

Floating!

I take a deep breath and feel my limbs bloom slowly outward like a rose. My eyes peel open, and I see him in my periphery, nowhere near me, wading backward toward the deep end with a smile on his face.

I lie there for a moment, staring up at the colorful morning sky and the loose row of willow trees lining the property. I see huge white-and-gray seagulls cruise across the sky and listen to my heartbeat in my ears.

I sense his approach and hear him say, "Now, stand up."

I follow the order, putting my foot down on the bottom in a surprising display of grace, followed by the second. Before I know it, I am standing again, this time with a big, dumb grin on my face. Warm water dribbles out of my ears, and I am elated.

He chuckles. "You did it!" He holds his hand up for a high-five, and I timidly smack it.

He checks his watch, and I see a glimpse of the cluttered display. "Boo. That's all the time I've got, but if you want another lesson, meet me here again in the morning. If you decide you want to get in the pool while I'm gone, just be careful and try to stay on this shallow end right here. I would never forgive myself if I found you out here, drowned."

"I promise. Shallow end only."

"And nothing past your calves out there in the Sound just yet, okay? There's a lot I still gotta teach you about the ocean. She's a beast. But she's a *fun* beast."

I follow him out of the pool, unable to stop staring at the way the wicking water makes his muscles glisten.

As he towels off, he nods back in the direction of the massive house. "C'mon. I gotta shower and get ready for work while you get things ready in the kitchen. I *believe* someone promised me some sort of potato pancakes for breakfast."

24

Ansel

Rinsing off the lather of spiced body wash, I'm disturbed by the presence of the goddamn *semi* between my legs. It pisses me off knowing what, or rather *who* brought it on:

Little-miss *Sarah, Plain and Tall* in the kitchen downstairs...

Making me potato pancakes, *whatever those are*, with fucking *applesauce*.

Being with her in that pool, feeling the warmth of her body in my hands, so small and delicate, so vulnerable and trusting... it stirred something in me. Something primal that wants to both *protect her* and *sully her* in the same breath.

I'm a fucking *creep*.

The girl is barely-fucking-legal, *and* now she's the help.

She came here to cook, not be fucking ogled by some thirty-one-year-old pervert.

I towel myself off and try to focus my mind on the meetings that I have today instead of how damn good her body looked in that painted-on rash guard or how those cold little nipples looked like they were trying to cut their way out of the spandex...

I dress and make my way downstairs, buttoning the sleeves of my 'monkey suit'-- *as my Dad always used to call it*. It's a tailored Zegna cashmere suit with flat-front pants, black with a hint of topaz sheen to it in certain lights. I always feel terribly overdressed in it, opting for casual board shorts and half-buttoned shirts with rolled sleeves every chance I get. My feet feel tortured when they aren't in sandals.

The aroma of breakfast has already surpassed my expectations. It smells fucking delicious, despite how horrible the combination of proposed foods sounds when spoken aloud.

Velda smiles at me over her shoulder, comfortable in her element. She looks good in the kitchen. And not just in the sexist *'that's where a woman belongs'* kinda way. But more like… *she* belongs. She looks confident, and at ease among the appliances, her grin reflected in marble surfaces and stainless steel as she plates the food.

Her braid is damp, and there isn't a single ounce of makeup on her face. She doesn't need any. She has a stunning, natural beauty, blessed with a pleasing bone structure that gives her a natural-yet-regal beauty.

I snicker when I realize she is wearing an apron, a joke gift from my distant aunt many moons ago. All she knew about me is that I like to surf, so the apron says, "I'm late for a board meeting," and features a silhouette of a man walking with a longboard.

I take a seat at the kitchen island and sweep my hands softly along the marbled top. Velda walks over with my plated breakfast, garnished and looking like something straight off the menu of a gourmet brunch spot.

"Potato pancakes and applesauce. This is one of my absolute favorite meals to make back home."

I smile. As she sets down a fork and butter knife on a napkin for me, I get a momentary glimpse of her husband's future: a smiling wife showcasing her love and affection through the language she speaks best: *food*.

I want to make a joke about the way to a man's heart being through his stomach, and then I realize how fucking weird it might sound to someone who hasn't heard the phrase before.

I slice off a bite of the pancakes, chew, and then moan. Just like her soup, it's *incredible*. Simple, yet hearty, somewhat like hash browns but more filling and tastier.

"Try some with the applesauce. I promise… it's good." She watches me with the steady eyes of a hawk.

I do, and she's right. It *is* surprisingly delicious.

"Holy *shit*," I groan pleasurably with a mouthful of food.

"What you were doing in the ocean this morning looked fun. You looked so happy."

I nod and shovel down the food in bigger bites, unable to recall the last time I had a breakfast *this* fucking good. I swallow hard, then speak. "I was surfing."

"How long have you been doing that?"

"Since I was about four or five. My Dad taught me right out there near those rocks, just a quarter mile down that beach. I really loved it. He and I would go out in the early mornings or on weekends all the time. He was really good, my Dad. Took second and third in a few competitions. Never could quite get the gold, but he had a lot of fun with it. It's easy to fall in love with being out there."

"I would love to learn if you ever wanted to teach me."

I look up from my nearly-empty plate to see her smile. It is optimistic and bashful at the same time.

"Once you learn how to swim, I'd love to teach you. I could start you out on one of our longboards, and if you liked it, I could make you somethin' custom."

"Oh, I couldn't... I don't think I would know what to do with it when I go back home."

When she mentions her eventual return to Pennsylvania, my stomach twists a little. Even though she's only been here a day and a half, the thought of her leaving kind of bums me out. It's been kind of... *exciting* getting to know her. Learning about her community's customs. Introducing her to new things at every turn.

"I could keep it for you." I shrug, feeling a little hopeful. "You know, for when you come back to Rhode Island for a visit."

Her smile falls the instant I say it, and her almost-sapphire irises settle on the countertop.

"I probably won't be able to visit once I go back. Once I am baptized, there will be no time. I will be too busy with marriage and children."

I see a moment of despair wrack her features. It is a private expression meant only for her, but I see it anyway.

I don't know what to say to that. Chores and children? She's eighteen. She's got a couple of decades or so to do all of that. I want to ask her follow-up questions about that, but it seems rude to pry. Instead, I change the subject as I finish the last of my food.

"So I was thinking…"

"Would you like some more?" She points to the stove where two more pancakes sit in waiting next to a bottle of oil, boasting about how heart-healthy it is and touting that it has zero trans fats.

"Oh no, thank you. It's all yours. I don't usually eat much the first half of the day. It's dinner when I'm usually famished."

"Then I will make you a nice feast tonight. I will make you a family recipe. You will love it."

"I'm sure I will." I dab the corners of my lips with the napkin and look at her as I toss it down. "So I was curious… the last few nights I was doing a little googling on my phone about your… er… *community*. And I saw something about how

147

the Amish only go to school until the eighth grade."

"Yes, this is true," she says, placing the remaining breakfast in a Tupperware and the applesauce in a foil-covered bowl. "Some Amish don't even go *that* long. Especially the girls. I had to beg my *Fater* to stay to the end. I loved school."

"Really?"

She nods firmly. "Even though there were lots of little children there, I still loved learning and reading. I would have stayed *longer* if they would've let me."

"Well, that's actually what I wanted to talk to you about. We, out here, usually go another four years, and then some people choose to go to college or grad school, and others go to a trade school."

"Oh, that must be so nice." She starts wiping down the tiles around the stove, scrubbing everything spotless.

"I was thinking, Velda... if you *wanted*, I could get you a tutor so that you could get your GED. You could basically pick up where you left off after the eighth grade. If you had one of those, you could do a lot of things, including audit some college courses if you wanted."

She laughs, but there is despair in it like it's preposterous.

"Why would I do such a thing? It will not help me back on the farm in Pennsylvania."

Fuck, she's got me there.

"Velda, the world is your oyster. You're young, and you have your entire life ahead of you. You aren't predestined for any one fate, even though it might feel like it."

"Ansel," she says shyly, "my life in Berks is all I have ever known."

"I know. And I'm not trying to disparage that. There's nothing wrong with the Amish way of life. If that's the life you *want*, then great. But when I was there, it really didn't seem like it. It seems like… you want more."

I can tell the words strike her hard, like I've hit the nail on the head. I continue.

"You are your own woman. And while you are here, the sky's the limit for you."

I set my empty plate on the counter next to her and crane my neck to get her to look at me. I want her to see that I'm not trying to shit on Amish life. I'm trying to show her that there is more in the world for her to see, more for her to do, before she settles down and has a litter of kids with some junior-high-educated schmuck she hates, having to hide torn paperbacks and cover her body like a woman in the Middle East.

"Velda, you can *be* anything. You don't *have* to be anything. But you *can be* if you *want* to, is all I'm saying. You have the opportunity to do whatever you want in this world, and as long as you are under this roof, I will bankroll any kinda education you *want*. I don't care if it's a fucking *watercolor* course at the learning annex or Spanish or typing."

She is considering it, but there seems to be a gravity to her face, to the heaviness of my proposition.

"I know you said you could only stay a while, but if you *did* get a GED and you wanted to stick around through the fall semester, there's a great university just up the coast and an art school that's just a couple minutes' drive from here."

She only stares at me, eyes glassy and blue.

"And, even if you got a GED and you decided you want to go back and settle down and have a family and work at your family's vegetable stand or whatever, I would be one hundred percent fine with that, too. I still wouldn't think of it as any kind of waste."

She nods solemnly, carrying a boulder on her shoulders as she puts some seasonings back in a spice rack inside one of the cabinets.

I check my suit for errant crumbs. "...And, Velda, your family wouldn't ever have to *know*."

"Thank you for the offer. May I think about it?"

"Of course!" I put my hands in front of me like a hostage in a stick-up. "I'll get off my soap box now. No pressure. If you are interested, I'll have Tom handle everything. Offer's on the table if you want it." I look at my watch. "I've gotta head out. I'll be home this evening, so plan for dinner around six."

She nods, her smile slowly returning.

"Did Tom set up your phone yesterday?"

"Yes."

150

"Did he program my number into it?"

"Yes, I think so."

"Good. I will text you if I'm running late or anything. Feel free to call Thomas or me if you need anything. I will send him over here today around one o'clock so he can pick up my lunch from you. There's an insulated lunchbox in the back of the cupboard with the Tupperware. You can send it in that."

"Yes, sounds wonderful." Her eyes glint with joy, and she pulls two bags of flour out of a paper grocery bag, setting them on the counter as I breeze toward the front door with my briefcase.

"Oh, and Ansel…?"

"Yes, ma'am?" I stop in the foyer and lean back so she can see me through the archway.

"I was wondering, do you have any stamps?"

I don't bother asking what they're for. I assume they are for correspondence with her family. They can't very well *Skype* each other, *can* they?

"Yep, my office in there." I point down the hall to a room that is half-library-half-office sporting no more than a wall of shelving crammed with books and my Father's old wood-and-glass desk with a brown leather chair in the middle of the room.

"Top left drawer of the desk. There's paper and envelopes in there, too, if you need."

"Thank you." Her smile is as warm as a cinnamon roll straight out of the oven.

"No problem. After lunch, feel free to take the bike in the garage and go explore. Or hit up Helena next door. She'd probably be stoked to take you clothes shopping." I pull my wallet out, peel out a wad of crisp twenties, and set them on the counter near her. "This is your *per diem* for today. I'll give that to you in cash every day, and Tom'll bring you all the paperwork around lunch today so we can get you on payroll and start getting you your paychecks."

She stares at the cash as if I just handed her ten grand.

"*Oh!*" I back up with a grin. "Last thing before I go. A delivery driver in a blue van will come today and drop off a bunch of little packages. Those are for you. Feel free to open them when they get here."

She stares at me, eyes as wide as they can possibly open.

"Consider it a welcome gift. A small token of my appreciation for you coming up to do this. You might be saving my life." I motion to my heart behind the lapel of my suit jacket. "It's the least I can do."

"*Danki!*" Her eyes twinkle as she smiles. "*Sehn dich schpeeder.*"

"What does that mean?" I ask with a grin as I step halfway out the door.

"It means... Thank you! And *See you later.*" Her voice is soft and puts me at ease.

"*Sehn... dich... schpeeder,*" I repeat, like a slow macaw. She waves and giggles, hearing me probably straight-up butcher her native language.

I soak her in for a moment before I leave, trying to burn the sight of her innocent smile into my brain for the half-hour drive into Newport.

25

Velda

I spend the morning rolling dough and making thin egg noodles by hand and boiling them for Ansel's lunch. I make beef stroganoff from scratch, careful to avoid salt as Ansel requested, replacing it instead with other herbs to give it flavor. I dish it into two Tupperwares and snap the lids on tight, placing some fresh garlic bread into a third once they have had a little time to cool.

The letter I've written to my parents sits folded on the counter, nestled in a plain white envelope with a stamp featuring a honey bee on it. It might as well be ringing an alarm bell in my head, and I feel dread wash over me every time I look at it, which is every ten seconds.

I cannot stand the idea of my parents being fearful that something bad has happened to me. I remember many years ago when I was only nine, one of my friends went missing from her family's field.

They never found her.

Many claimed that she had been taken by an Englisher, a predator with bad intentions. Others said that she ran away and left the community due to the abuse at the hands of her *Fater*, committed on a regular basis.

I knew her *Fater*. We *all* did, as he was heavily involved in our church. I had seen the way he looked at her. Not like a *Fater* should at all. I remember how he talked lowly into her ear, *touched* her...

I *know* she ran away.

Still, I need *Mamm* and *Fater* to understand that this is what this time to run around is *for* and that even though my siblings never did anything *remotely* like this, I am not *them*. I need them to understand that my being here doesn't mean that I love them any less.

I search the front of the house, roaming foolishly along the wrap-around patio, looking for a mailbox. At my home, the box was always next to the front door, connected to the house. But I can't seem to find Ansel's. I think about sending him a text to ask, just to try it out, but I feel intimidated by the phone, and I'm too nervous to bother him for something so trivial while he is at work.

It occurs to me that one of our Englisher neighbors back home had a dome-shaped mailbox with a little red flag on it out by the roadside at the end of her street. I decide it's worth a shot to venture out to see if that is the case here.

I stroll through the thick grass, shorn short like a lamb. I try to silently name the flowers planted along the path, but I can only recognize a few. The others are foreign to me. I make a note to try to use my phone soon to look up their names. If any are edible, like the nasturtiums, zucchini flowers, or cabbage... I can use them in my meals.

At the end of the path, much to my relief, there is a mailbox near the rock wall at the entrance to the property, and I feel a slight sense of relief when I close my letter inside, thankful that I no longer have to look at it or think about it again.

"Hey." I hear a voice to my right, hollering through the line of willow trees.

I turn and see her, a blonde girl wearing next-to-nothing in a chair. She is sprawled out fully with her arms behind her head, black sunglasses engulfing her face. On her chest are just two triangular pieces of fabric connected in the middle by a string and tied behind her neck, similar to the suit Ansel first offered me this morning.

Her underwear has ties, too, and is an identical match to the top. I look away, feeling a brief sense of shame on her behalf. She is nearly nude and on full display where anyone driving on the tree-lined road could see her.

"'Sup?" She nods.

I wave, feeling myself start to blush for her.

"You Ansel's niece or something?"

I shake my head.

"Huh. I thought Wolf was into cougars." She snickers. "Didn't know he liked 'em young, too, or I'da taken a run at him already."

I don't understand what she means. I have only seen a cougar once in my life, and it was stuffed and long-deceased. I don't know how that is relevant here.

"You working, visiting, or movin' in?"

I shrug, unsure how to answer since all three options are applicable. Finally, I settle on, "Ansel just hired me."

She giggles. "Shit, you don't look like any escort I've ever seen."

I don't know what an escort is, and I feel uncomfortable right now seeing so much of her bare skin.

"What is an escort?"

She slowly lifts her back from the chair until she's sitting straight up. "Where are you *from*?"

"Pennsylvania," I say quietly, unsure if she is about to bully me.

"What's your name?" she asks.

"Velda Yoder."

Her tight belly judders with laughter. "What the hell kinda name is Velda Yoder?"

"I..." My cheeks feel like they are on fire. "I am Amish."

"No fuckin' way."

"I was just trying to find the mailbox."

"This all makes a *lot* more sense now. *Nobody* writes fucking letters these days. It's all just texts, dick pics, and emails." She yawns, bored.

I feel frozen in place, excited to see another female, and simultaneously terrified at how foreign she feels even though her face and hair look like anyone I might meet back home.

"Why don't you *dress* all Amish? Like with the big froofy pastel dresses and the little white hat thingy?"

"I…" I don't know what to say. My heart is in my throat.

"Helena." She's too bored to wait for my answer. She waves lazily. "Rubio. Wanna come over?" She waggles a phone that looks almost exactly like mine in the air. "I was just about to make a fuckin' stitch video, but *this*," she motions to me, "seems *way* more interesting."

Before I can decide, my feet shuffle through the grass toward her.

On one hand, I feel totally out of my element and a million miles from home. I remember a long time ago, an Englisher neighbor kid told me a story about a girl who was sucked up in a tornado and woke up in this colorful new world where she made friends with lions and scarecrows and a man whose body was metal.

That is how I feel right now, here in this strange place. It is as if the whole world is vibrant and different, and people could be randomly made of metal. Maybe Helena could be my scarecrow in this new world.

"I need to change. Come on. I'm gettin' scorched." Helena waves for me to approach faster, and I make my way through the dark patches of shade from the row of looming trees overhead toward her.

She leads me across her own lawn, up a sweeping outdoor marbled staircase, unlike anything I've ever seen. She laughs at me, and I realize my mouth is open in an expression of wonderment. Her place is just as big as Ansel's. Together they could house nearly everyone I went to school with comfortably.

"I know, right? It's so grandiose it's fuckin' disgusting. My Dad is never home, and he owns a house so big that it's an eyesore. Meanwhile, homeless veterans are sleepin' in the goddamn street."

My head spins toward her as if it has been slapped that direction. She just took the Lord's name in vain.

"People are drinkin' brown water in Flint, Michigan, and we might as well have *Dasani* comin' out of our bidets." She rolls her eyes and throws open the front door, breezing through the massive checkered-and-marble foyer like she's royalty. "You want anything to drink? We have beer, wine, scotch, Perrier… I make a mean bloody Mary."

"Do you," I pause to keep from stammering from the nervousness raging within me, "have any soda?"

She barks a laugh that echoes wild through the space around us. "Yeah, if that's what you want. What kind?"

I shrug. I don't remember all the options that exist. "Surprise me."

Helena reaches into the refrigerator, and I glimpse her body again, barely covered by a couple of tiny swaths of hot pink spandex and black cord. Though I have never seen so much skin on another woman before, I am surprised and relieved to learn our bodies look a lot alike.

She lobs a red can of soda to me and grabs a beer for herself, cracking open the lid on a screwed-in piece of metal on the counter with a level of skill that says she's done it a hundred times before.

"Come on, my room's upstairs." She races toward another awe-inspiring staircase just beyond the entrance, taking the steps two at a time, galloping toward the top.

I follow closely behind, one slow step at a time, taking it all in. The walls are all adorned with black-and-white photos like those in Ansel's living room. Floating high above everything dangles a gold chandelier with what must be thousands of tiny, shining crystals hanging from it like raindrops off a tree.

Helena's door is taller than any I have ever seen before, and her room is an inviting explosion of pink in every shade.

"Your crown braid is tight, girl. Can you teach me how to do that?" She tucks a strand of fallen blonde hair behind my ear, and I suddenly remember that it is not hidden by my *kapp*.

"Sure," I say. I take a long sip of my soda, and in an instant, my mouth is alive with the carbonation and sugar. I hold up my can. "Thank you for the drink."

"No prob." She flops onto her side on the bubblegum-colored bed next to me, looking at me like a toy she's not sure she likes playing with yet.

My eyes roam around the room, and I feel Helena watching me, imagining what I might do next.

"So what do you do for fun where you're from?" Her voice isn't enough to draw my eyes from her bookshelf, one with at least two dozen paperbacks, one of which I also have. I am almost giddy at the revelation that we have something in common already.

"I like to sew."

"Did you make this?" She motions to my salmon-colored T-shirt and rose-patterned pants.

"Oh, no. Ansel's assistant bought this for me yesterday. Do... do you like it?"

I don't know why I feel the need for her approval at this moment, but I desperately do.

She giggles. "No. If I'm being honest, that's something my grandma would wear to bingo. Although the color looks nice on you." She looks me over like I'm a horse she's deciding to purchase. "What are you doing tomorrow? I am volunteering in the morning, but for the rest of the day, I don't have any classes. We should go shopping and get you some new duds, show you around the area a bit."

I think for a moment. "I'd like that."

"Great!" She looks down at my shoes and tries to hide her distaste for them. "First stop, new footwear."

I slide my feet beneath her bed, embarrassed.

"We can get you some sexy little heels. Some makeup... you'd be a catch."

"I have never worn makeup before."

"Oh, fuck yeah, we can do a makeover!" She acts like I just gave her an exciting gift. "And we will get you some stuff that shows off your figure a little more. I like showing a little cleavage, even though I don't have much."

She cups her breasts and hoists them up and together in one fluid motion, changing the entire landscape of her torso into something completely different. "What are you, a B-cup? I'm flat as a fuckin' board. I'm gettin' a boob job next year for my birthday, though. I'm not going like... *comical*. Probably like a full B, like you, or a C."

"What's a *boob job*?"

I have never heard of this line of work before.

She giggles like a chipmunk. "It's where they cut you open and stuff in these bags of silicone and sew you back up so you have big tits." She stands and marvels at me. "Wow, you really *are* Amish, aren't you?"

I nod and blush, feeling about an inch tall in her confident presence.

"Yours are cute. Put you in a push-up bra, and I'll bet those puppies would *pop*."

"I've never had a bra before."

Her jaw drops. "No way! Like, not even a training bra? Or a sports bra?"

I shake my head and watch as she shuffles over to a little box on her dresser. She opens it, stuffs a roll of something that looks like paper in her lips, and burns the end with a lighter. She inhales, holds it for a long time, and blows it out. It doesn't smell like any tobacco I have ever smelled before.

"I don't know about Pennsylvania, but it's legal here, and it has been for a *while*." She takes another drag and then lets it out with a heavy cough. "Oh, fuck. That's gonna hit hard." She meanders toward me. "You smoke?"

I shake my head. "What is it?"

"It's a joint."

"What's a *joint*?"

"Wow. You're really quizzin' me on some basics here." She chuckles again. "It's like… the dried-out flower of a marijuana plant. Some people call it weed. You wanna try it? It's an indica. Nice and mellow."

I'm scared to try it, but at this moment, I also remember that I am in Rhode Island, hundreds of miles from my home, on a mission to see what this world holds.

After a few seconds of silence, I nod almost imperceptibly.

"Atta girl." She grins. "Maybe you're cool after all." She hands it over and takes a seat on the bed next to me. "Start small. Just do one puff and hold it. If you decide you like it, you know where to find me. I've always got, like, a fuckin' variety."

Nervous, I place it between my lips and draw a deep breath in. The end burns red-orange, and it tastes awful on my tongue. I can only hold it for a moment before I start coughing, hacking like I'm about to die.

She giggles again and takes it from me, drawing in another breath of it in before snuffing the joint out in a crystal tray. "Fuck, you're about to be high as a kite, girl. Just let it relax you."

I finally manage to stop coughing and chug some of my soda. The smoke has made the flavor of it change and it is overriding the sugar completely.

"So. Are you and Ansel fucking?"

"What?" I cough again, feeling the burn in my chest.

"Oh, girl, I ain't judging. He's hot as *hell*. If I knew he was into younger chicks, I'd have already been knocking on that door."

I don't know what to say to that. "No, it's nothing like that. I came here to cook for him."

"*Oooookay*," Helena says it like she thinks it is weird and leaps off the bed. "I'm gonna change. You're cool with that, right?"

I nod and swallow hard, my throat feeling a little raw from the fit.

"You're not, like, lesbian or anything, are you?"

"What?" I scrunch my brows.

"Like, I don't care if you are; I just don't swing that way, and I don't wanna, like, lead you on or something if you are."

"No, I'm not."

As soon as the words come out of my mouth, she unties her top and drops it to the ground, standing before me in nothing more than her stringy bottoms. My eyes dart violently in every direction but hers.

Out of my periphery, I see her putting on a black bra and yanking her breasts up into it until they are shaped exactly how she wants them. She turns to me.

"See, you need one of these bad boys." She motions to the bra. "Shit hikes my mosquito bites to the moon. I look like I actually have cleavage."

She isn't wrong. Her breasts do miraculously look much larger in what she is wearing. She reaches into a drawer and tosses one to me. I catch it.

"You look like you're close enough to my size. It might be a little tight, but it's worth a shot. This one is a little big on me. Gives me a gap. Try it out later."

"Thank... you." I feel strange. Thoughts swirl in my head, and my heart pounds a little faster at the act of kindness. I have only known Helena for a few minutes, and she's already been kinder and more generous than any of the girls I went to school with.

"So… you like to sew. What else do you do for fun?" She stares at herself in the mirror some more, examining her body from various angles.

"I…" I feel a little lightheaded. "I cook. I clean—"

"Sewing, cooking, cleaning… girl, here those are called *chores*." She laughs. "Most people consider that stuff, like, *work*. What do you do for *fuuuuun*?" She draws out the last word, talking to me like I'm a young child, even though she's clearly roughly my own age.

"I… *read*."

"Oh, yeah? Okay, that's better. I can work with that." She has changed into underwear now that is nothing but a string in the back and shows even more of her butt than what she was wearing moments before. "What do you read?"

"I read… anything I can get my hands on, really. But I really like to read romance books."

"No. Fuckin'. *Way*." Helena gallops toward me. She reminds me of my neighbor's horse as she kneels on the bed beside me. "Sweet or spicy? And, yes, there *IS* a wrong answer."

I think she might be making fun of me.

"I don't know what that means. They are books. They don't taste—"

"*No*," she groans, "like, do you like your romance all chaste and Hallmark-y where the most they do is, like, *kiss*? Or do you like 'em with some raunchy *sex*?" She grins fiendishly at the last word. My face flashes with heat like I'm

166

too close to a campfire, and my eyes dart away quickly.

"Yesssssssss. Okay. So you *do* like 'em sexy."

I nod, mortified.

"Dude, why are you acting all *embarrassed*? Sex is fuckin' awesome." She bounces up to the edge of the bed by me. I don't say a word.

"Oh my God." She gasps and clasps her hands over her open mouth for a moment before lowering it in revelation. "You're a *virgin*, aren't you?"

"*What*?" I wring my hands, feeling anxiety from this line of questioning.

How could she tell just by looking at me?

"Oh my God, a real-life *virgin*. At your age, that's impressive. What are you? Nineteen? Twenty?"

"Eighteen."

"Okay, I guess it's not *that* crazy then. And we aren't that far off. I'm nineteen. Twenty in December." She snickers. "So. Million-dollar question... you saving yourself for marriage, then?"

"No," I say meekly. I know my family would be appalled at my answer.

"Ohhhhh, really?" She looks me up and down. "*Interesting*. Well, if its a matter of just finding an opportunity, I can hook you up, girl. I probably got ten dudes in my phone that'd be more than happy to punch your V-card." She snickers again. "Shit, probably a couple girls, too, now that I think about it."

167

I could not blush any harder than I am now. "No, thank you."

"Suit yourself." She shrugs.

"Are... *you*... one?"

"What? A virgin?"

I nod.

"Oh, *hell* no." She laughs. "You kiddin' me? I lost that shit back in junior *high*. To a little weasel named Matt Ringhouse. Stupid fuckin' bowl-cut hair-do. Braces. Dick so little the condom kept fallin' off. Oh, that poor boy couldn't find a clit if I drew him a *map*. The next guy, though, *Brad*... mmmmmmmm. Now, *he* knew what he was doin'."

"You have had sex with more than one man?"

Helena laughs so hard she doubles over. "Wow, you're adorable. You're like one of those movies where people unfreeze someone from a block of ice and introduce 'em to the modern world. I'mma start calling you my *Encino Woman*."

I stare at her blankly.

"Yes, I have been with more than one man." She walks over to her bookcase and scans through the titles. "You're not gonna start *slut shaming* me, are you?"

I shake my head. "No. Not at all."

I do feel a little shame for her. But... she also feels like she could be a friend, and that is something I desperately crave, being this far from everything I have known.

"Good. I thought you were gonna go all goody-two-shoes on me. I was gonna tell you to take the Coke and get lost."

I feel my shoulders close in on themselves, my body folding thin enough to disappear.

"Have you ever done other stuff?" she asks, still looking at her books.

"Like... what?"

She waves a pink paperback at me. "You know. Fingering, dry-humping, making out, blowies... any of the other bases."

Cheeks red, I shake my head.

"Oh wow. Pure as the driven snow." She makes a sharp *tsk* sound and turns back to her books. "Part of me envies you. You probably dodged a lotta *turds*. And I guess you still have the chance to make your first time with someone, you know, special."

When she says it, my mind flashes to *Ansel*. I think about the way he looked at me in the *Waffle Hut* with his shirt unbuttoned, tan arms covered in ink beneath his rolled silk sleeves, his hair a mane of perfect waves. I think about the sincerity in his tone and the look of curiosity in his eyes...

Ever since, I have fantasized that he would be the first man I would ever experience that level of intimacy with.

I feel the air leave my lungs, and a faint wave of intoxication blows through my head. I think whatever I inhaled is playing with my mind. Like I am in the pool again, floating on the water's surface.

"Okay," she holds up a book, "You read this series yet by Score?"

I shake my head. I've never seen the book in her hand before.

"Wild plot. Maybe a little too wild at times, but it's a lot of fun. You might dig it. Got some good spice in it toward the end." She holds up another. "Oh, better yet... what about this? Huang's *Deadly Sin* series. Read it yet?"

Again, I shake my head.

A smile creeps up her face. She hands me the book. "Oh, damn, it's *soooo* good. Here, give this one a shot. It's *Wrath*. When you're done, if you like it, I'll loan you the others. If not, I'll give you Score's."

She stuffs the other book back onto her shelf and I clutch the one she loaned me against the bra in my hands like they're both the greatest gifts I have ever received.

"Thank you." I don't know what else to say. Nothing else feels good enough for how nice she is being.

"All good. When you're done, we can talk about it. What we liked, what we didn't. We'll start our own little beachy book club."

Helena yanks the book back out of my grasp, walks it over to her desk, and writes something inside on the first page. She hands it back. "There. My number's inside in case you wanna shoot me a text when you're ready tomorrow. Or you can just come over."

I smile down at the numbers. Even though I don't really know how to text yet, I feel connected to her.

Between Ansel and her, I start to wonder if everyone here in Rhode Island is this generous and outgoing.

"So, what do you have planned for the rest of your day?"

"Just settling in, I think. This has all been... a lot. Two days ago, I was harvesting vegetables and cleaning up from my sister's wedding. Now I'm many states away with all of... this." I hoist up my book and bra.

Suddenly, I feel extremely giddy and can't stop myself from giggling.

"What's so funny?" Helena starts laughing, too, even though she has no idea what I find humorous.

"I got my first swimming lesson this morning. Me!"

She bursts into full-blown laughter, and it makes me laugh harder. What I said wasn't exactly funny, but I can't seem to stop laughing.

"I had better get back. Ansel's assistant will be coming over soon to pick up his lunch." I shift the items in my grasp to shake her hand. "Thank you... for *everything*."

She scoffs and wraps her arms around me in a big hug, nearly spilling what remains of my soda and smooshing the book and garment into my chest. "Welcome to the neighborhood, Encino Woman."

She releases me, hurdles herself back onto her bed, flops back on her comforter, and cups both of her hands together in the air in the shape of a heart.

26

Ansel

"Okay, what have we got?" I settle into a high-backed rolling chair and slide toward the massive conference room table. The smell already has my mouth watering.

"She said it is beef stroganoff," Tom says as he enters with a container on a tray. He sets it carefully in front of me. Steam curls up toward my face. The smell of the fresh gravy makes me moan like I'm getting a blowjob.

"She said she 'hopes it is okay, but she made enough for me, too.'"

"Sure! Great. Sit. I gotta multitask. I have a Zoom call with Clarence in a bit," I say, lunging for a fork and napkin. "Sarah, Plain and Tall's done it again."

"It smells so good. My stomach was growling the whole way over," Tom forks some broad, twisted noodles and blows on it.

I take a bite, and my mouth feels *alive*. It tastes even more divine than it *smells*. "Oh, fuck." I point at it with my utensil. "That's fucking *good*."

Tom eats his forkful and groans, bobbing his head in agreement. "Wow... now it all makes more sense."

"What do you mean?" I shovel another bite in my mouth and resist the urge to pound my fist into the conference table. *It's so damn good!*

"No. Forget I said anything."

"No, I'm curious now."

"It's none of my business, Mr. Wolf."

"Well, you've got my curiosity piqued. You can be real with me right now."

Tom looks around, hesitant. Suddenly, he pops up in his chair, eyes bulging like he just remembered something. "Oh, shoot."

He scurries off and returns, bouncing a foil-wrapped wad from hand to hand like he's playing hot potato with himself.

"Holy Madonna, that's hot. Careful, I just heated these up in the toaster oven."

"What are they?" I sit straight, trying to catch a glimpse, but I can smell it already. It smells incredible.

"She said after she made the noodles, she had time to make you fresh garlic bread. She said she left out most of the salt and went heavier on the garlic because it's good for your heart."

"Oh Christ. Gimme, gimme." I flutter my hand impatiently. Tom forks one onto the lid of my Tupperware.

"Smells so good."

"Yes, it does. Thank God it's a *video* conference and not a meeting," I chuckle and then gnaw into a piece, savoring the garlicky bite. Once I swallow, I repeat my question. "You're not getting out of it that easy. Finish your thought.

What'd you mean when you said, 'Now it makes a lot more sense?'"

His shoulders slump a little when he realizes I'm not letting the subject go.

"Well, please forgive me if I'm way out of line." Tom takes a long sip of seltzer water before continuing. "I just meant that you brought her back when she doesn't have, like, any formal training or, really... *anything*. No car, phone, license, or diploma. You could've hired someone local with a culinary degree for a fraction of the cost and effort."

He pauses for a second, debating whether to continue as he blows on his noodles.

"It just... seemed strange at first, is all. Now, it makes a lot more sense. She's *clearly* good at what she does."

I listen intently, savoring what are *clearly* handmade noodles from scratch. I don't think I've ever even *had* handmade pasta before. Here I was, expecting basic-ass salads and sandwiches and stuff. Velda has already far exceeded my expectations.

Now, I'm curious about what she's making for *dinner*.

"It just seemed like maybe it was a," he tries to choose his next words wisely.

"—Like a *mistress*-type thing?"

Tom nods, apologizing with his eyes. He holds his hands up, fearful. "Not that I would ever judge you for that. That's not my business in the slightest."

175

I shake my head and tap the gnarled remainder of my piece of garlic bread against the plastic. "No. My doc said it's imperative I change the way I've been eating, like... stat." I shrug. "When I was down in Reading, Velda was there working at one of those little farmer's markets. I had a bowl of her soup, and it was fuckin' delicious."

I stuff the rest of the bread in my mouth and chew, talking again as I swallow.

"She's on her Rumspringa or whatever right now, so, to me, it made sense."

"It was stupid of me. I should've known better, anyway." He smiles. "I've only ever seen you pursue... you know... *older* women."

I eat another forkful. "Don't get me wrong, she's pretty and all, but she's way too young. The girl is barely legal."

We eat for a minute in silence, and my words ring back in my head.

Pretty and all.

What an understatement.

Velda is the feminine embodiment of all that is sweet and pure in this world. I don't know why I'm downplaying her looks to Tom. Or maybe I'm doing it for my own benefit, to try to convince myself that she isn't stunning.

As I eat, my mind drifts to how she felt in my arms this morning in the pool. Blue eyes cast skyward. Freckles like a faint constellation of ochre stars across her fair cheeks. Pale, flawless skin bobbing along the surface, warm in my palms despite the cool water lapping around us. I think about her shy smile, and my mind drifts to a few days ago when her eyes glistened in the darkness of the movie theater. I think about how she held my hand in the seat as she sobbed for the characters, breath hitching through the orchestral swells. I drift to the image of her bare breasts, bathed scarlet by my taillights. I feel my dick harden in my boxer briefs, battling against the rigid starch of my slacks as it tries desperately to right itself.

Velda is absolutely off-limits.

She's an employee.

And a fucking eighteen-year-old one, at that.

Fucking her is *never* going to happen, but there is no telling my strained cock that right now.

"Oh, I went up to the D.M.V. this morning." Tom's words cutting through my silent fantasies, startle the absolute fuck out of me. I jolt in my seat. He continues, never noticing. "I got her signed up for driver's ed so she can get her learner's permit. It's a thirty-three-hour course, so if you want, I can do pick-ups and drop-offs for that."

"Yes. Please do."

"They do require a birth certificate to issue one. Velda says she doesn't think one exists for her, but this afternoon, I plan to call around down in Pennsylvania and see if someone can point me to where to get one for her."

"Jesus, I didn't even think about that."

"Yeah, they really do things very differently."

"No shit," I shake my head.

"I also picked up some study materials for the G.E.D. prep course. I picked up a pamphlet from the learning annex and ordered some of the recommended reading for it. Looks like she can take the actual test online when she's ready. I'll ask around and get a tutor hired for her right away."

"Great." I bob my head as I fork up the last of the noodles, surprised as hell that I ate all of it.

"I've scheduled pick-ups and drop-offs twice a week for this week and next to take her to get groceries. I put it on our shared calendar as well in case you need me to run any other errands while I'm out."

Tom thinks of everything.

"Right now, she's set through the end of the week."

"Awesome."

"Have you approved the banner art for the New Smyrna Beach surf competition yet?"

"Yeah, I went with the one of Alex in the maroon board shorts."

"Okay, good. Clarence was asking me to follow up with you."

"Clarence can blow it out his old ass. You're *my* assistant. You don't answer to him."

"I know. It's just... he's relentless."

"I know. Why my Dad ever became friends with him, I will never know. There is nothing redeemable about that impatient fuck."

Tom leans back in his chair and looks at me. "Do you want me to call the *Elation on Sea* and book accommodations for Ms. Yoder? I believe their villas have full kitchenettes there."

I think for a moment. "Yeah, that's a great idea. Or see if we can upgrade to the beach house this time. I think the one they have is two stories if I remember correctly. Oh, and call and inform my pilot that there will be an additional in the jet for that trip and tell him that I'm bringing a couple boards with me and that they better not get dinged up this time."

"Gonna try to catch a few waves?"

"I'm not going down to New Smyrna and *not* surfing. Tom," I poke the back of his hand, "never lose sight of your passions in this world. That's when you stop living and start dying."

Tom nods dutifully. "I'll keep that in mind, sir." A knowing grin morphs his face into something almost ghoulish. "You gonna be meeting up with *Miranda* while you're down there? If so, I can make you a reservation for Fire Rock again if you want."

Oh, Miranda. My Central Florida booty call. Jesus, her name hasn't crossed my mind in months. Hell, not since the last time I was in the Daytona area.

Miranda is a divorcee in her mid-forties with a sex drive that could rival a horny twenty-one-year-old male. The last time we fooled around, the cops were called by the neighbors, and we got a stern warning about violating the local noise ordinance. The police ordered us to keep down the ruckus, and I was sure I was going to wake up to a shit-show of local papers talking about '*TwinFin* surf mogul's scandalous sex romp.'

Shortly after the cops left, Miranda crawled apologetically back to me on the floor with a black rubber ball gag clenched between her teeth, offering it up to me like a forlorn puppy, pendulous breasts swinging, tramp-stamped ass bearing several perfect red outlines of my right hand.

I love to dish out a good spanking or break out the fuzzy cuffs as much as the next guy, but there was something about her being so over-the-top and theatrical that was a little off-putting. Like it was just a stage show with a ton of fanfare. Like being kinky was all she had to offer to keep a man interested instead of being something she really enjoyed.

I chuckle. "We'll see. Don't make any reservations yet. If I see her again, it won't be out in public."

Tom nods, eyes wide, and he smirks. "Okie dokie."

I think about Velda, innocent and sweet, wading in the shallow end of my pool with doe eyes, nipples at attention. I feel my dick stir again. I think about what it must be like to be with someone so innocent. She probably doesn't even know what a ball gag *is*.

Jesus, Ansel. Get a fucking grip.

I tidy up my space, pack the containers back in the insulated tote, and slide it toward Tom.

"This afternoon, I want you to sit in on Larry's meeting with the bank and give me the Cliff's notes when you're done."

"Got it."

I look at my *Panerai* watch, the thirty thousand dollar three-hundred-meter submersible timepiece I bought to celebrate *TwinFin* hitting the ten million mark a few years ago. I bought it because, not only is it beautiful, but it has functions for surfing. It was also the *exact* amount of a full year's salary at my first full-time job out of high school, so I considered the price tag a sign. I know the doctor told me to wear my smartwatch, but today, I needed a little reminder of how far I've come in the past decade.

"I'm gonna run. God forbid I make *Clarence* wait." I say his name as if it is sour milk on my tongue.

Tom rises from his chair and whisks away the trappings of our meal. "Good luck, Mr. Wolf."

***

"Clarence, you ol' hound dog, how are you?" I wince at the fact that I said *hound dog* like I'm some zany asexual neighbor in a '70s comedy. What I really want to say is: *You man-sized ingrown ball hair. You ice cream headache in human form.*

You perpetual pain in my ass...

"Ansel." He nods, and the ugly glare off his bald fucking head nearly blinds me through the

181

screen. His cold, stern voice sends a sensation through me that reminds me of how it feels to step on a burr with a bare foot. "I hear you've been a busy man."

I feel a blast of cold chill me to the core like I just dove headfirst into the Sound in December. I *know* he's referring to Velda, which is none of his fucking business. I don't care who he is. He doesn't have the right to tell me who I can and can't bring on my own personal staff with my own out-of-pocket money.

"The boys down in Reading seemed quite upset when they called the other day. Said that you tried to cancel the contract when you went down there and pull all future production."

My momentary relief that his comment wasn't about the Amish woman in my employ is replaced by a bubbling venom for what I know this chrome-domed prick is about to say.

"They shit the bed, Clarence. They had one job, and they couldn't fucking do that. They aren't the only board manufacturers in the world. Hell, they aren't even the only ones in this neck of the woods."

"I hired them *back*. Told them the order is still on. I negotiated their contract for next year at a reduced rate. Seventy percent of what they originally quoted." He smiles. It's tight and smug, and I feel my blood begin to boil. "A 'thank you' would be nice."

"Thank you? I'm supposed to thank you for undermining me with our manufacturers? Fuck that!"

"Woah, language, Ansel."

"You can't *do* that, Clarence."

"Maybe so. But I already talked it over with Alan, and as C.O.O., *he* can. It's a done deal. Next time, you need to *talk to us* before you do something so rash. Alan, Larry, and I all should have been part of this discussion."

"This isn't a democracy, Clarence. You don't get a vote. This is *my* company. I started *TwinFin*. If I say these motherfuckers are fired, then they're goddamn fired."

Clarence draws in a deep breath, and his shoulders raise like they're stuffed with shoulder pads. He sighs like he's annoyed, talking to a petulant child. "You may have started *TwinFin*, Ansel, but you are not our Lord and Savior here. You need to take a page out of your father's book. See, Hans knew how to *play well with others*."

"*Hans* didn't *build* this company—"

"No, but his *life insurance policy* sure did."

The comment enrages me far more than it should. I can't help but think back to that image ingrained in my skull, the heartbreaking one of my father, lying on the floor of the shower in the fetal position. Naked through the steam.

More still than I've ever seen anything be.

I'm gonna go take a shower...

It's true that the payout from my inheritance was the seed money for *TwinFin*, but Clarence

183

acts like I didn't do a fucking thing beyond putting up the capital.

This geriatric weasel never saw the nights I was up bumbling my way through sewing wetsuit prototypes and the hours spent over cold Cup-o-soups and leftover pizza as I hand-designed the sketches for our first line of boards, found other investors, sought out manufacturers, and put my business plan into action. He never saw how hard it was to fumble my way into filing our company's paperwork or felt the thrill of getting our first retailer to agree to carry our line of board shorts.

He will never know the anger that I felt when my own Mother asked me to give this pathetic old bag of bones a job at the company as a favor to her and my late father. As if Dad *cared* anymore. He was fucking *dead*. And now, Old-Man-Judgement has glommed on and made himself a fixture with Alan and Larry, burrowing down like a damn *tick*.

"Let's get on track, Ansel. Shall we?"

I ball my hand into a fist, thankful that the dickhead's screen only shows halfway down my tie.

"As you know, we have a shareholder meeting in August at the *Bon Temps* conference center. They're expecting your pitch for the new ladies' wear designs."

No shit, Sherlock. I know what the fucking meeting is for. We do this twice a fucking year.

As he yammers on, I fantasize about slapping this douche so hard his dentures go flying.

"...They seem less than impressed with the sales figures from the new Grommet line."

"That's why I fought against it, Clarence. I *told* you guys it wouldn't do well," I growl, wanting to pound a fucking dent into my polished oak desk. "I fucking *said* that parents aren't going to go out and readily buy their kid a twelve-hundred-dollar heated wetsuit. It made no fucking sense to go that far with it. Kids need shorts and sandals and boogie boards. You rejected the majority of my designs and trademark suggestions. I told you that Irving was way off-base with his pitch. If you'll recall, *I* told you that we needed to focus on a *women's* line."

"Of course, hindsight is always twenty-twenty. I refuse to bear the brunt of the responsibility for the Grommet line." He sighs and leans back in his chair.

Thank *God* he isn't in Rhode Island because I would yoke him up by the lapels of his tacky fucking suit and—

"Look, I just wanted to check in and see if you needed to outsource anything for your pitch. I got a contact for a local designer that you might like. Studied at URI, my *Alma Mater*—"

"Clarence! I don't need to work in tandem with anyone. We got to one-point-two billion because *I* had a vision. And I *executed* that vision. I backed myself," I grumble. "You're way out of line on this."

185

"Fine." He huffs and looks down at his desk. "Ansel, I hope you really wow us in New Orleans. That's all I've got to say."

At this moment, I opt to not further inflame or taunt him. He's the type of person to dedicate his entire life to forming a successful *coup* that would force me to step down and do nothing but draw a fat paycheck. Unlike me, he has that kind of downtime.

His eyes meet mine with a cruel, wrinkly gaze.

"I am anxious to see what you come up with. I have to run. I have another call scheduled in a few minutes." He smiles, but it's as fake as his wife's misshapen tits.

I don't say a word. I just wait for him to sign off, feeling pressure tighten in my chest, coiling through my ribs and around my lungs like a boa constrictor. My head pounds.

I close my laptop, stand, and slam my closed fist right into the top of my desk with a force that splits the skin of my knuckles open instantly. Pain radiates through my hand. I growl like a grizzly as I punch the wood again, leaving a second brick-colored stamp of blood on the polish. I hit it a third time, imagining Clarence's withered face in place of the wood, taking the beating.

Hand shaking, I close my eyes and breathe.

This kind of anger isn't good for me.

Behind my eyelids, I see my Dad again, water beading off of his skin, into his open eyes, snaking around his drained-looking lips.

Dead without warning.

Dead without a goodbye.

A relationship tether sliced clean with a sharpened Ginsu. An impossible message to relay to my Mother, who was downstairs watching people duke it out on small claims court as she diced butternut squash for bisque.

Clarence isn't worth me meeting the same fate, I assure myself, trying to calm my nerves. But it's all just words swimming in my head. Things I *ought* to do versus what I *want* to do.

Breathe, Ansel.

Breathe, or it could be you that E.M.T.s are scraping off the wet tile floor and loading into a body bag.

27

Ansel

A rush of exhilaration courses through me as I carve up and down the barrel of the left-breaking wave, fins slicing through with precision. My body is relaxed, and I feel that flood of chemicals hit me like the best drug in the world.

I pivot, careful to avoid a kook charging for the wave directly in my path. I deftly carve up, catch air, and miss clipping the apparent newbie by inches. I regain my composure, relax my body, and let the wave carry me almost the entire way to the shore.

I shake my hair like a shaggy dog, remove my ankle tether, pick up my board, and start down the beach toward the house. I debate kicking sand onto the kook's phone, wallet, and clothes when I pass them, but at the last minute, I decide against it. I had to learn the etiquette once, too. Sometimes, it's hard for me to expect others to not display the same courtesies in the water.

Upon my approach, I see Velda there, smiling and lovely, waving like a shy child with something in her other hand.

"I made you a smoothie." Velda presents me a Waterford crystal glass of something the color of ice-blended sangria. Her hair is out of the crown braid now, brushed and straight, sporting just about as many individual shades as the sand beneath us. Her tresses flutter in the wind. I've never seen her with it down until now.

She looks older, maybe even a touch more mature. Like someone you'd see on the street and think that she'd had a normal American upbringing.

"Aw, thank you." I'm breathing hard, saltwater dripping down my mess of hair like drizzling rain. I unzip my wetsuit, fold the top half down, and let it hang at my waist.

Velda's eyes paint themselves up and down my chest in long strokes and then dart away, cheeks reddening once she realizes I caught her doing it. It's cute.

I keep forgetting that this much exposed skin has got to be a shock for someone who grew up in a chaste place where dresses practically touch the floor.

"Thank you. It's very... *red*. What is it?"

"Beet, pomegranate, and strawberry." She smiles.

I resist the urge to wince. The thought of drinking *beet* juice is unappealing to me, but I feel an obligation to at least give it a try. I'm certain it'll taste pickled.

"It is good, I promise. Beets are very good for the heart. I have been learning about ant-i-ox-i-dants." She says the last word awkwardly like it is the first time her lips have ever had to form its syllables.

"Yeah?"

She nods. "On the phone. Thomas showed me how to ask someone named Siri questions."

"That's great!" I smile, still stalling on taking a sip. "Just... word of advice, not everything on the internet is true."

...Like whoever said putting beets in a drink was a good idea.

She frowns, and it's adorable. "Is there a way to know what is true or not?"

"Kinda. Yeah... well, no. Story for another time." I force a smile at the drink she's prepared and raise it to cheers. "*Prost!*"

I take a solid sip and...

I am once again *pleasantly* surprised.

Not only does it not taste like I remember beets as a kid, but the combination of flavors weirdly *works*. It's sweet, but not overly so, and earthy.

Had I not known what was in it and ordered it at a smoothie shop, I would buy it again *in a heartbeat*.

I moan into the glass and chug as much as I can until I'm teetering on brain freeze. I lick it off my top lip, tasting the salty brine of the ocean mixing with the juice.

"That's *delicious*."

Hell, maybe being on this healthy diet will be a lot less terrible than I thought.

I toss my board down in the sand and hand her my glass. "Hold this, please?"

She nods, and I see her eyes drift down my damp chest again. I cross my ankles and spin myself until my butt is planted in the low dunes beside the board. I raise my hand for the glass, and she hands it over, sweeping her bare legs in a similar-but-awkward fashion until her round, little ass is parked in the sand next to me.

I down another third of the drink, loving the juxtaposition of the warmth of the setting sun and the icy beverage wrestling for dominance throughout my stomach.

Finally, I break the tranquil silence with a declaration.

"I'm going down to New Smyrna this weekend. My company, *TwinFin,* hosts several surf competitions a year. We give out prizes to the winners. It's all televised. The media comes out. Everyone takes photos and videos. They're a lot of fun."

I fiddle with the beveled edges of my crystal glass.

"The beach house Tom booked is huge. Two stories. Full kitchen on the bottom level with two ovens. I know you just got here, but... you feeling down for another little travel adventure?"

She hugs her bent knees and nods with a smile. "Where is New Smyrna?"

"Middle of Florida, on the Eastern coast. Near Daytona. They have a lot of motorcycle fests and stuff around there, too, but it's one of the best surf breaks in America."

She laughs. "*Motorcycles?*"

"Yeah." I chuckle. "Ever seen one?"

She nods. "A few times. From the buggy. They are loud."

"Yeah, they are. We can get you a leather jacket while we're there if you want. You know, *when in Rome…*"

"When in Rome?"

"Yeah, it's… a saying. When in Rome, do as the Romans do. It just means that it's okay to try to fit in and indulge in local customs when you are someplace new."

I can see her computing my words as if the saying actually resonates with her.

"I like that. *When in Rome.*"

"It'll be a fun trip. You'll get to go on the jet again."

"I love the jet." She beams her smile out at the water. "It is so amazing to wake up in one state and to fall asleep in another. I have a hard time wrapping my head around this." She clutches her head like she has a migraine.

It is only *then* that I realize her shirt sports a very familiar pattern, one I special-ordered a bolt of two weeks ago.

What are the chances?

It has long sleeves and seems to be fastened tightly to her on the side. I see the red bead of a quilting pin in the middle of the fern print.

192

"I like your shirt." I chug the last of my smoothie, keeping my eyes glued to her.

"I..." She can barely look at me. "I made it. You said that I could use the machine."

"Wait, you *made* that? Today?"

I feel shocked. She's been in town for so little time, and now she's already teaching herself how to use the sewing machine and making clothes with it.

"Yes. Is... that okay? It isn't perfect. One of the sleeves is a little longer than the other. But... I found a few patterns in a box, and I saw this fabric. It was not like anything I had ever seen at home."

I don't say anything. I'm still taking it all in.

"Are you... *mad*?"

I smile. She is so sweet. So meek. So mild. So considerate.

"No. God, no, Velda. I'm definitely not mad. If anything, I am extremely impressed." I point to her side. "You're gonna poke yourself though. You left a pin in it."

She chuckles. "Oh... back home, that is how we fasten our clothes. We don't use buttons."

"Huh. Seems... *painful*." I scratch at the bevels on the glass again, and she reaches out and takes my palm in her hand, suddenly alarmed.

"You're hurt!"

Her fingers are feather-soft as they manipulate my palm for a better view of my scabbed knuckles, now looking gnarly and pruned from the water. As her hands slip across mine, for a moment, I can't help but imagine how they would feel wrapped gently around my cock.

I twist my head and crack my neck to try to segue myself out of the momentary fantasy. "It's nothing."

"What happened?" Her eyes are huge with alarm and blue as gemstones.

"Well, Velda, when you play stupid games, you win stupid prizes."

I chuckle and see that my self-deprecating joke has gone right over her beautiful little head.

"I got mad. Punched something. It was dumb. I shouldn't have let myself get that worked up."

I'm sure she thinks I'm one of *those guys* now. Those 'Kyles' who love to display their fragile egos and toxic masculinity through cratered drywall and misdemeanors.

But just then, she does the damnedest thing.

She leans down and places a soft kiss near my marred joints, pats the back of my hand, and says, "All better."

I snicker and slowly pull my hand away, trying to make my dick forget about the single second of motion where she leaned in like she was about to give me a hummer and to try to overlook the saccharine-sweet display of affection.

"I should get back inside," she says softly, pulling the sandy glass from my hand, blissfully unaware that the discontinued four-glass set it belongs to cost me a little over a grand.

"Supper will be ready in one hour. Roasted chicken with seasoned vegetables and fresh bread."

I nod, mouth watering at the mental image of it. I watch the cider-colored sheen of the setting sun bathe her sandy ass as she leaves and return my gaze to the churn and froth of the Block Island Sound before me.

The sets are strong, and if I can get back out there and catch one or two more waves, I can let the water wash away the last of my Zoom with Clarence and the wholly inconvenient attraction I'm starting to feel toward the barely-legal Amish girl who just had her warm little mouth on me.

God dammit.

What have I done?

28

Velda

"Alright, you settled in? You good?" Ansel leans into the aisle of the jet and stares at me with those eyes of his, a dizzying mix of colors I get hopelessly lost in.

I nod, a buzzing blend of nervous and excited being in the jet again. I am anxious to see a new state, one I have only ever read about in books.

"You want a soda or anything?" He points to the curtain that the man in the strange tie passed through moments before.

"Yes, please," I say, and then crack open one of my brand new books to my bookmark, the receipt from the *Waffle Hut* with Ansel's phone number on it. I have already read and returned the one that Helena gave me. Now, I'm starting one of the ones Ansel bought me.

I know it seems weird, but I lift the book to my nose and inhale deeply. It smells so good.

Ansel flags down the man, and he returns quickly with a can of something blue. I thank him, but I am still uncomfortable being waited on, especially by a man. At home, it is *our* duty to wait on them. Fetching them things, bearing their children, scrubbing their homes, cooking the food they have grown, sewing their clothes...

It is what the Bible wants us to do. After all, woman would not exist without man.

Only men have the wisdom to read God's word to us, to tell us what it means, and to interpret his message for us. The roles being reversed like this, having a man serve me in such a way, makes me feel strange and guilty. Like I don't deserve it.

The flight is only a few hours and in that time, my book made me blush several times at the graphic acts described on some of the pages. Reading some of the scenes made a dull ache swell between my thighs, growing to a painful level until I found myself squirming in my seat.

I have never had a book make me feel this way before.

Though it is sinful, my mind drifts to Ansel, and I find myself curious, wondering if he ever does these things. And if he would ever do them with someone like *me*.

I know it would enrage my *Mamm* and *Fater* to know that I am having such immoral and impious thoughts about an Englisher, but there is so much that I want to experience before I go back. Part of me wishes that I could act out these abominable acts with his body. Part of me wishes he would defile my body the same way as the man in the book.

If wanting to do these things with him is truly a sin, I am doomed to smolder in the ashes of Hell for eternity.

I close my book and sit for a moment, clutching the armrests like they are going to fly away, staring forward at the blank wall, sucking in slow breaths.

The pangs of guilt in my impure heart clang in time with the slow pulses of my thighs, squeezing and releasing. I revel in the feel of friction from the seam in my shorts, feeling the maddeningly delightful sensations from it against my most intimate parts.

I have never touched myself there except to wash, but the thought of his large hands on me right now is enough to nearly rip me out of my leather seat.

"Velda?" Ansel's voice snaps me out of my shameful fantasy and back into reality like the slingshot Atlee used to hunt squirrels with as a kid.

"You okay? Are you feeling motion sick? You're all pale and dewy. You need to throw up?"

I panic, my heart racing, and then I nod. Ansel calls the man in the tie back over and asks for motion sickness medication.

"No," I interrupt them, mortified, feeling heat rip across my remorseful face. "I will be fine. It… is passing." My heart thumps like a jackrabbit's foot at the lie I've just told, and an avalanche of shame buries me. I shift in my seat, feeling a strangely uncomfortable dampness between my legs.

I want to scream, but I don't make a sound. I just clutch the seat tighter.

As the man disappears behind the curtain again, I feel Ansel's hand slide into mine and hold it firmly.

I look over, and he offers me a weak smile.

"It's gonna be okay. We land in less than an hour. Just breathe. Shut your eyes and try to relax."

I do what he asks, melting at the way he is holding my hand, offering me comfort right now in this secretly immoral moment. As I sit and breathe, I feel another crushing wave of shame crash around me...

Because all I want to do is to pull his fingers down between my legs to ease this awful ache.

29

Ansel

We reach *Elation on Sea*, and the beach house and villas have undergone a major overhaul since I was here for last year's competition.

Velda makes her way up the sweeping staircase with a grouted, blue mosaic inlay of glass refracting the unforgiving Florida sun. She fans herself with her book and looks around, eyes wide with fascination, soaking everything in.

The limo driver retrieves our luggage and my boards and I stuff an obscene tip in his hands and mumble my gratitude. He leaves, unable to hide the beaming smile beneath his white Sam Elliot mustache. I grab all I can carry, and Velda follows me up the winding stairs to the second floor with my smaller board.

"Not bad, eh?" I say, unlocking the suite door in the upstairs breezeway, a beautiful vantage point of nearly a mile of beach. A stifling wind wafts through, riffling through a shaded window planter full of creeping pothos. They've attached themselves to the stucco and are making an ever-so-slow getaway to the roof.

"It's beautiful!" Velda gasps, batting her head around like she's watching a slow-motion tennis match, trying to take everything in. It's kind of adorable how enamored she is with the simplest things.

The door creaks open, and I follow her in, dumping everything carefully inside the room. Velda does a slow sweep around the space, admiring the bevy of nautical decorations in white, sea foam, and sapphire blue, giving the place a very beachy Florida feel.

Through the sliding glass doors, she bolts onto the terrace and smiles over at a bubbling hot tub that could comfortably seat four. Beyond the railing, on the first floor, is a private swimming pool with the mosaic of an azure sea turtle in the middle, the same new *Elation on Sea* logo that seems to adorn everything after the revamp. Mouth ajar, she looks back at me, pointing down to the pool.

Waves crash along the beach behind her, and she is a vision among it all. Poseidon's flaxen daughter. The rightful heir and future queen of the ocean.

"Look! There is water, and water, and more water!" She points to each body of it as she shouts. It's the first time I've heard her raise her voice over the meek inside-voice level.

"Yep. I'll be able to give you another swim lesson or two while we're here. Maybe test your skills out at the beach, too."

I watch her for a few minutes, soaking in all the new things around her before I finally put her duffel on the floor. I'll carry it down for her in a bit. I don't think she even realizes that there is a whole bottom story to the building yet, all of which is hers for the entirety of the weekend. As the duffel flops down, I realize it barely has any clothes or toiletries in it. I'm sure it's just loaded with books.

I check the booze cabinet and pour myself a whiskey. Velda is still exploring. Now she has found the television remote and is jamming her fingers against its buttons. The large flat screen shifts through channels, and her eyes are alight with fascination. Though there is a television in my room at the house, it is the only one in the dwelling so I forget that she hasn't really had access to one until now.

I sip the whiskey and roll my shoulders back, trying to switch gears out of 'travel mode.' Meanwhile, her eyes never blink as channel after channel flit across the screen. Finally, she sees one where the actor and actress share a long kiss. The actor's hand slides down to the woman's tit and gropes.

Velda is frozen in place. She reminds me of how I was in grade school when I saw naked human forms writhing in channels of staticky snow.

As saxophone music starts to play and the man's hand slides between the woman's legs, I speak, scaring the absolute bejeezus out of Velda when I do.

"They have a lot of porn channels here. Those channels are free for all the beach villas.

Last year, they had some kind of seventies marathon. It was more bush than you'd ever want to see in your life."

Velda turns the television off as soon as clothing starts being shed, and she looks at me, cheeks rose-red with embarrassment. She blinks hard as if her brain is trying to compute a difficult equation. Finally, she asks, "Bush?"

I laugh.

"You know, the *hair*... down *there*." I point to my crotch, remembering how sheltered this girl really is.

For a moment, I think about how fucking hot it would be to introduce her to all the toys and kinks she's never even heard of. And as quickly as that thought rushes in, it is replaced by the cold reality that she is just a girl at heart, still learning about the world. She is only eighteen *and* an employee who is beholden to me for a job.

I feel my phone vibrate in my pocket, and as I fish it out of my jeans, I am thankful for the momentary distraction.

It's Miranda.

MIRANDA: Heard ur in town for the surf thing or whatever.

I chew my lip and consider what to say to her.

ANSEL: Just got in. Literally.

I contemplate whether I should try to facilitate an easy booty call. Maybe it might do me good to get my mind off of... *everything*.

MIRANDA: I just got some new nipple clamps. Dying to break them in. U down?

Then, she follows the message with a picture of them splayed out on her comforter next to a black lace garter set.

Ahhh, and there it is.

That classic Miranda brazenness that I've come to know. She always skips straight to the point, like she's only got a few days to live. Like she can't be bothered with pretending to be anything other than what she is, even for the sake of having a little fun with the chase.

The thought of her huge breasts strung up with black-and-chrome clamps, draped like some kind of dark Krampus-style string lights, excites my cock. But the fact that she so willingly sent the message to me -- with a *picture*, no less -- makes the whole interaction reek of crude, unsubtle desperation. The woman has a stellar body, but her approach leaves absolutely nothing to the imagination. I wish she'd understand the journey can sometimes be hotter than the destination.

ANSEL: We'll see.

MIRANDA: U know u miss this kitty.

As the emojis of cats and peaches and eggplants start to come through, I roll my eyes and stuff my phone back into my pocket before she can bombard me with updated photos of her bald cunt vulgarly spread like a Penthouse model.

Sure, if I meet up with her, there's a guaranteed release. But there's no *chase*. It feels no different than getting a severely discounted escort. Her casual nature always makes me cringe a little. If she is this forward with me, I can only imagine how she is with the Florida locals. One busted condom and…

Shit, some STDs, even *penicillin* won't cure.

"I'm gonna change into some shorts. It's hot as Hell here. After that, I'm gonna take a walk down the boardwalk if you wanna join me."

Velda whips her head back to look at me from the sliding glass door, where she's gone back to watching the waves like she will have to draw them from memory later. I can only imagine how someday when she's in her forties or fifties, the imprint on her mind of this very view might be enough to get her through a hard day on the farm.

"Yes, please." Her voice is soft and sweet. See, Velda, on the other hand, is the very *definition* of the word demure. Pure and untainted. She probably doesn't even know what a fucking *eggplant* emoji is, much less a nipple clamp. She's probably never received a spanking that wasn't some kind of corporal punishment.

She doesn't view her body as a commodity to be traded in exchange for attention or affection.

And to me, *that* is sexy.

She is going to make some man *very* lucky one day.

***

The boardwalk is packed with throngs of beach-going Floridians and vacationers in scanty bikinis and board shorts. As we window-shopped, I made a note of how many *TwinFin* articles I saw on people, whether it be sunglasses, shorts, footwear, or wetsuits.

Thirty-seven.

Not bad for only two hours of strolling.

Could be better, though.

Velda swings her bag of newly-acquired goodies like an excited child, full of energy. She glances around in a big, floppy sun hat that still has the price tag on the brim. She eyes the people who pass us with a smile that seems permanently fused to her face.

Every store that she's lingered at the window of, I have urged her to go inside and ultimately bought her something. All in all, I've spent less on her this afternoon than I did the limo driver's tip, and she's smiling like I spent a hundred times as much.

Near the little corner grocery store on the way back, we stop in front of another retail window on the boardwalk, one she breezed past

206

the first time because she was too busy watching parasailors cruise over the waves behind a mooring commercial boat.

"You still need some shoes."

"But I have shoes." She points down at her feet. "Helena helped me get these."

"Those are sneakers, Velda. You don't wanna walk around in the sand in sneakers. When you're on the beach, you need sandals."

"At your house, I always just go in my bare feet."

"Yeah, but if you have sandals, you won't cut yourself on shells or burn yourself on hot pavement." Some of these things have just been second nature to me since before I could even talk, ingrained in the rest of us like DNA, so the fact that she doesn't quite grasp it baffles me a little.

"Trust me on this. Sandals are good to have. What do you say we stop in here before we grab the food," I ask, pointing to the cluttered shop next to us.

"Okay." She nods sweetly and slinks inside past circular racks full of discounted novelty t-shirts that say things like "Straight Outta New Smyrna" and "Fuck You, You Fuckin' Fuck." I picture her Dad, presumably some old bearded Amish dude in a pastel shirt and vest, looking at this, about to pass out.

Velda drags her hands along the fringe of a colorful article and smiles.

"Get it," I order with the hint of a smile.

"What *is* it?"

"It's a sarong. You wear it around your swimsuit bottom like a skirt."

She stares at it for a moment, dazzled by the strings and array of bold colors. I pull it off the rack and drape it over my arm. She smiles with gratitude, and it melts me a little.

I love spoiling her like this. She acts like the two hundred or so I've spent might as well be a million.

Even just walking alongside the beach has been fun. Just being together, that human contact, that rare connection with someone. All the contact I ever seem to have with people since my folks died is either *TwinFin*-related or the occasional fleeting booty call.

Velda wanders onward, and her hands and eyes linger on a holographic, purple bikini for a long time. She wanders further into the store, and I snatch up the swimsuit quietly and add it to my pile.

I nod at the Latino man perusing a magazine about motorcycles at the register. "Excuse me, do you sell sandals?"

"In the back." He points to the rear of the comically long rectangular shop, past glass displays of snowglobes and trinkets, and into a part of the store that looks like it has a lot more than the usual run-of-the-mill boardwalk junk.

"Do you carry any *TwinFin* stuff?" I ask, just for shits and giggles.

The man shakes his head, and his eyes return to a Harley V-twin soft tail spread across two pages like a metal centerfold.

"*...Be a lot cooler if ya did,*" I mumble quietly to myself, mocking McConaughey's Texas twang.

I follow Velda into the back, past display racks of everything from gaudy mood rings to leather jackets to lidded kitchen containers with hideous macaw parrots printed on them.

But Velda is glued into place, and as I near her, I see what has frozen her stiff.

A wall of cheap sex toys towers over her, offering everything from cheaply made floggers to lace one-size-fits-all body stockings to a wide variety of 'personal massagers' and wands. Beyond her, sits an array of cheap sandals, but she doesn't blink, because nothing beyond this wall exists to her in this moment.

I try to hide my smile as she drags her hand along the tassels of a clearance-priced flogger and down over a discounted paddle that has the cutout of the backward word 'DADDY' across it. I think about what the letters would look like in raised welts across her cute little ass, and my cock stiffens at the thought of it.

I lift a package of something from the rack just over her head and examine it. It's a small silicone-sleeved vibrator. It comes with a one-size-fits-all cheetah thong that has a mesh pocket for the toy. It's Bluetooth-operated, syncs with a phone app, and touts being waterproof up to three meters, which is actually a huge selling point for me.

Miranda can make a bit of a mess.

"Don't judge me," I snicker as I put the package in my arm atop the beach apparel.

"I wasn't." She says with a devious grin that she is desperately trying to hide.

"You, uh… see anything you want?" I ask, trying not to sound fucking sleazy. I just know she grew up on a farm and didn't have access to this kind of stuff.

Jesus Christ, what am I doing trying to bankroll this girl's future orgasms? What the fuck is wrong with me?

Reel it in, Ansel.

"I couldn't." She shakes her head and presses on toward the sandals.

***

Three bags of groceries and two pairs of sandals later, we return to the beach house.

"I'm gonna go take a nap upstairs before things kick off. We have a meet-and-greet mixer with the competitors this evening at eight o'clock at the marina, so I'll meet you back down here for a light dinner at seven, and then we will head over. Sound good?"

"Yes." She smiles, nods, and stuffs all of the food into the refrigerator in her ground-floor suite.

"If you need anything, just text or knock or whatever." I place the last of her things in a pile on the counter.

She nods again, and I am off, making my way up to my suite with my own paper bag of goodies. Once inside, I pull out a few pairs of board shorts I liked the patterns of and toss them onto the dresser. I throw my new flip-flops on the floor and smile down at the packaged toy lying all on its own in the bottom of the bag. I pry it open, ravaging the sun-yellowed plastic shell it's encased in, and unfurl the cord. I plug it into the wall to charge and flop on the bed with my phone.

The Florida heat is assaulting, and I feel my skin tingle with the familiar sensation of a touch too much sun. I breeze through the barrage of nudes Miranda has sent, photos of her recently tied up in Shibari ropes like a fly caught in a web, double-D breasts purple from the pull and strain of the artfully twisted bondage material.

There are more of her, too, including a shot of another girl going down on her made into a meme that says, "Wish you were here," along with a blob of text detailing her recent experiences at a Central Florida sex dungeon where she alleges she had the absolute time of her life.

I scroll back up to the "Wish you were here" meme and wonder how many men she has sent that to in the days or weeks since it happened.

Still, there is a part of me that desperately wants to fuck someone, anyone, to clear my head and think straight before I make a huge mistake and say or do something that I can't take back with Velda.

I can't unring that bell once it sounds.

I brought her out of Pennsylvania so she could see more of the world beyond her farm. And more importantly, I genuinely brought her to Rhode Island because I don't want to end up dead on a goddamned *shower floor* in another ten years. *Not* so I could isolate or destabilize her or make her into some little plainclothes geisha.

That settles it. I text Miranda.

> **ANSEL: Should be free after the meet and greet tonight if you wanna get together.**

It takes less than thirty seconds for her to respond.

> **MIRANDA: Great. Text me the address later. I'll get a sitter.**

Yeah, there are other fish in the sea. But the one positive about Miranda is that she doesn't come around for my *money*. She comes around for my *cock*. And that may not seem like it's that much better, but those two types of people are worlds apart.

Miranda loves sex. She doesn't give two fucks that I have a mansion or a black Amex with no limit. She only cares that I get hard as a goddamn rock, spank the living hell out of her, and fuck her until she's damn-near unconscious.

I reach into my shorts and massage my dick, hoping I'll nap harder if I can cum and clear my head of all the fucking nonsense swirling in it.

I glance quickly at the nudes that Miranda sent as I stroke. But moments later, I find my fingers scrolling through my camera roll to a photo of Velda on the boardwalk today, skirt waving in the wind behind her like a flag, tank top clinging to her sun-kissed skin, face smiling beneath the wide, striped brim of her hat. I pump my dick harder, bearing down with more pressure, hearing nothing but my staccato breaths slicing through the silence of the room.

I only look at the photo for a split second, but it's all I need to burn it into my memory.

I toss the phone down, and suddenly, Miranda's thirsty photos have vanished from my mind, replaced with the fantasy of what it would be like to defile and corrupt the sweet Amish girl cooking for me downstairs.

I think about how sweet it would be to press her into my bed, to hear my name moaned into the decorative sea turtle pillow beside me as I slowly filled her, pistoning in and out of her tight, immaculate pussy. I think about how divine it would be to hear her whisper for me to fuck her harder, *deeper*, feeling the warm, slick sign of her body's emphatic consent around my girth as I oblige.

A moment later, I am a geyser. A mess of spilled seed and heavy panting, dick throbbing beneath my clenched, healing knuckles.

I groan. It's an angst-filled lion's roar into the silence. Only the muffled crash of waves answers back through the double-paned glass.

But it is only a few seconds of bliss before my mood shifts. Now, there is a storm hanging over me, ironic for such a picturesque summer afternoon. The storm, it presses down on me with barometric guilt.

She's *eighteen*.

She's my *employee*.

I am a sexual goddamned deviant. A piece of fucking shit.

She's downstairs in a kitchen like Suzie Homemaker, making pot pie from motherfucking scratch like something out of a wholesome 50's sitcom. And here I am... with a cum-covered hand, a racing heart, and a sweaty head full of perverted thoughts about how unbelievably amazing she'd feel to be inside.

30

"Damn. Velda, the pot pie was incredible. Thank you." Ansel pats his stomach and smiles as he leans back in his chair at the table until it is on its back two legs.

He hasn't made much eye contact with me since his nap, and I wonder if it is because he is ashamed of me. I wonder if it is because he knew I watched a few minutes of one of the... *films...* while he was asleep.

A girl named 'Anne Chovy' was delivering pizzas in tight shorts and roller skates to a shirtless man with a thick mustache and gold chains. He invited her inside, laid her on his bed, slid his head down between her legs, and put his tongue inside of her while she moaned.

I watched in stunned silence, forgetting to breathe for what felt like two whole minutes. Eventually, I turned it off because I heard a noise. I was scared I would be caught watching it.

The man never even took a bite of the pizza.

"Would you like dessert? I made whoopie pie." I smile and take Ansel's dishes to the sink.

He laughs. "Oh, God, no. I can't be looking like Homer Simpson in front of all of these svelte surfers."

I want to laugh, too, but I am confused. "I'm sorry. I don't know who that is."

"He's... a cartoon character. Pop culture icon." He shakes his head and picks at a chip in the tabletop. "Don't worry about it. It's not important. He's got a big belly."

I nod.

"Maybe later, though. I'd like to try it." He checks his watch and stands. "We should head down there, though."

Ansel looks so handsome tonight. His shirt is white with almost imperceptible beige squares in it, unbuttoned to his sternum with a corded necklace of a figure surfing surrounded by the tan skin of his chest. His shorts are khaki, and the ensemble makes his tattoos really stand out. His arms are so muscular; I just want to snuggle up in them and feel small.

"Am I dressed okay?" I point to my clothes, nervous because I am still so new to how the Englishers dress.

Finally, he looks at me, and a genuine smile graces his face. "You look amazing."

I shyly smooth my hands over my new clothes, eyes darting away.

"C'mon." He nods at the door, and I follow him out.

I catch him staring at my legs, hips, and waist as he locks the door with his key, and I feel a flush of warmth spread through me. I hope that *Gott* can forgive me for all these compounding sins when I am baptized, but... I want him to do more than *look*.

I want him to *touch* me.

And I have absolutely no idea how to tell him that. It's the opposite of everything I've been taught. We are told not to tempt men and their carnal urges and desires. But he has been so nice to me and so attractive, and it is everything I can do not to keep imagining him doing to me the things I saw in the movie today.

A movie that felt sinful to watch.

A movie I couldn't look away from.

A movie I imagined myself being *in*.

Outside, the air is so much warmer than I imagined, and it does nothing to cool the heat of my cheeks as we make our way to the sand.

He walks beside me, careful to look away whenever he sees me look at him.

"Hopefully, you'll like some of these guys. Hopefully, this doesn't bore you to death."

"What is this again?"

"It's a meet-and-greet. Some people call it a mixer. It's where the surfers competing tomorrow all get together and mingle with the people putting the event on, as well as the other competitors and the press."

"And... you're putting the event on?"

"Yeah, my company is sponsoring it and putting up the prize money and all that. In exchange, we get to advertise our brand and have it splashed all over everything so that people see our stuff or our logo in the media and buy our products."

"How did you start a company like that? That seems... hard."

We trudge through, passing smashed shells and crumbling sand castles. I stare down at my new sandals as we walk.

"My Dad and I always used to surf together. I grew up by the beach and spent every waking hour that I wasn't in school in that water. My mom eventually left the restaurant to become a seamstress." He chuckles, "Believe it or not, I used to help her tailor wedding dresses and stuff all the time. She eventually taught me how to use the sewing machine, and I started sewing my own rash guards and board shorts. Got a lot of compliments on 'em in high school."

Ansel steps around a large, deep pit someone has dug into the sand and grabs my hand to guide me around it safely. "Careful. Don't want you falling in."

But his hand lingers in mine, and he smiles at me. The wind ruffles through his hair, and the amber glow of the nearing lights on strings bathes his skin. I feel like I can't breathe when I look at him.

My mind cries out for him to kiss me, just once, a kiss that I could never forget decades later as I tend to root crops and crying children.

But my lips say nothing. Frozen shut in this dumb smile of mine.

When he realizes he is still holding my hand, he apologizes quietly and lets go. When he does, I feel like I shatter a little inside, parts of me breaking into something irreparable.

I hear the crowd up ahead and the cackle of drunken men as we make our way through the last leg of the trek.

"When my dad died, I got an inheritance." When he says it, it startles me a little. I forgot he was even telling me a story.

"I don't know if the Amish have it, but we have something called life insurance here. If someone passes away, under most circumstances, you get money from the policy."

"Okay." I'm trying my best to keep up, both physically and mentally.

"So, I took the money I got when my Dad died, and I invested it in myself. I used it to start making surf products. It felt like the right way to honor him." He bobs his head and looks at me. "Then, a couple years later, mom passed, too. And I did the same. I put her money into expanding the company, and now... here we are. Ten years later, it's a 1.2 billion dollar empire."

"Wow." I shake my head. "What do your *bruders* and sisters do?"

He laughs. "Nothing. They don't exist. I'm an only child."

"What?!" I stop in my tracks.

"Oh, don't look at me like that. There's no pitying the poor little *billionaire* orphan boy."

"No, it wasn't pity. It was… shock. Did your mother have…" I point to my stomach, *problems?*"

"What? No." He starts to walk again, this time never taking his eyes off me. "She just only ever wanted one kid. Hell, some people choose to have none at all. They use birth control or get vasectomies and stuff."

"Why?"

"Well, because… sometimes people don't want kids. Sometimes people can't afford them or want to do other stuff with their lives, like travel or invest more time in their career."

The concept has me truly stunned. I have never really heard of such a thing.

"In my community, it is every woman's duty to have as many children as possible."

"Is that so you guys have, like, just a lot of free little farmhands running around?"

I can't tell if he's joking.

"It is to help expand our community and make sure the Amish beliefs and values live on."

"Can't help but notice you said 'the Amish beliefs' not '*my* beliefs.'"

I don't know what to say to that.

I suppose I *did.*

"So, I take it you have a big family," he says.

I nod. "If you are an only child, I doubt you would believe me if I told you how big my family is."

"Try me. Name 'em. Lemme have it. Gimme the whole list." His pace slows, and he places an

220

arm around the small of my back as we approach the crowd of people on one of the piers in the marina.

"Okay. My *Mamm* is Susana. My *Fater* is Menno…"

"Menno? That's a *name*?"

I nod. "Then, my *bruders* and *schweschders* in order from oldest to youngest…"

"Lay it on me, girl."

"Atlee, Abram, Hannah, Rebecca, Lavina, Saloma, me, and then Levi."

"Holy fuck."

"Abram has three children. Stephen, Isaiah, and Anna. Lavina is pregnant with her first child. Atlee's wife is barren, unfortunately, but Hannah has a son named Daniel and a daughter named Rachel—"

"*Damn.*"

"And that is not counting my grandparents, aunts, and uncles."

"Shit, that's like the entire population of some Midwestern *towns.*"

I stop to look at how many people are on the pier. It is a sea of faces, and the only one I know here is Ansel. His hand flattens on my back, and I feel myself pull toward him as if he is a shield from all of the anxiety I feel right now approaching this horde.

Like the flip of a switch, Ansel's eyes turn from me to the first person he recognizes.

"Scooter! How *are* you, man?"

His hand slips off my back and into the hand of the stranger. I focus on his knuckles, which are healing but are still dark where he broke the skin. I force my face to smile at the stranger.

"I'm great! Good seeing you here! I was wonderin' if you were going to come out. Glad to see you're not too busy for us little guys."

"No, man, never. Any excuse to leave that office to go be on the water, I'm there." Ansel chuckles.

"You bring your stick?" Scooter asks.

"Of course I did. Are you crazy? Brought two. Brought a new pintail I just finished and the ol' Mini Simmons for shits and giggles."

"Nice!"

"How's the surf back in Cali right now?"

"Oh, man, lately it's been total goddamn chunder, but they're calling for a tropical storm next week, so that'll be good. Hopefully, I can catch some then."

Ansel nods and turns to me. "Scoot, this is my friend, Velda."

I feel bittersweet about the term he used to describe me. On one hand, I love that he considers me a friend and not just his cook. On the other, I hate that I will probably never be seen as anything but. After all, he's kind and handsome.

He could have any girl in the world.

"Velda, this is Scooter Maggard. He's a big surfer out of…" He pauses.

"La Jolla," Scoot says with a nod.

"La Jolla?" I ask.

"It's in California," Ansel clarifies, then looks at Scooter. "She's Amish. This is her first time out of Pennsylvania, if you can believe it."

"For real?" Scooter looks at me like he's suddenly filled with intense fascination. I feel like an animal in a petting zoo as he leans in. "Like Amish as in… no electricity and all that stuff?"

I nod. Some communities *do* allow it. Mine does not.

"Ho-lee-fuck. Yo, Gnarly, come over here! Bring Ben!" Scooter yells over his shoulder.

"This fuckin' *Quimby* right here…" Ansel shouts and wraps his arms tight around one of the other men. Then he shouts, "Ben," at the other. "Holy shit, I didn't know you guys were signed up for this one."

Ansel turns to me to introduce them. "Velda, this is 'Gnarly' Charlie Miller and Ben. We call him 'Hang-Ten' Ben."

I shake their hands, suddenly feeling as if the streetlamp above us is a spotlight and this pier is a stage. I don't know my lines. I freeze, paralyzed in front of a captive audience.

Scooter looks at the other two men, both with shaggy hair of different colors with shirts unbuttoned all the way, open enough to expose strips of their chests. "Dude, she's Amish."

"No *way*!" Ben's eyes widen.

"Do you... *wait*," Gnarly Charlie shoves his way to the front of the group. "Do you guys use outhouses, or, like, do you have indoor bathrooms?"

223

I swallow hard and force myself to speak, but the word comes out in a warble as meek as if it came from a fledgling sparrow. "Outhouses."

"That's *wild*," Gnarly Charlie mutters to the ground before looking up at me with another question a split second later. "Hey, do you guys really drive the... the horse and carriages?"

"Buggies? Yes."

"Yeah, *buggies*. That's it! You ever see that show *Amish Mafia*?"

Ben hits him in the shoulder. "You moron, how would she have *seen* it? They don't have T.V.s."

"Oh, yeah." Gnarly Charlie giggles. "What about *Kingpin*?"

Scooter leans forward and locks eyes with me. It sends a shiver through me.

He's looking at me the way I wish Ansel would look at me.

With a *hunger*.

"Forgive him, Velda," he says lowly as if it is our little secret. "For he knoweth not how goddamn *stupid* he sounds. Guy's absolutely faded."

Another man bumps into Ansel, and again, they greet each other like long-lost friends. Seconds later, he is swept into a group of men, all beaming and happy to see him.

The other day, I saw the wind take someone's inflatable beach ball into the ocean behind Ansel's home. With every wave, the ball

224

was sucked further away from the shore, out into the horizon.

That is Ansel right now.

He is a shiny ball cruising away with the rhythmic flow of the water.

Scooter wraps an arm around my lower back, right where Ansel's was only minutes ago. He sweeps me in an opposing direction.

"Come, darling. Let's get you a drink, shall we?" Scooter looks over my shoulder and flashes a glare at Ben and Charlie, one I think they both take as their cue not to follow.

We wriggle through a huge mass of people. A man with a camera flashes brilliant, white lights at some of the men and women. Every time, the people pose and hold still until the light blasts. Then, they go back about their business, chatting in small groups, all nearly shoulder-to-shoulder.

Scooter's hand sits lower than Ansel's sliding down my back to the top of my butt. I feel a shiver rip through me as his hand warms me through the fabric of my dress, although it seems like he doesn't know he is doing it.

"Wow, it's a zoo here tonight." He smiles back at me as we make our way toward a long countertop with lots of bottles lined up all along the top. "Didn't realize everyone and their mother was going to turn out for this one. They're so hit-and-miss, you know?"

But I don't know.

I have no idea what he is talking about.

225

I timidly nod, hoping he will not know how disoriented and confused I am. I'm not used to being around quite so many people all at once. Even though the beach seems massive and endless, there have to be well over a hundred bodies packed into this one square patch of sand.

"Ahh, we made it." Scooter grins at the man behind the countertop, one dressed far nicer than anyone else attending the party. "Yes, hello! Let me get... an Old Fashioned."

The man nods, and Scooter looks at me. Banners flap in the breeze behind him and I recognize Ansel's company logo splashed on it in huge letters.

"What would you like, doll? My treat."

"Oh, I... I don't know," I stammer. But my voice is just a whisper, lost among the notes of the strange music overhead and all of the loud conversations behind us.

"How about..." Scooter brushes the tip of his nose against the shell of my ear and mumbles, "a *Sex on the Beach*?"

"*What*?!"

I am shocked that he would ask something so forward like that. "Absolutely not!"

He sees the outrage in my eyes, and he laughs. "Oh, honey. It's the name of a *drink*."

I look at the well-dressed man and he nods, lips pursed as if he is annoyed.

"Oh." I swallow the lump in my throat.

The well-dressed man speaks again. "If you want one of those, I'm gonna need to see your I.D."

Here we go again.

"I'm sorry. I don't have one," I mumble.

Scooter points to me, and a tuft of straight blonde hair sweeps down around his eye and hardened jaw. He smiles with a row of gleaming teeth and I can see where a faint scar mars his mouth. I never would have noticed it if I wasn't this close. He looks back up at the man behind the bar.

"She's Amish. You believe that? Like, legit *horse-and-buggy* Amish."

The man behind the bar doesn't think it's as funny as Scooter does.

"Sorry. If you don't have an I.D., all I can do is water, soda, or a Shirley Temple."

"Oh! Soda, please."

It is the first good thing about this party.

"Regular or diet?"

I don't know which is which, so I just blurt, "Surprise me."

The man in the bow tie shakes his head a little and uses a strange nozzle to fill up a glass for me. I drink the contents fast and set the empty cup down.

Scooter cackles. "Wow. You are just like... a whole new breed of woman." He looks to the man behind the bar again and pulls out a small wad of cash. "One more for the road."

The man nods and fills it again with a forced smile. Scooter hands him the cash, puts a couple of dollars in a cup marked TIPS, wraps his arm back around my waist, and walks me through the throng of people to the pier.

I feel relieved to be away from the chatter and all of the strange faces. Once we are at the end of the pier, he removes his hand and leans against the railing. He peers down over the edge at the black water. I do the same.

The moon glistens off its surface. It's beautiful.

"So, tell me, Velda." He twists to lean on a bent elbow, gazes into my eyes, and smiles softly. He nods in the direction of Ansel. "What's a pretty little thing like you doin' with the big, bad Wolf?"

31

Ansel

I scan the party, looking for Velda. As the moments tick by without seeing her, a low hum of anxiety percolates in my chest. I know she's her own woman and can go where she pleases, but I'm the only one she knows here. It feels irresponsible not to be able to account for her whereabouts. I got swept away in a cloud of familiar faces and quickly lost track of time. It isn't until a waiter hands me my third glass of champagne that I feel it imperative to peel away and go off to search.

I want to give her some freedom to roam and make new friends, but I don't intend for her to end up on some future episode of 20/20 with the boardwalk photo of her in my phone splashed on the news as the last known photo of her alive.

I wander around frantic, eyes scanning the crowd for her. I down the glass of bubbly and set it on the tray of a passing waiter. I feel my feet move quicker, with urgency and guilt and a sense of responsibility.

"Have you seen Velda?" I murmur into Charlie's ear.

"Yeah, she walked off with Scoot. I think I saw 'em down on the pier."

I take off, half in a brisk walk, half in a jog down to the edge of the water. I see two human figures amid the darkness, silhouetted by a horizon of moon-bathed ripples bounding gently in every direction.

As I move closer, their bodies become clearer in the dim light of a waning moon.

They're close.

They're... *kissing*.

That piece of shit silver-medal surf bum has her face cupped in his hand as their heads bob like buoys.

"Hey!" I holler. The word comes out stern, far more powerful than I feel with what I see before me.

Scoot yanks himself away, and Velda's whole body stiffens, rigidly turning to me with a look of shame painted on her porcelain-smooth face.

"Um, *excuse* me," Scoot hollers. "Do you *mind?*"

I growl, growing more threatening as I near him. "Get your fucking hands off of her!"

My hands snatch Scoot by the collar of his open shirt and yank him backward, arching his back over the wooden railing.

He looks at me with a glimmer of fear, as if I am about to push a touch harder and topple him into the black water below.

And I just fucking might.

"Jesus Christ, we were just kissing! Fuck! What *are* you, her *Dad*?!"

I roar again and shove Scooter toward the edge of the pier, away from Velda. He hisses from the drag of the splintered rail.

I scoop Velda's bare shoulders into my hands and turn her gently toward me. I'm shaking, vision tunneling, vignetted with rage. "Are you okay?"

"Yes." She nods. Scared like I've never seen before. Possibly of *me*. "I'm fine, Ansel."

"See, *Dad*, she said she's *fine*." Scooter grins. "So… let me ask again… do you *mind*?"

"Did he *hurt* you?" I ask, frantic, searching for the answers through the darkness.

"*What*?!" Scooter hollers loud enough to be heard all the way down the pier. He timidly makes his way back toward us, clever enough to stay just out of my arm's reach. "What the *fuck*? *No*, I didn't hurt her! Jesus, we were just fucking makin' out. Last I checked, that wasn't a crime."

My face whips toward him, and I feel a pounding in my head, the too-familiar thrum of growing fury. "She's *eighteen*, you twat."

"So-the-fuck-*what*?" Scooter steps to me.

I look Velda in the eyes, expecting a 'save me from this man' look in them.

Instead, I see *fear*…

Fear of *me*.

Mixed with *shame*.

"You act like I *roofied* her. She's *sober*, Wolf. She's been downing diet cokes like they're water. Take a goddamn *sip* if you don't believe me. I'm not taking advantage of anyone."

I eye what's left of her bubbling beverage on the railing and then her. "Did he... *force* you to do this?"

After a long moment, Velda shakes her head. "No."

"Jesus Christ, she leaned in and kissed *me*, motherfucker," Scooter shouts.

I ignore him and stare only at Velda. She looks like I just told her she was grounded for three months.

"Is that true?" I am quiet now, pleading in my head for her to say it isn't.

She nods, and my stomach twists.

I am appalled, although I have no fucking clue if there is anything to actually be appalled *at*. I didn't realize she had it in her.

Maybe she's not the demure little daisy that I assumed she was.

"Yes." She says it this time, and her eyes rise to mine, displaying a glimmer of fierceness and mild defiance, things that have been hidden deep within her, finally released like an animal that's been trapped in a cage its whole life. "Am I in trouble?"

The words come like a punch to my fucking gut. One stiff breeze could knock me into that churning water right now, and I'd be too stunned to swim to the surface. I'd drown from the weight of those words alone.

"No. Jesus, no." I step back and take my hands off of her like her soft, dewy skin is made of molten lava.

What the fuck am I even doing?

"You're not... no... you can do what you want."

I run a hand through my hair, mortified by my actions. I don't know what to say. I have already said far too much. Instead of speaking, I turn and head back toward the raucous gathering.

Moments later, I hear the *click-clack* of Velda's flip-flops approaching.

"Wait! I'm sorry, Ansel."

"Great," Scooter yells. "Just great. Thanks for the cock-block, Ansel."

I feel like I'm on some kind of carnival ride, slightly dizzy and off-kilter. Velda's hand wraps around my forearm, gentle fingers clenching like she's going to be left for dead in a foreign land.

"Don't be mad. *Please*," she begs.

"I'm not, Velda. I thought..." I look down at her pleading eyes, so soft and sincere, "something else was going on. I thought he was... *never mind*."

She pulls tighter, pressing her breasts against my arm. "Can we please go back to the beach house?"

I nod, unable to say more. We leave the party without so much as a single goodbye to anyone.

***

The walk back to the beach house is painfully silent, neither of us uttering a word. As we approach the building, the breeze rustles through the villa's palms and blooming mandevillas, caressing them like a loving hand. I make my way up the stairs to the top floor.

"Ansel." Velda's tone is so small from the base of the stairwell. "Can we talk?"

I look down at her over the balcony. Capulet and Montague, our worlds vastly different. I, with salty ocean water coursing through my blood, and her, the loamy earth. Rich and poor. Worldly and sheltered. Fury and pacifism.

We are *worlds* apart, though the distance is only fourteen feet.

"I'm sorry," she says again, as if she has *anything in the world to be sorry for.*

"Don't be."

I feel deep regret for how I acted, quick to anger, just like the ugly side of my Father, the side I don't like to think of out of respect to his memory.

But it was there.

Eating him alive from the inside like caustic acid until the day that it finally ballooned through his valves and left him forever stilled. It was fury he clung to like an old friend, an all-too-familiar jump from calm to fearsome in two seconds flat. I always feared that if I let that same rage simmer inside of me, the toxicity of the trait would eventually kill me, too.

"Please, can we just talk?"

"That's not a good idea," I mutter before entering my room and shutting the door quietly behind me.

The truth is, if we talked, I don't know what I'd say. I'm ashamed to say that I don't know if how I acted back there was because I was *really* afraid for her safety... or if it was jealousy.

The latter scares the living shit out of me.

She was kissing someone. Pure and simple.

And I just made her feel like that was the worst thing in the world, shaming her to the point where she might as well be back under the rigid rules I thought I was getting her away from.

The truth is, she deserves to experience the world. The poor girl's been sheltered all her life on a farm.

Hell, she said she'd never even seen a *vibrator* until today.

The thought of the toy makes my brain shift into another gear completely. My eyes find the panty-vibe on the charger, bathed in the lime green light, indicating that it is fully charged.

My thoughts shift to Miranda.

A good, sweaty fuck would help me ease my tension and clear my head right now. I need to forget Velda, forget fucking Scooter, and most of all... forget the unmistakable pang of *envy* I felt when I found out she'd kissed him on purpose.

I text Miranda the beach house address and implore her to bring her toys. All of 'em. The more, the merrier.

The two minutes I wait for a response feel like forever. My body buzzes with nervous energy. It bubbles with the excitement that I'm about to get laid for the first time in probably two months.

And also dread about what to say to Velda when I see her next. And also a fierce hatred for Scooter for thinking he was good enough to…

No. I need to stop that.

She's young, but she's still technically an adult. She can make her own decisions. Like she said, by her age, the lion's share of girls in Berks County are already married and starting families.

I hear the slosh of water outside, but not from the ocean. Something closer. I slide the glass door open and make my way out to the rear balcony. I lean against the railing, vined thick along the sides with trumpet-shaped flowers and lush leaves like something out of a stage play.

I see the source of the noise.

It's *Velda.*

She's in the shallow end of the pool, practicing the freestyle stroke I taught her yesterday. Her top half is in the bikini I bought her today, but she's wearing it upside down so that it is pulling strangely.

Around her waist is a block of lavender. It looks like she is wearing a skirt or something in the water. I fight the urge to laugh.

Still, she swims peacefully, enjoying the water and the silence, clearly anxious to learn the basics well enough to explore deeper waters.

My phone vibrates and interrupts the tranquility of the secretive moment where I am drinking her in unbeknownst to her. The buzz of it scares me so much that I damn near drop it off the balcony.

MIRANDA: Can't make it. At a walk-in clinic. My spawn got a jelly bean wedged up his nose, and we can't get it out.

The text is followed by a photo of a toe-headed four-year-old crying in a waiting room. Then by another photo of Miranda's face, frazzled and annoyed.

MIRANDA: Raincheck.

I pocket the phone and watch Velda again swimming slow, careful laps across the shallow end with a giant mosaic sea turtle lit up by underwater lights on the floor of the pool just beyond her. It looks inviting, and I decide, perhaps against my better judgment, to join her.

I strip out of my clothes, throw on some swim trunks, and head down the back stairwell that bleeds out into the concrete perimeter around the pool.

"Hey." I want to apologize but I can't find the right words, so I just ask, "Mind if I join you?"

The rest of the people along this patch of beach seem to all have gone to bed for the evening, making it feel like we have all of New Smyrna to ourselves.

She shrugs, and it's the most aggressive I've ever seen her be. She's not happy with me.

I tilt my head, certain that my eyes are not deceiving me now. "Are you... wearing your sarong in the pool?"

I have to fight the urge to laugh.

She's not finding any humor in the question. "Yes."

"Why?"

She looks at me like I have three heads. "You said to wear this around the bathing suit bottom like a skirt."

Now I actually *do* laugh.

"On land, Velda. Not in the water."

She only stares at me as I make my way down the stairs and into the water.

She looks like she can't tell if this is my idea of a cruel joke or not.

"People usually wear it on the beach to cover up a little. Not in the water." I fight my smile. "Sorry, I should have been more specific."

I wade a little closer to her, letting my body adjust to the shock in temperature.

"You're also wearing your top upside down. You've got the torso string around your neck and the neck string around your torso."

She looks mortified, lowering deeper into the water until only her face is above the surface. I see her arms fold across her chest beneath the ripples.

"It appears I can't do anything right."

"No," I sigh and wade a little closer. "That's not it at all. Look, Velda, I'm sorry for how I acted tonight. I thought he was taking advantage

238

of you. I thought he might have drugged you or was making you do something you didn't want to do."

After a long silence, she wades backward a little, putting distance between us. Her eyes are glassy, like she is on the verge of tears.

"Back in Pennsylvania, there is a boy named Amos Miller. He is not handsome. He is not nice. He is not smart or funny. He is not nice to the horses on his farm or the frogs in the pond. And he has just as little money as many of the rest of us."

I wade backward slowly into the deep end to tread water in place. Her gaze follows me.

"...But Amos Miller is not related to me, and he is not married. And that is all my *Mamm* and *Fater* care about in the end for me. They have made it clear that when I get baptized and make my commitment to the Ordnung, I need to settle down with him."

I swallow hard, trying to imagine what it would be like to have your whole life basically hand-picked for you by others. I can't fathom it. Since my parents died and my bank account fattened, I've had nothing but unfettered freedom.

"I will be expected to be with only Amos, or someone *like* Amos, for the rest of my life, bearing as many children for him as my body will allow before I turn into the husk of who I am today."

"*Jesus,*" I mutter. I think about how bleak her future is as lukewarm ripples lap against the facial hair on my jaw.

"I kissed that man tonight because I *wanted* to. Not because I love him, but because I do not want Amos Miller to be the first... or the *only* lips to ever touch mine."

The second she says it, I feel my dick awaken from its cold, shrunken slumber, grateful that it is hidden underwater where it cannot betray the stoic expression on my face.

"The truth is, Ansel, I do not like the idea of Amos Miller being my first... of *anything*. While it is my time to run around, I want to know what it is like to do these things with someone else. I watch the women around me working in the fields, sewing quilts, quietly miserable in some of their marriages. I am sure they wish that they had fonder memories of times before to carry them through the hard times."

She sighs, and the heaviness of what she is saying sinks in.

"You'd never been kissed before tonight?" I don't know why it is the first thing from my mouth, but it is.

"No." She dips below the water and glides up slowly, a foot closer to get the mess of blonde hair out of her eyes. She surfaces with it slicked back, and her blue eyes sparkle from the bright, white pool lights.

"So... you've never... done *other* stuff? Like *sex*?"

She shakes her head, but not apologetically. Firmly, expression serious.

"I want to, but I don't really know how to. They don't tell us anything about it in my community."

"Nothing? You guys don't have sex ed or anything?"

"Sex ed?"

"Like the class when you're a teenager where... they tell you about the birds and the bees?"

"I know a lot about birds and bees."

I know from her expression that she missed the euphemism completely. I laugh. It's too loud, but it just sort of comes out of me.

"No, Velda, not *actual* birds and bees. It's a saying. It means sex. In sex education, that's where they teach you about condoms and penises and periods and vaginas and all that stuff. You never had that?"

"No." The shake of her head is so violent that her hair nearly splashes me. "There is nothing like that in my community."

"Holy shit."

"There was a booklet they gave me when I was eleven. But it only told me not to encourage lustful desires in the men around me by dressing improperly and such."

"Jesus Christ." I shake my head, almost alarmed by the amount of negligence in not teaching people such basic things. In making it a woman's duty not to *entice* men, as if men are not created with any semblance of self-control.

"I'm sorry, I'm fascinated now. So you're saying you've *never...*"

She inches toward me in the water, treading to keep her head and shoulders just above the surface. "Never *what*?"

"So... you've never had *sex*."

"No."

I assumed she was chaste, but only in my wildest fantasies did I think she was still a virgin at eighteen. Her confirmation sends another thick pulse of blood to my dick, and now I'm fully hard at the thought of her body being *untouched* and *pristine*.

"What about..." My tone is quieter, and my face scrunches. I know I'm crossing a huge line with these inappropriate and probing questions, but I'm equal parts turned on and fascinated right now. My voice is almost a whisper when I ask the question.

"What about *orgasms*? You've like... *masturbated* and stuff, right?"

An instantaneous bloom of red ravages across her face and neck like red ink spilled in milk.

She shakes her head and inches toward me again, making her way into deeper waters. She looks at me as if I will tell her to return to the shallow end at any second, but when I don't, she keeps coming. It seems we are both toeing the line of our boundaries.

242

"No." She confirms it verbally.

My cock is painfully engorged now at the thought of it all, at our close proximity, at the fact that she is close enough to reach out and feel how fucking hard she is making me with her honest admissions. I can't even feel my body treading.

The thoughtful angel on one shoulder tells me to be a good boy, tells me to jack myself off and put her on the first plane back to Pennsylvania before this world can corrupt such a sweet young thing.

But that Devil on my shoulder, *oh that sly little Devil*, it is telling me, *yelling at me,* to plant that flag, to be the first man inside of any and all of her orifices, to be the first name screamed from that perfect little mouth...

To be the first person, including herself, in the entire fucking *world* to ever make her cum.

I could be the man she reminisces fondly about for the rest of her life in Pennsylvania...

But I don't say anything.

I plunge myself beneath the surface, hoping the water will miraculously cool me or infuse some sense into me through osmosis, hoping the pressure around my chest and head will remind me that she's *thirteen* years younger than me and my fucking *employee*.

I don't want to come up for air.

I want to drown here, with my clear view of a soaked sarong and an upside-down bikini top covering the most beautiful, untouched body I've ever seen.

243

When I finally surface, Velda is closer now, wading into the deep end with a surprising proficiency. I would rejoice with pride right now if I weren't so distracted by the information I've just been presented with.

"I wasn't entirely truthful tonight," she says, looking down at the sea turtle beneath us and wading inches closer.

"Yeah?" I want to faint. I don't know how I am forming words with my brain so devoid of blood. "How so?"

"Well," she says it shyly now as if she is admitting something embarrassing. "I… didn't exactly want to kiss *him* tonight."

I swallow hard, hoping she's not about to say what I think she is going to say.

And then she says it.

"I really wanted my first kiss to be with *you*."

The lap of the water and the whip of wind feels like it is deafening in my ears. For a moment, I am lost in her blue eyes, unable to find my way home.

"I like you, Ansel. I was wondering if…"

She doesn't even need to elaborate. I know exactly what she is inferring: She was wondering if I will be her first for *other* things.

For a moment, I think I died. Just for a split second, I am ping-ponged back and forth between Heaven and Hell and then extruded through some kind of black hole back into my mortal body.

"Velda…"

The word hurts me, but what I'm *about* to say already feels like a fucking *knife* in my gut,

"I can't. I'm thirty-one. You're barely eighteen. *And* you work for me. That would be... so fucked up of me."

"Please," she begs, and I almost fucking faint at the word. If I were standing, my legs would have crumbled beneath me.

She could bring an emperor to his knees with a plea like that. Halt wars. Get anything she wanted in this world.

Anything but *this*.

"I want my first time to be with someone I like, someone I trust." She swims closer still, nearly touching me now. Close enough that I could pull her to me and show her what a *real* fucking kiss is supposed to feel like.

"Would you... at least... *think* about it?"

A laugh burbles out of me. As I look away, I think my face is now beet red, too.

How could I *not*?

There is no way on God's green earth that I will *not* be able to think about it...

Every second...

Of every coming-fucking-day.

"I won't... *tell* anyone if that is what you are worried about." The way she says it is so innocent and pure.

Jesus Christ. The fact that she is a virgin *and* wants to be my dirty little secret is a new level of sexy that I didn't even think *possible* right now.

I wish I had never come down to this pool. I wish I had stayed upstairs and masturbated furiously to my favorite bookmarked internet porn and never heard a *word* of this.

My voice squeaks out of me, something I've never heard my body do before. "Mayyyyybe you should find someone closer to your own age."

Velda stares at me for a moment and then slowly wades backward with a slightly dejected look on her sweet face.

And then, that sneaky little Devil rears his head again as I add, "For the *sex*."

She swims in place, looking confused.

"...And the *kissing*."

"I don't understand." She cocks her head sideways, and drops of chlorinated water trickle from her chin. "It seems like you are trying to say more."

"I... am." I hesitate for a moment, debating whether or not to permanently blur that line, to sound that bell.

I tell myself: *It's still not too late to turn back, Ansel.*

And then my fucking mouth opens.

"*Come with me*." As the words slip from my lips, I have sealed my own fate.

Into the darkness, I fall...

32

Velda

My towel is soaked through, dribbling water all along the stone staircase to the top floor, soaking the grout between the thousands of carefully placed pieces of broken blue glass. Toward the top step, Ansel holds a palm out for me, and I take it in mine, feeling my heart hammer in my chest. I am scared and excited, and all I can think about is how relieved I am that he's holding my hand.

I cannot believe all of the things I just told him. Never in a million years did I think I could manage to say the words aloud. But there, in the water, it just seemed... *right*.

Ansel opens the door and pulls me into his room. I think for a moment that maybe I have misunderstood him. Maybe he *is* going to take my virginity right here... right *now*. I feel a wave of panic and terror wash over me, wondering if I am ready, wondering what it will be like.

He turns on a lamp, and I watch as water beads down his strong chest and muscular abdomen. Part of me is ashamed to say that I want to lick it right off of the tattoos there.

He steps close, and I can feel the heat of his body as I stare up into his eyes. He has to be nearly a foot and a half taller than me and nearly twice as broad in the shoulders.

"I won't touch you, but I'll be your first at something."

I don't understand, and it must be written all over my face because he speaks again to clarify.

"I'll be the first to give you an orgasm."

The way he says it, I feel my right knee shake. He tucks a wet bit of hair behind my ear, and I feel my body tremble.

He lifts the pair of cheetah print panties in the air on one finger. It has no back, just a string like Helena's was. I recognize the print on them from the shop on the boardwalk today.

He twists them inside out and shows me a three-inch pocket in the front. Then, he pulls the blue device from the charger and slips it into the underwear.

"Go to the bathroom. Leave your top on. Take off the sarong and your bikini bottoms. Wear this."

His voice sounds different now than before. Dominant. It is an order, not a question, and the way he demands it starts an ache between my thighs.

He points to the side strings. "These sit on your hips."

He stares down into my eyes for a long moment, and I feel my heart beat in my throat.

"Come out once they're on."

His tone is authoritative and firm, and I feel gooseflesh light up every inch of my skin.

I nod -- *at least, I think I nod* -- and disappear into the bathroom to do as I'm told, replacing the cold, wet sarong and bikinis with the underwear he just gave me that makes me feel even more exposed.

I stand poised at the door with my hand on the knob, feeling my pulse throb through me into the cold metal. I am scared to open it. Scared to show this much of my body to him... to anyone. The outfit I just peeled out of is the least amount of clothing I've ever worn around anyone.

And now I am about to stand in front of him in this.

Finally, I breathe deep, twist the knob, and take small steps out into his room, feeling a mix of fear and excitement in equal measure.

Ansel is on the bed and studies my body for a long time without ever blinking once.

He isn't smiling. In fact, he looks serious, almost mad.

He points to the cushioned fabric chair in the corner of the room.

"Go sit."

Slowly, I follow the order, taking a seat in the chair and clenching the arms tightly, as if it can offer me some comfort.

I feel exposed. He has changed back into dry shorts and an open button-down, and I feel even more under-dressed because of this.

"If you want to stop, say so." His voice is low, his eyes gravely serious. "I won't be mad. We can forget any of this ever happened."

I feel my body tingle for a moment, and I shake my head. The faintest trace of a smile touches his lips as I do.

He holds up his phone to show me something that I cannot see well from where I'm seated.

"This is an app. This app links to the vibrator in your thong via Bluetooth."

App? Thong? Vibrator? Bluetooth? I don't know what any of it means. He might as well be speaking another language right now.

"What this means is, if you're wearing *those*, and I am in range with *this*, I have full control over the toy inside of it. Like this…"

He slides his finger across the screen of his phone and, like pure, terrifying magic, the device in my underwear whirs to life, shaking on its own, sending shockwaves through my entire lower half.

I shriek, and the buzzing stops.

"Are you okay?"

"Am I… being *electrocuted*?!" I am angry and scared. I feel like he might have just tried to kill me.

"No," he cracks a smile, which fades quickly. "The blue thing in there is a tiny vibrator. It vibrates against your clit—"

"Clit?"

"It's short for clitoris. It's like a little bean at the top of your vulva with more nerve endings than the lips on your face. It's one of the most sensitive parts of your... *you*."

I breathe heavily, still clenched onto the arms, not wholly sure what just happened to me.

"I'm going to turn it on again. I'll start it on the lowest setting. Relax your body," he says softly. "Okay?"

I bite my lip and nod, furrowing my brows in preparation for this thing again.

"The more you relax your body, the better it'll feel."

I swallow hard. My throat is parched, and I can't tell if it's the pool water or sweat trickling down in time with the rapid rise and fall of my breasts.

The vibrations start again, this time much lighter, and my whole body flexes again from my jaw to my toes to my fingertips. The device between my legs sends a tiny, sustained shock through me. Against my will, my pelvis squirms and bucks, sensation differing depending on my position. Terror and pleasure mix in my body. I feel my nipples harden, rubbing against the wet fabric of my top as I writhe.

I make sounds, quietly fearful at first, similar to a bleating animal. I close my eyes and bite my lip so hard I think I might draw blood.

"Velda, relax your body." Ansel's voice is soothing.

A moment later, I hear the ruffle of covers, and I open my eyes to see that he has crawled across the bed to the corner closest to me, a few mere feet from my nearly-naked lower half.

I try to relax my body, but the feeling is so intense that I feel it pulse and tighten instead.

I moan and grunt, clawing the woven fabric of the chair with my nails. I realize that I have forgotten to breathe, that I've been holding air in my lungs for a long time.

The vibrations slow to a stop, and I feel my chest heave. My eyes are finally able to open, but my mouth is unable to form any words that would make sense.

"Are you okay?"

I take a moment to breathe, to register the question, and then I nod.

"You want me to stop?" Even though his voice sounds genuine, his body looks like it is at war with itself, hungry for more. His eyes silently beg for me to decline the offer.

I consider his question for a moment, but the longer the pause goes on, the more I realize that I am alright, that I am not hurt, or in any pain.

Finally, I shake my head, and he flashes a smile so gorgeous that I melt into the chair, becoming one with its fabric.

"I'm going to turn it on again."

I nod, clenching my toes in preparation.

It starts again, low, resonating through my flesh and bones, feeling like a warm current radiating outward through every fiber of my body, dissipating at the end of every extremity.

I clench my eyes as the sensation intensifies, and I feel noises coming from my throat again, behind my nose. Ones I can't seem to stop. Ones my throat feels like it's making all on its own.

"*Breathe*, Velda. Deep breaths."

I suck in deep lungfuls of air until I feel lightheaded.

I open my lids, and Ansel is studying me, staring at me like I'm his favorite painting in some small, secret gallery.

"*Jesus Christ, Velda,*" he whispers, edging his way even closer to the end of the bed. "*You are so fucking sexy.*"

There is adoration in his words, and the moment he speaks them, I take back some control over myself. I force my muscles to relax one grouping at a time. First, my thighs, then my calves, my hands. I feel my back arch, shoulders digging into the cushioning of the chair as if my breasts are reaching out, begging for Ansel to touch them.

"*Mmmmm. That's a good girl,*" he coos softly, and I melt, feeling the quiet, buzzing vibrations in my very soul.

"Put your feet up on the bed. I want to see you better," he orders.

Trembling, I slip one foot onto the bed by his elbow. My body heaves and judders with the new and different sensation of the device. Slowly, I slide the other on the bed, feeling so much more exposed now that he is close enough to reach out and feel me, one slip of the foot away from touching him.

"Spread your knees for me."

I do. Slower than anything I've ever done in my life.

When they are fully parted, Ansel smiles, and I am filled with warmth.

"You're so wet," he says, licking his bottom lip with a moan of satisfaction, never blinking as his eyes dance from my pelvis to my face and back again.

Something in me builds to a point of no return, and suddenly, I think I am *dying*. I cry out, screaming into the night air. Ansel doesn't silence me.

My body lurches like I'm a limp marionette being tugged into the air by a string around my waist. Every muscle in me tenses to the point of being almost painful. I feel my calf cramp, toes curl. My vision darkens. My eyes fill with tears, and my mouth howls like I'm in mourning for a loved one.

The vibrations slow, and with it, my butt drops back to the chair. As the device stops completely, my body has no fight left in it. My muscles are no longer under my control. My head and heart pound in unison. I pant, unable to suck air in fast enough. I'm dizzy.

My entire self has gone slack and blissfully unaware of my surroundings.

Moments later, the darkness recedes, and Ansel's lamp-lit face smiles wolfishly at me.

"Are you alright?"

I don't know how long it takes me to answer. Maybe seconds. Maybe minutes. But in that time, Ansel doesn't move. He just stares from the bed, watching my body slowly recover.

"Yes," I finally say, even though I can see my ribs jump in time with each slam of my heart. "I think so."

Ansel stands, grabs an empty glass off the dresser, fills it with water from the bathroom, and hands it to me. I take it, unbelievably grateful for every drop. I gulp down the entire thing without stopping, dragging my wobbly legs to the floor in a limp attempt to stand. But they are working about as well as the limbs of a newborn calf, and I stay seated to keep from falling.

"You should sit for a minute. Just enjoy it." Ansel smiles and sits on the edge of the bed in front of me. As he does, I notice the obvious bulge in the front of his shorts where the fabric is tenting, and my mouth goes drier still at the thought that the night is not over and there will be an obvious need for me to reciprocate to soothe his animal instincts.

"What... was that," I finally mutter. I have never felt my heart bang so hard in my life.

"Well... you just had your first orgasm." He tries to hide his stunning smile but can't. "Congratulations."

"I thought I *died*," I manage before shaking the last remnants of water from the glass onto my tongue.

He laughs at my comment. "The French call the orgasm '*Le Petite Morte.*' It means 'The Little Death.'"

I hear the palms rustle outside with another slow gust of wind, and I close my eyes to listen to it. I feel like I could fall asleep to it.

"It's pretty spot-on, isn't it? It does feel a little like you're tasting death."

I am still not entirely sure what *world* I'm on or if I should feel shame, gratitude, horror, or joy. Maybe I feel them all at once. A powerful blend that scares me more than anything tonight.

Ansel stares at me for a moment and then covers the bulge between his legs with a decorative sea turtle pillow. It reminds me of Adam's fig leaf in the Garden of Eden, there because he felt shame after eating the forbidden apple.

I stare at the sea turtle, trying to find the right words, but I am scared. Finally, my clumsy, parched mouth settles on, "Do you want me to…?"

To what? I don't even know what I am trying to ask. The acts all still feel like a mystery.

He looks at his lap and laughs. There is a silence between us, one in which he looks like he is struggling to find his own words.

"No. I'll handle that." He smiles softly, and his eyes meet mine. "But, thank you."

He checks his watch. "We should get some sleep soon. We gotta be there for eight o'clock."

I nod, willing my legs to do as I command: *move*!

They don't. They feel temporarily out of my control.

Ansel stands again, retrieves my wet clothes from the bathroom, and puts them in one of the bags from the boardwalk. Then, he holds a hand out to help me stand. My legs feel weak. One has a mild burn as I flex it from the way my muscles cramped. Once I am up, Ansel wraps my body in a warm, white robe. With the wet paper bag in one hand, he holds out the other for me. I take it. It's warm, and its grip makes me feel secure like he is not going to let me fall.

He walks me down the outside steps, and warm air caresses my damp hair. We take every step slowly, carefully. He never lets go of me. Once inside my part of the beach house, he eyes the fridge.

"You hungry?"

The question stuns me. I thought he was anxious to get some sleep.

"A little," I say, fidgeting with the belt of the robe.

"I've never had a whoopie pie before."

It all rushes back to me that I even made it. Waking up in Rhode Island, the flight, the boardwalk, the party, the pier, the pool, and then, of course, what just happened in Ansel's room. The entire day seems like an incredible blur. A week compressed into less than twenty-four hours. I forgot I even made food.

"It's delicious. Let me make you a plate."

"How about you go and change. Get comfy in some dry night clothes. Meet me on the back patio. I'll plate up some pie."

I nod, unsure what to say, and disappear into my bedroom. I change slowly, surprised by the warm feeling of bliss in every inch of my body like I have just soaked in a hot tub. I peel off the underwear with the toy, and the tiny device feels almost mystical in my palm. I make a note to scrub it all in the morning until there is no trace of my sin left on any of it.

Once in my nightclothes, I exit the room. The whole level is quiet except for the hiss of the trees outside.

Ansel is slightly reclined in a beach chair with a whoopie pie on a plate in his lap. Another plate of dessert sits on the empty chair next to him. I pick it up and settle in, grateful for the soft pajama set Helena gave me that feels like Heaven on my skin right now.

"This is absolutely delicious," Ansel says, motioning to the last bite of chocolate and creme in his hands.

I smile. "Thank you."

I pick up mine and eat it just like a tiny sandwich. It tastes even better than I remember back home, and I moan a little as I chew.

Ansel laughs at the sound and stares out at our lit-up private pool, the palms, and the waves of the ocean rushing in through the darkness. They never have to sleep.

As I finish my dessert, a huge smile comes across my face.

"What?" He giggles a little, putting his hands behind his head, arms winging out beside his shoulders like an eagle. "What's so funny?"

I wave for him to look away. I'm embarrassed, but it's making me smile even more.

"What?" he asks again, wiping his lips. "Do I have chocolate on my face?"

"No," I giggle now, too. I lay back in the chair. "I just feel really good."

"Oh," he snickers. "Yeah, I don't know if you know this, but when you…" he tries to find the right word, "have an orgasm, your brain releases chemicals that make you feel… I dunno, euphoric. It's great. It's a huge part of the reason why people love sex. It's like a drug. But one that makes you happy and usually doesn't have you out there pawning your uncle's T.V. to get more."

"It is so strange to hear you say that. Where I come from, it is not at all the same."

"No?"

"No. I don't know anyone who says they love it. Or any woman who says she does it for fun."

"Well, maybe those people aren't having orgasms." He shrugs. "You can have sex and not have an orgasm."

"Do you," I am sure I should not be asking a man such things, but I do it anyway, "remember your first?"

"What? First time I had sex or first orgasm?"

259

I am shocked by the question. I guess I had assumed they were one and the same.

"Both."

He chuckles. "Oh yes. First time I ever had an orgasm, I think I was nine or ten, somewhere in there. I remember I was in the shower, and I had the body wash, and I was scrubbing myself. I was washing my dick and," he laughs harder, and I can hear it disappear in the wind, "I thought I got electrocuted. I collapsed against the wall. Almost fell on the floor. I remember feeling scared. Like I had just had a near-death experience. In my mind, I thought something shocked me. Like there was some kind of open wire or something. For six days, I refused to shower. I thought I was going to get shocked again. Finally, my mother tells me I have to. And I get in there thinking I could die. You know, as a kid, when no one tells you about this stuff, you're really on your own trying to figure it all out without a guide. It would be another couple of years before anyone would have any kind of talk with me about that stuff."

Another gust of wind bends some of the trees. They look like they're waving at us.

"So I'm checking the shower for wires, looking everywhere for what could have shocked me. I don't see shit. Not one wire. Nothing. So, I decide it must be a fluke, and I start washing myself again. I get back to my crotch, and it happens again. Less scary this time but just as... electric. And that's when I realized I wasn't being shocked at all. I was causing it."

260

"And then what?" I ask after a pause.

"And then, I realized I really liked it, no, I loved it, and I started doing it all the time. Sometimes a couple times a day."

For some reason, this story brings me peace in all of the excitement.

"What about the first time you ever had sex?"

"Oh, God." He blows a raspberry. "Jesus, I think I was sixteen, somewhere in there. It was this girl I met on the beach in Australia. My Dad took me there to go surf for my sweet sixteen."

"Sweet sixteen?"

"You don't do those in Pennsylvania?"

I shake my head.

"It's just a big birthday party when you turn sixteen. Some people get cars and stuff. I got a trip to Bells Beach in Victoria. It's this gorgeous place with a long right-hand pointbreak that I had seen on the *Rip Curl Pro* competition on T.V." He wags his hand.

"Doesn't matter. Point is, this girl was a local surfer girl. Really attractive. And she... ended up punching my V-card."

Almost as if he could read my confused mind, he clarifies.

"That's just a euphemism for taking someone's virginity."

I nod and then look at him. "Were you scared?"

"*Shitless.*" He laughs. "I was scared *shitless*. And I was terrible. I think I unrolled the condom and put it on inside out at one point. I was a mess.

261

I didn't know what I was doing at all." He sighs. "But, you know, it was exciting and fun. And, then later, throughout life, the more I did it, the more fun it was."

We sit in the quiet for a moment, and I imagine his story as if it were a movie in my mind.

He looks at me and smiles. "How are you feeling?"

I smile and snuggle into my chair. "Very good."

He grins. "Good."

Ansel checks his watch, sits up, and gathers our plates. "It's getting late. I'm going to head to bed. Do you need anything?"

I shake my head with a smile.

"Okay. If you need anything, just text me. Or knock."

"Okay."

"See you in the morning. We gotta be over there at the pier at eight. So... breakfast around seven-thirty?"

I nod. "Perfect."

"Good. Okay, well... goodnight, Velda." Ansel beams down at me.

"*Gut novid*, Ansel."

Ansel sets the dishes in the sink and heads upstairs. I stay for a while and think about this whirlwind day as I listen to the quiet crash of steady waves upon the shore as the ocean sings me its lullaby.

33

Ansel

"Who is next?" I mumble to Alan, one of the Floridians coordinating the competition. The sun is vicious today, roasting me beneath its intense rays.

"Next up is Taylor McCarthy. After that, 'Hang-Ten' Ben. Then, the judges will confer, and we'll have you present the medals at the ceremony. We'll all take a few press pics, as usual, and call it a day," Alan says, never prying his leathery eyes away from his clipboard. The man has never heard of sunscreen, and his tough, sun-baked skin is starting to resemble my grandmother's old couch.

"Great." I pat him on the back, fold my arms, and walk toward the line of competitor tents.

Velda mingles serenely with some people at the radio station's pop-up booth, conversing with an air of tranquility about her that I haven't seen from her before. Normally, she's mousy and shy, but today, she's holding her body straighter, seemingly with a little more confidence in herself. She radiates joy as one of the announcers tells her something that makes her laugh. It's a belly laugh that judders her whole top half. It makes me think about last night, her body's convulsions. I have to look away quickly because I feel myself starting to harden again at the thought of it.

No amount of cold showers will ever be able to soothe the excitement I felt watching her body writhe against the upholstery, nipples stiff through the triangles of her spandex top, face contorted in ecstasy and confusion as her first-ever orgasm wracked her petite body.

I would have given anything to slide inside of her after she came, to feel her pulse around my girth, to push through her hymen like a marathon runner at a finish line, feeling her pussy swallow me up, wet and tight from her arousal.

Goddamned stupid fuckin' conscience...

I'm half-tempted to turn on the app and push the power button just to see if she's still wearing the toy. But instead, I walk away. If I don't stop thinking about it, I won't be able to disguise the fucking lump in my shorts soon with any alteration to my posture.

I see Ben and the others and wave. Just beyond them, Scooter towels his hair off under the furthest of the row of colorful tents.

There's the fucking boner-killing distraction I need.

I make my way down the row, throwing the shaka sign to some old friends while mouthing 'hang loose.' I breeze past excited spectators, eager cameramen, bright surfboards, product-laden banners, canvas folding chairs, rumpled beach blankets, half-grated bars of sex wax, and ice chests full of drinks.

I step beneath the last awning next to Scooter and adjust the four thousand dollar Ray-Bans on my face. He stops toweling and glares at me, his eyes snakelike, expression venomous.

"Great job out there. Beautiful 360 kick-flip there in the middle. Nice job on the rock dance at the end, too."

"Can I *help* you with something?" The words slither through his tensed jaw.

"I'm sorry about last night." I turn to him, speaking sincerely. "She's *sheltered*. I didn't think she knew to be wary."

"Wary of *what*? You act like I *drugged* her or was about to sell her into some *sex trafficking* ring. We were just swappin' spit. It wasn't a big fuckin' deal."

Those words from *his mouth* about *Velda* make me furious all over again. The image of it makes me want to hurt him.

…Hurt him to the point where he forgets she *exists*.

I look out over the water at the smattering of people standing on the shore, taking photos of McCarthy as she glides effortlessly along the edge of an eight-foot barrel. Storm clouds darken the sky, and shore-bound winds ruffle through my hair. I clutch my own biceps tight, mostly to keep from knocking Maggard's front four teeth right out of his piece of shit mouth.

Scooter watches McCarthy, and I step toward him, brushing my shoulder against his, speaking lowly into his ear.

"Touch Velda again, and they'll be finding pieces of you wash up from Ponce Inlet all the way down to Miami for the next ten years."

Silence.

His eyes flash to me with a look of hatred, shining like polished steel.

"Understood?"

He doesn't move. Doesn't speak.

I pat him on the back a little too hard to be a friendly tap.

"Good talk, Maggard."

As I walk away and mingle with the guests, Scooter only stands there, grinding his molars and feeling the weight of my threat.

Hours later, when I place the gold medal around his neck, he looks everywhere but in my eyes. We smile broadly for the cameras, for reporters and amateur photographers alike. But all the while, my eyes are vacant, mind preoccupied with the memory of Velda's toes curling around the wrinkle in my sea turtle comforter, the glistening crotch of the vibrating panty, the rise and fall of her panting chest, and the inhuman lurch of her perfect little body as she experienced her first -- *of hopefully many* -- little deaths.

34

Ansel

The stars are masked by a thick veil of clouds, and the wind howls through the warm night air. The palm fronds sound like the sweeping of a straw broom as they rub together around the beach house. Our bags are packed for the early morning flight back to New England, and I'm now seated in a lounge chair on the upper balcony, studying Velda's face as she moans into the froth of the churning hot tub.

I swipe the dial on the app, turning up the intensity of the vibrator between her legs, truly testing its claim about being submersible.

Her head lolls back against the headrest, mouth open in a silent howl as the tiny, shaking submarine in her panties edges her toward another climax.

Her bikini top is on right tonight, and the bubbles caress her tits as she takes turns biting her bottom lip and inhaling and exhaling deep gasps of air.

I fucking love watching her like this.

I love to watch the pleasure etch into her face. Or hear the soft, sweet moans escape her lips. I love the roundness of her back when her body arches. I love the taut skin of her throat as her head falls back.

And, Jesus Christ, do I adore the lost look in her eyes as her body flexes, like she's been thrust back into consciousness from a black void, blue irises darting around yet taking in little visual information beyond the ceiling of the balcony and the insides of her fluttering eyelids.

She is pleasurably intoxicated from the cocktail of chemicals her contorted body is producing, and I am high, too. High off the feeling of power that I wield over her all from feet away with the touch of my screen.

Best twenty-five dollars I have ever spent.

I want nothing more than to unzip my shorts and stroke my cock in tandem with her body's movements, imagining that it's the gentle nudge of my engorged head pressing into her entrance bringing her this elation.

But to do so feels like it would be a violation in some way, an even grayer line to cross than I already have. I've muddied the waters enough with this perverse act, something that has brought her to orgasm three times already and probably will at least once more after she recovers from her current one.

If she wants, I'll even give her one on the jet tomorrow, too.

I'd love to order her to hold her G.E.D. study guide as the vibrations ripple through her lower half.

That ought to help pass the time on the four-hour flight.

I'm extremely jealous of whatever lucky bastard gets to fuck this multi-orgasmic little angel first. But because of her age and because I brought her away from her home under the pretense of work, it simply cannot be me.

It wouldn't look right. It wouldn't *be* right.

Even though she *wants* me to.

Even though she asked without any sort of prompting.

Whipping out cash for her *per diem* the next day could feel disgustingly transactional, like some form of prostitution. I don't want her to look at me like a fucking John. Hell, one lie to the right lawyer about how I extorted her into sex with the promise of a paycheck, and I'm sure she could own half my fucking mansion.

Plus, she is only eighteen. Just turned, not even on the cusp of a less-gray *nineteen*. Physically, a gap of thirteen years, but mentally, possibly moreso due to her sheltered upbringing.

The entirety of the list of cons devastates me, but I know it is for the best.

For tonight, though, I will enjoy myself, watching her blushing face crow with pleasure until the vibrator runs out of energy... or until *she does*.

269

35

Velda

"Helena, can I ask you something?"

"Shoot," she says, eyes studying the *Cosmo* she's flipping through.

"What is a *blowjob*?"

My heart thunders as I ask it. I feel like she is going to laugh at how foolish I am.

"You've never heard of a blowjob?" She seems surprisingly unfazed, flipping through to another page. I guess after spending a few weeks with me, she is more used to my strange questions than I thought.

Despite telling her all about my kiss on the pier with the surfer, I haven't ever mentioned a word about the vibrator -- *or Ansel controlling it* -- in the two weeks that I've been back from New Smyrna Beach. I don't want anyone to know, and I certainly don't want to do anything that will make him stop. Having an orgasm is one of the best things I've *ever* experienced.

We've done our little ritual almost every night since the return from Florida. A few times in the privacy of my bedroom and a few times in the living room with the curtains pulled wide open, the ocean our only witness.

Never once has he touched me, and I have been far too nervous to ask. He always just *watches* me, eyes wide with fascination, like I must have looked when I saw my first movie at the cinema.

But now… I want him to do *more*.

I want him to *kiss* me.

I *desperately* want him to *touch* me.

And I want to do the same to *him*.

If I could only just find the words…

"Well, people call it a lot of different things. Hummer, head, blowie, blowjob, suck-job, slobbin' the knob…"

That makes me chuckle. I roll onto my belly on the flat lounge chair next to her, rest my cheek on the glossy cover of my test prep book, and drag my fingers through the sun-dappled grass of her backyard.

"Don't call it *slobbin' the knob,* though. That's a euphemism that doesn't belong in any sexy situation," she adds.

"Okay." I take a mental note of this. For only being a year or two older than me, Helena has so much wisdom on the subject. The thing I like most about talking to her is that she not only isn't appalled like anyone back home would be, but she always seems happy to inform me without judgment. Even though, back in Berks County, someone like her would be under the *bann* or dubbed a heathen for speaking of this stuff the way that she does.

Talking about this with her feels...

I don't know...

Healthy.

"A blowjob is just oral sex... on a *man*. It's called *cunnilingus* on a chick. But people usually call that 'eating a woman out' or, like, clam-diving or muff-diving. There's, like, a million sayings for it."

"Wow," I mutter, adjusting my gleaming bikini as the sun warms my shiny skin. The smell of the cream Helena told me to put on smells like coconut candy.

"A blowjob is just when you take a man's dick in your mouth and suck. It's, like, really easy. Men love it. *Obviously*."

"You *suck*? Why is it called a *blow* job, then?"

She laughs so loud that her voice rings out through the neighborhood.

"That's honestly a good question. Who the hell knows." She holds the magazine out to me. "You should make something like this little summer dress. You have great shoulders. You could totally pull off these straps. That shit would look hot as hell on you."

I look at the image and smile. It's such a simple design. I make a mental note to find a pattern later that I can alter when I do my afternoon sewing.

Then, it hits me that my question doesn't seem fully answered. "Wait, *then* what?"

"For the blowie? Then, nothing. Then you just suck and bob until he cums, pretty much. In the end, you just gotta choose whether to *spit* it, *wear* it, or *swallow* it. I always spit because I can't fucking stand the taste of it, and I don't want it all *Somethin' About Mary'd* in my hair."

"*Spit* it?"

"Guys tend to like it more if the chick wears it or swallows it. They think it's hot. Probably 'cause they aren't the ones who have to taste it or clean it up."

"What does it... *taste* like?" I am both a little scared to know and highly intrigued.

"Everyone says it tastes like something else. And what they eat definitely makes it taste different. Like, *coffee*... ugh, never let a guy splooge in your gullet after coffee. That shit is bitter and *nasty*."

I just stare at her as she flips pages.

During her silence, I watch a flock of small birds flit by, and a breeze rustle through the willows between the property. For a mere moment, I feel like I am in Pennsylvania again.

"It's not *bad*, usually. It's just not *good* either. Mostly, to me, on a regular day, it tastes like if you soaked a rubber band in warm water and then drank it."

"Why do people do it then?"

"Because it's hot. It makes them feel good. When you're giving a blowjob, *you* have the ultimate power. Even if you're on your knees looking like you're groveling like a slave, you're a Goddess. You're in full control over whether he cums or not. To *me*, that's hot."

She shrugs and flips through more pages.

"Takes a lot of trust with some guys, too. Imagine putting the most sensitive part of your body in the most dangerous part of a woman's. It's like *Fear Factor,* but with an orgasm prize."

She finally looks at me with a wide, devilish grin. "Wait... is Ansel asking you for some sucky-sucky?"

"*What?*" I feel appalled.

He has never once asked for anything sexual from me, a fact I find frustrating because I really wish he *would*.

Oh Lord, I know it's wrong to have these kinds of lustful desires in my heart. I don't know what's wrong with me. I hope you'll forgive me.

"No, absolutely not," I say quickly.

"Oooooh shit, is it that fine-ass G.E.D. tutor of yours? What's his name? Giancarlo? Giuseppe?"

"Giovanni."

"Mmmm, yeah. I knew it was a *Sopranos*-type name. I saw him leaving your place the other day. He is a *fine* little piece of ass."

I force a smile.

Giovanni *is* good-looking, I won't lie.

But he is *nothing* like Ansel.

"Okay, so when you take Giovanni's little Italian sausage into your mouth," she says, rolling her magazine into a tube in front of her face, "you wanna wrap your lips over your front teeth like this."

She curls her lips in for a moment, mouth in a tight "O."

"Then, you wanna be careful not to drag any of your molars on their dick. The skin is really sensitive. It basically feels the same as your clit, but for like their whole damn rod. That's why a lot of 'em cum way too fast. It's all just like one big sensory overload."

I realize that I haven't blinked in almost a full minute. I am soaking in every bit of it and doing my best not to look surprised. I think about the orgasms that I have had with the toy, about my *own* sensory overloads, and fight the urge to uncomfortably squirm in my lawn chair.

"Then, you just bob up and down on it and suck. Start slow, then pay attention to their body. If they start getting excited, you can ramp up the speed a little. It's, like, *super* easy." She giggles and unrolls her magazine.

"They usually give you a little extra praise if you can work the tongue right or if you play with their balls while you're doing it. But honestly, bob and suck and watch the teeth. That's all there is to a hummer, girl."

She flings the magazine carelessly on the grass, adjusts her Prada sunglasses, and takes her top off, a regular occurrence for her, often followed by a comment about not wanting tan lines. Every time she does it, I can't help but look at her breasts and study our bodies' similarities and differences. It makes me feel like I am normal, like everything is where it should be.

275

I admire how confident she feels in her own skin, and I want more than anything to feel that way about myself.

She chuckles and lays back in her chair again, this time, her whole upper half on full display. "Where'd you hear about blowjobs anyway?"

"They mentioned it in two of the books I have read. I just didn't know really what it was."

I don't tell her that I also saw it on my television in New Smyrna because I still feel a little ashamed that I watched it.

I also don't tell her that I desperately want to learn how to tell a man that I want to experience more than just a vibrator, no matter how much I love the feeling of the little death that comes with it.

36

Ansel

"Jesus, Wolf, you look like shit," Larry Cummings says, plopping into the armchair across the desk from me.

I smile. "You're looking great, too, Larry."

"No, seriously. Have you been sleeping? You look like a fucking *shell* of yourself, man."

Last night's voyeuristic adventure plays through my mind. From the doorway, I watched Velda, arched backward over the sewing table like a rainbow, pale hands clutching the bolt of fabric beside her like hawk talons, cheeks flushed to the color of bubble gum as the panty-vibe purred quietly in her shorts. It was the perfect vantage point for a vista of pleasure as another violent orgasm rocked her body.

I could have sworn when she climaxed, she murmured my name… *twice.* Surely it was only my deceptive brain tricking me into thinking I was hearing her beg for me, but my cock responded as if it were true.

I've had to jack myself off at least twice a night lately just to go to sleep because my perpetual hard-on keeps me too wound up.

Worth it, though.

It is getting harder not to touch her. Harder not to kneel down before her and replace the Bluetooth toy with my eager tongue.

"You ready for Nola?" Larry asks, ripping me back to reality.

"Hmmm? No. Not at all. I keep second-guessing everything. I know Clarence is just going to shit on anything I pitch. These last few years, it's all he does. I'm half-tempted to pitch the board a bunch of shit first and then wait for him to knock it all and then bring out the real designs."

"Don't do that. Come on. He's not that bad."

I tap my *Montblanc* on my desk and sigh. Every time Larry stands up for Clarence, it feels like he's gaslighting me.

"We gonna go alley-catting around the French Quarter again? Like last time? Remember that?"

I smile. "How could I forget? Last time was a blur of curvaceous Cajun strippers, lime-green hand grenades, and a river of beads. Jesus, how many beads did we throw last time?"

"Probably six hundred dollars worth over the course of two days," he muses. "This time, I'm steering clear of the hand grenades. I can't handle throwing up toxic-looking sludge again. It was like a scene out of the fuckin' Exorcist."

"I'm sticking with the sixteen-dollar bottomless mimosas this time down at Duke's."

"I can't wait."

"Neither can I. Velda's never been. I'm trying to picture how mind-blowing the Quarter is gonna be for someone Amish."

His smile sours. "Wait, you're bringing the girl?"

"Of course." I furrow my brow at him. "Why wouldn't I?"

"You're going to the home of the best fucking food *in America*... and you're bringing your *chef*? Are you insane?"

The word chef sounds weird since she has no formal training, but I don't correct him.

"I don't stop having high blood pressure just because I'm out of town."

"Oh, for fuck's sake! Come on! It's *two days*! How are we supposed to fuckin' get black-out drunk and wing-man each other if you're babysitting a Mennonite the whole time?"

"She's not Mennonite, she's—"

"You're missing the point, Wolf. This is New Orleans. When we aren't in stuffy board meetings, we should be out there picking up bitches at jazz bars or walkin' around, tanked, with a drink in each hand."

"*You* can still do those things, Larry. No one is stopping you."

"Are you fucking this chick?"

His question makes me panic, even though I haven't touched her. "What?"

"You... are totally fucking her. That makes... wow, it makes *so* much more sense now. Oh my

God. Has it been the *whole time*? Was she, like, your *Tindr* hookup in Reading?"

"Fuck you, Larry. I'm not screwing my cook."

I'm not.

Barely, but I'm not.

He doesn't need to know that I've imagined what it would feel like to fuck her in literally every fathomable position. Multiple times...

"Mmm-hmmmm. I'm not buyin' it." He smacks the desk a little with his hand. "Good on you, though. What is she? Nineteen?"

I feel an inch tall when he says it. Like I'm a monster for even *imagining* it. I don't dare correct him on the age, either.

"Hey, you know what they say: If there's grass on the field... play ball."

He stands.

"I never would have thought you the type to shit where you eat, but, hey, if your little Amish concubine can cook, too, I'm fuckin' jealous. My frigid bitch of an ex couldn't make a fuckin' *sandwich* to save her life."

He cackles crudely, hanging on the door jamb with his feet already in the hall. I lean back in my seat, feeling a low surge of anger seethe through my body. Him talking about Velda like she's my fucking subservient prostitute is making my blood pressure rise.

"It's why she's the *ex*-wife. Well, *that* and I walked in on her with the dick of her twenty-two year old assistant in her fuckin' mouth on *my* bed."

I nod, lips pressed tightly into a thin line. I want him out of my fucking office. I want the stink of this conversation to dissipate. I want him to go away before I lurch across my desk and knock his fucking lights out for talking about Velda like a goddamned sex toy.

He shrugs. "Eh, *good riddance*. I'm better off now." He slaps his hand hard against the door and lazily waves. "Later, Wolf."

Then, he howls at the sky, like the idiot always does, and makes his way down the hall.

37

Velda

"Hey, Lenny! How have you been?" Helena says it like she and the dirt-covered man in front of her are old friends.

"Hey, Helena," he mumbles through a mouth full of missing teeth. "I... I... I just remembered a story I... that I... that I wanted to tell you."

"Do tell."

I know my eyes are large when I look at him, but I can't help it. Never before have I seen someone that looks like him. He looks... bad. His skin looks like it is smudged with soot, and his clothes are torn and mismatched.

Helena looks unfazed in the slightest. She leans in like he is one of her friends from college or something, even though he has got to be an elder of at least three times her age.

Helena ladles a big spoonful of chicken noodle soup into the bowl on his tray and looks around. When she sees that the coast is clear, she gives him another half a ladle's worth and winks at him.

"I was... I was just gonna say that... well, that since you're from Montana, once I was driving through," he raises a shaky hand and points over his shoulder. His other hand tremors hard enough that the soup nearly spills. "I stopped at a bar and... ordered a drink..." he looks around, confused, and then remembers what he is saying, "and this guy... he sits next to me at... at the bar... and he says I'll have a Jack Daniels ditch, please. I says, what the heck... is... is a ditch. It's water. Apparently... in Montana, if you order a ditch, it means water."

"Wow, I'll have to remember that next time I go, Lenny." Helena smiles brightly at him. She looks like she's actually sincere. Like she's having fun.

"Fruit cocktail?" I ask, holding up a giant strainer spoon of grapes and melons.

"Yes, please." He nods, and I place it in an open compartment on his tray. "Okay, it's good seeing you, beautiful ladies. See you again soon, Miss Helena-Montana."

Lenny shuffles off, and I look at Helena. I feel like we both look silly in these hairnets, but I suppose to an outsider, a *kapp* must look just as strange.

"You're from Montana?" I whisper it like it's some kind of secret.

"No, a long time ago, I told him I was conceived there, hence the name, but he committed it to memory wrong, so he's always giving me little factoids about Montana. For example, did you know that sometimes mountain goats smash horns so hard that their hooves fall off?"

"No," I say, smoothing the apron over my new clothes, feeling sad that that man's shirt was full of holes.

"Or that no state has as many different animal species as Montana."

I nod. Then, after a moment, I ask, "Why do you come here?"

Helena looks at me strangely. "Because it feels good. Because helping other people is a nice thing to do. Some people donate money. We do that, too. My Dad gives about three hundred thousand to different local charities in a year. But I know a big part of why he does it is the write-off. For me, it feels good to give my time. Feels more valuable than money. Money comes and goes. You win some, you earn some, you lose some. But time, time you can't get back."

Another man comes through our line, and she greets him by name, too. They chat for a moment, and he waltzes off with his food.

Helena points to him with a ladle once he is out of earshot. "He was a Marine. Fought in Bosnia. Got a Purple Heart. Lost everything in a house fire a while back. Nice guy."

She points across the cafeteria to a couple. "Sherry and Paul. Paul's got a couple of conditions. Medical bills bankrupted them a while back. They've been coming in a while."

"You must come here a lot," I say quietly.

"It's good to give back." She looks down at the big pot of soup in front of her. "Whoever oppresses the poor shows contempt for their Maker—"

I interrupt. "...But whoever is kind to the needy honors *Gott*."

"Proverbs." Helena straightens her back and smiles at me.

I cannot believe she just quoted the Bible. All this time, all these weeks, she seemed like the kind of person that *Mamm* and *Fater* feared I would become, a promiscuous heathen. A heretic. A member of the flock that has strayed from *Gott*.

I am stunned to learn that despite her positions on *promiscuity* and *electricity* and *independence* and *photographs* and *vanity*... she still believes in the Bible and in *Gott*, after all.

It is the first moment of my life where I am starting to think that maybe my community is *not* somehow closer to the word of the Lord despite all of the pleasures we deny ourselves. Maybe we are *not* more holy simply because we fight to become a faceless mass. Maybe we are not better than the Englishers just because we deny ourselves the freedom to explore carnal desires.

Helena has done many things that the Amish would abhor, but at the end of the day, she is still going out of her way to do things in the service of *Gott*.

"Hey, Helena, Velda, he was the last one. You guys are all set if you want to split."

"Cool," Helena shouts and then grins back at me. "Come on, there's a sale today at the *Briny Babe* in Newport, and we are getting you a new outfit so you can go out on a date with Giancarlo."

"*Giovanni*," I correct her with a chuckle. I think she is saying his name wrong at this point on purpose. "Plus," I add, "we haven't talked about going out yet."

We haven't.

Sure, Giovanni has been flirtatious during my tutoring sessions, and he seems nice enough, but my thoughts have been *far* too preoccupied with Ansel lately to take the tutor seriously.

"Yeah, sure, whatever. *Giovanni*." She pokes me in the chest lightly. "And I don't care if we have to shut the plaza down, by God, we are getting you your first pair of high heels if it *kills* me. With legs like those, you're going to get a damn *fine* if we don't start showing those bitches off."

I laugh and take off my hairnet and apron, mentally calculating the amount of cash I have saved from my last three weeks of *per diem*. I still have no idea how much shoes cost. I only hope that it is enough.

38

Ansel

"Mother...fuck," I whisper, examining the shorn needle, snapped off just above the presser-foot of the Bernina. I look down at the neoprene and dig out the sharp metal remains. The thickness of the material is a bitch to sew, and the 3mm width is no match for the denim needles I keep going through.

The chipper lyrics of *Men At Work's* "Overkill" burble out of the room's built-in speakers, and although it's one of my favorite songs, the noise -- *any noise* -- right now only seems to agitate me more.

"Alexa, turn off the music."

A moment later, there is silence.

I groan and slump back in the seat. I pop up the presser foot, shear the string on the built-in razor, and pull the mock-up out completely.

It's not bad. I'm excited to see Velda try it on for the photo shoot with the neighbor girl on Tuesday, but at this rate, I'm never going to finish it tonight if I keep snapping shit.

I need a break to stretch. A quick walk on the beach. A stiff drink. Literally, anything to keep the rage for this fucking project stuffed down in my internal organs where it belongs.

I hear soft laughter downstairs, male and female, and suddenly I wonder what could *possibly* be so goddamn funny about mathematics.

I toss the wetsuit onto the sewing table, and it falls into a position that reminds me of Velda in that same spot two nights ago, grinding her molars and hissing from the intense pleasure as I increase the intensity of her panty-vibe.

The laughter continues, and I follow it down, hearing bits and pieces of a story about the tutor's high school math teacher and some stupid geometry *faux pas* that's making Velda giggle like she's listening to a stand-up comedian.

Despite how beautiful it sounds when she laughs, I feel irritated knowing the cause of it is the kid I'm paying to *teach* her.

A kid much closer to her age.

A kid who graduated with honors and made the Dean's List and is now attending URI on a full scholarship.

A kid with thick hair and cocky swagger sitting at my kitchen island leaned in far too intimately for such a dumb fucking story.

As they both come into full view, I bite my tongue and nod cordially. Velda sits straighter, pulling subtly away from him as I make my way to the fridge for a bottle of water.

"Hey! 'Sup?" Giovanni asks with a nod.

"Not much. Just taking a break." I grab a Fiji and purse my lips, annoyed.

With *him*.

With the *neoprene and the needles*.

With *New Orleans*.

With… *everything*.

"Cool." Giovanni clears his throat and turns back to Velda. "Anyway, that was it. He got fired shortly after that. They brought in a new teacher, Mrs. Henley. She was *great*. She was the one who ended up making it all sorta click."

I step out of the sliding glass doors and suck in a lungful of ocean air. It's therapeutic, the air here in New England. Good for the soul.

Still anxious, I take the short walk down to the sand. I watch the neighbor's gardener hustle, ever the busy bee. Their yard is starting to look like the sort of botanical garden you'd pay an admission fee to walk around in.

Tonight, it looks like he is diligently burying the roots of what looks like a new fruit tree in their miniature orchard, trying his best to get it in the ground before the last of the day's light vanishes, plunging the area into velvety darkness.

I watch the surface of the water ripple unnaturally as a school of minnows leaps and flutters out, their entire school under the threat of attack from a larger predator beneath the surface.

I sigh, still feeling the tightness of anxiety in my chest, constrictive and useless to me despite how hard it is working to do… *whatever the fuck it is supposed to do*.

I consider for a moment that this lingering irritation isn't from the wetsuit at all but instead from the proximity of Velda and her tutor, their flirtatious gaze, and the way he made her laugh.

I told her that there were certain things I wasn't willing to do.

Because she's so young.

Because she works for me.

Because we exist in different worlds.

Because this is all just... temporary.

I told her to find someone her age, and now she has. And, for the life of me, I can't understand why I felt such a twist in my gut when I saw them together.

Too close.

I make my way back to the house, wondering if the craft store will still be open long enough to grab a few more packs of needles. Maybe a drive will do me good.

But as my fist clasps the handle of the slider, I see it there. Giovanni's hand on her bare thigh, pinky finger nudging the bottom hem of her shorts.

The feeling in my gut wrenches, twisting so hard I can feel it radiate out through my limbs.

I slide the door open, and Giovanni's hand subtly retreats to his own jean-covered thigh. Velda's laughter dies down, and their eyes, once again, settle on me.

"Velda, can I see you upstairs right now, please?" I say it quietly, unable to hide how annoyed I am. Something about the image of him touching her is making my blood percolate to a fucking boil.

I make my way upstairs, knuckles nervously cracking as I turn into the second-story hall. I cross my arms in front of my chest.

Velda follows, wrenching one hand with the other. She stands before me, and I catch a whiff of her scent. It is something delicious, like citrus and cream. Her blonde hair is wild, and I have the urge to smooth it, to tuck it behind an ear that I know for a *fact* turns the shade of a pink carnation when she's aroused.

But I know if I touch her, I am going to lose myself. After all of our intimate sessions and fighting to keep my hands -- *and my goddamn cock* -- to myself, to finally do so would shatter me in a way that I would not be able to be whole again.

"W-what did I do wrong," she stammers, blue eyes darting around the polished wooden floorboards.

My shoulders slump because, although I want to yell or growl or chastise, I know I have no fucking *right*. After all, it was my mouth that told her that if she wanted more, she should seek out someone her own age.

And she did.

Or maybe it wasn't conscious.

Maybe it's just the natural way life is supposed to work.

I don't know why I fucking hate it so much, why it's making my hands shake.

"You didn't do anything wrong," I finally manage.

"You look... mad," she finally says.

"Velda, it's just," I point at the stairwell. "Why are you letting him touch you like that?"

Her eyes bolt up to mine, but her voice stays soft. "Because... Ansel, I want... to be *touched*."

"You can do better than him. *Look at you.* You're so fucking beau—"

I stop myself.

I can feel myself getting dangerously close to sliding further down the rabbit hole.

"I told you, Ansel. I am trying to make the most of this time that I am here. I can't stay forever. When I go back to Pennsylvania—"

"Velda, I *know*." I stop her before she can remind me that she will soon have to settle down, have to marry young, have to mother children.

The very thought of her lying with another man makes me feel sick at the thought. The thought of her meals made with love being gluttonously slurped down by some fuckhead in a wide-brimmed hat and a weird beard make me want to smash every knuckle on my right hand repeatedly into concrete.

"Ansel, this is my only-one chance to experience all of what this world has to offer." The way she says it, I am reminded that English was not her first language, something I find strangely exotic and endearing. Something I know her future husband cannot possibly appreciate.

She edges toward me, and I feel her sandals bump the front edge of mine. Her chest-length flaxen hair is dangerously close to brushing against my crossed forearms.

"Ansel." The way she says my name, there is a hardness to it. A firmness and confidence I have never before heard from her. "I *intend* to use it wisely."

The words feel like they suck all of the air from the room because of what she is implying. I feel my vision vignette darkening everything in my periphery... until there is nothing else in this world right now *but her*.

"I do not know how long I can stay. Where I am from, women are already settling down with families. One of my sisters already had two children by my age. Even though you say I am too young, I am old enough to know what I want."

I have never heard her talk like this.

So... *assertive.*

"He is not worth your time. Those kind of boys, they just screw you and leave. That's why they're called *fuckboys*."

But what she says next surprises me.

"I don't *want* him to stay. I don't want to start a life with him." She leans even closer. I can feel her nipples brushing against my arms through the fabric of her tank top, crying out for attention, hard enough to cut sheet metal.

"I want to experience... *everything that I can*... before I go back."

"Goddammit, Velda, I am..."

I quiet myself down, shouting in whispers so that the tutor doesn't overhear. My words wad in my throat like a jammed sock, strangling every syllable.

"*I am giving you what you want. Am I not?*"

Without so much as a blink, she finally says, "No. Not *everything*."

Her lustful look says more than her words ever could, and, with it, I know *exactly* what she is implying. The primal part of me desires to be that for her. Every fiber of my being wants to claim her, to be inside of her, to sully every pure-and-innocent inch of her gorgeous fucking body.

"*Velda*," I plead, the word coming out quieter than I've ever heard myself be. It is one word, but with it, I am trying to convey everything that I feel at this moment without saying too much.

"*What*?" There is defiance in the question. She's taunting me now. Trying to get me to bite.

And God help me, I want to bite…

"Giovanni asked me out on a date."

Every word of it feels strangely painful to hear from such cruel, beautiful lips.

"Give me one *good* reason why I shouldn't go," she traces the lilies on my chest with the feather-soft touch of her fingertip, "and I won't."

As if my arms are betraying my mind's orders, I feel them slip out from their folded spot across my chest, removing the safe barrier between our bodies. I watch, unable to override, as my hands slide up against the sides of her face, burying themselves in the blonde hair behind her suddenly pinkening ears. They move slow and with intent, and Velda gasps quietly. I press her against the coral-colored wall behind her, into the shadows of the hall. I step forward, and the charged chasm between us disappears again. My lips hover dangerously close to hers, and my waves of hair close in around us like a dark veil.

"Velda, please, I'm begging you."

She uses her nose to tilt my face away, and her whisper seeps into my ear as clear as a bell.

"You look so hot when you beg."

The words send a current from my throat to my cock, springing it to life with voltage like some Mary Shelly creation. It strains against her, through the fabric of my board shorts, like it's trying to reach out and touch her without my consent.

Further down I go.

Descending into this deepening pit of erotic madness and angst.

I can't take it anymore…

My lips crash against hers, and for a split second, as I savor the taste of her cherry chapstick, I feel the hunger of her body's eager response and the withering death of my willpower as it blinks out of existence.

As our tongues entwine, I feel like I'm falling, careening from a great height straight toward unforgiving ground.

I feel like the world I have known is at an end.

Her hands are in my hair, pulling me closer, feet clawing my calves like she is trying to climb me like a tree.

My body is not my own, hands foreign to me as they memorize the perfect curvature of her face, her neck. My body is helium, and the passion of the kiss is all that's keeping my body grounded.

I taste her tongue and suck her bottom lip, pressing against her so hard that I fear she might become one with the wall. My cock throbs, aching for her touch, pounding at the thought of being buried in her warmth.

We have crossed a new line.

A line that, for several weeks, I have been able to stay *firmly* on the right side of.

I pull away, but Velda is not ready to part. But I pull harder until what was once *one* is now *two* again.

She leans back against the wall, rose pink splashed all across her lightly freckled visage.

I stagger back, hopelessly stunned.

Jesus Christ, what have I done?

"*That*... cannot happen again," I finally manage, unable to wipe her balm from my lips because then it will be gone. Then, it will be *truly* over.

She catches her breath and straightens her clothes. She smiles brightly, the brightest I've ever seen her face. Like a light has turned on inside of her.

"That was all I needed," she finally says. "My one good reason."

"No, Velda. I *cannot* be your reason."

I want to scream. I *know* I'm giving her whiplash with my mixed messages. I want to punch myself in the face for the words coming out of my mouth. And I want to punch myself *harder* for not saying them sooner, for muddying everything in our worlds for good at the top of this stairwell.

"Velda, you *should* go out with him."

"But you said—"

"*Forget* what I said."

Fuck, forget what I did, *too.*

"If you need *more*, then… you should go out and get it."

Half a smile flits across her reddened lips, ones puffy from drawing them between my teeth with soft bites only moments before. She touches the railing to retreat back down the stairs and looks over her shoulder at me.

She is flawless grace, like a Vermeer oil painting. She is my *Girl with a Pearl Earring,* one with eyes that pierce like loosed arrows.

In seconds, she is downstairs, and I hear Giovanni's voice asking, "Everything okay?"

Banished here in my upstairs hallway, I think about the mistake I've just made, one just as cruel to Velda as it was to myself.

I must rid myself of this oppressive desire to be her *first*, to fuck her in a way that will brand my body into her mind for the rest of her life. To be the first mouth on those perfect, hardened nipples. To be the first tongue to lick that excitable little clit of hers to a screaming climax. To be the first curled fingers to massage that untouched G-spot. To be the first man to feel her orgasm grip his cock...

39

Velda

"Have you ever thrown an axe before?" Giovanni asks, tightening his grip around my waist.

I shrug. I am more focused on how strange my feet feel in the tennis shoes we had to rent because the lady at the desk said my heels were inappropriate.

"Don't worry, I'll show you how."

We follow a man in a uniform to a caged-in area with a large wooden bullseye mounted to a wall. Two axes are buried in a large hunk of severed tree trunk in the middle of a black, chain-linked area. The spotlight above is unflattering, beaming down on the employee's thinning hair as he explains the rules of the activity to us.

I can barely concentrate on anything he is saying because, behind me, Giovanni's hand drifts slowly south until it is gently on my right butt cheek. The feel of it sends a shiver through me, and I can't tell if the air conditioning is too high or if I am just excited to have a man's hand touching me this way.

"You're up first," Giovanni says, motioning to the axe on the right as he withdraws his hand from my body.

I timidly pick up the tool, similar to the one I have used countless times on the farm for chopping heaps of wood for warmth for our family in the winter. The moment its handle is in my grasp, I think about the farm. I think of Lavina, Abram, and Atlee. I think of my *Fater*, Menno's, stressed face as he poured over the bills. I think of Saloma's wedding.

And then I think of the moment I crawled out of the window and left everything I knew behind. My heart is heavy from that decision. I know that I have to go back eventually, but I want to hold on to this day and my kiss with Ansel as hard as I am holding onto this axe right now.

"Yup. Just... whenever you're ready. Take your time," Giovanni says, his tone sounding slightly impatient about how long I am taking.

I whizz the axe through the air, planting it squarely in the bullseye.

Giovanni and our instructor look shocked, but I am not. I could easily hit that thing from three times this distance.

"Jesus! Um, alright." Giovanni laughs nervously, picks up his axe, and prepares to throw it. "I *knew* I should have taken you to an arcade instead."

***

My tutor's car idles in park at the far end of Ansel's curvy driveway. I can see the house lit up

300

in the distance, the moon glistening off the rolling waves behind it. The sky is a deep indigo through the weeping willows.

"Well, tonight was… fun," Giovanni says. He seems a little deflated after losing all of the various games at the axe-throwing place.

I nod and smile, looking at him for a moment before staring down at my hands in my lap. I don't know what to do to get Giovanni to kiss me. I don't even know if I really want *him* to kiss me.

I want *Ansel*.

Ever since yesterday's kiss, my fantasies have been in overdrive.

But my days here are numbered, and I cannot fathom the rest of my sexual experiences belonging only to someone like Amos Miller, the boy who used to kick girls in the shins for no reason in the second grade. The boy who has darkness in his eyes sometimes…

In this moment, *Giovanni will have to do*.

"It's hard to turn around up there. Do you mind if I let you out here? It's easier to back out this way."

I nod, disappointed that this date won't be going any further.

Giovanni stares at me for a moment. He looks like he's debating something.

Finally, he leans forward, and the creak of his jacket against the leather interior is all I hear before his lips meet mine.

He kisses me.

With tongue.

But it is… *uninspired.*

Nothing like how Ansel kissed me against the hallway wall. This kiss doesn't take my breath away. It feels like an *obligation.* A *nicety.* My body doesn't respond to it at all like I thought it would. I thought I would be excited again. I thought my cheeks would feel hot or the area between my thighs would be wet like they were in the hallway.

He pulls away and taps the wheel. "Had a fun time with you."

"Me too. Thank you," I say, tugging at the handle of my door and placing my high heels into the loose gravel of the driveway.

"See you Monday for more test prep?"

"Yes." I feel the chilled night air kiss the sliver of thigh showing through the slit in the dress Helena talked me into buying for this occasion.

I shut the door and wave as Giovanni backs out of the drive. Salt and seaweed fill my senses as I make my way carefully up the lawn, trying not to fall on my way to the front door.

40

Ansel

I hear Velda's key click the deadbolt, and I look over my shoulder from the couch to see her enter the kitchen.

Her hair is pulled up tight and clipped. She looks *dangerously* fucking good, clad in a strappy black dress with a slit all the way up to her mid-thigh. And those high-heeled *fuck-me* pumps.

Christ almighty.

She reapplies her chapstick near the kitchen island, and her eyes meet mine as she does it. I haven't been able to stop thinking about the sweet flavor of that balm haunting my mind all damn day.

"How did it go?" I ask, unable to hide my disdain for the weasel she spent the evening with now that I am a couple fingers of whiskey deep. My eyes return to the crumpled designs on my coffee table, ones the board is going to shit on at my presentation in New Orleans in two weeks.

"It was fine," Velda says quietly, opening the refrigerator.

I crane my neck again to catch her expression as she notices the piece of cake I brought her back

303

from my dinner out with *TwinFin's* C.O.O. and his wife.

"It's for you," I say, unable to mask my sullen tone. I'm fucking frustrated.

About the kiss.

About their date.

About the anniversary of my Father's death tomorrow.

I haven't been able to get Velda out of my mind since the kiss yesterday, even moreso than usual. I half-assed my way through dinner with a lot of *Mmmm-hmmm's*, and *You don't says*, and *Wow, reallys*.

Velda appears by my side with the to-go container of cake and sets it on the table. She takes a seat on the couch next to me, touching my leg with hers when there is an entire couch at her disposal.

We both stare at the white frosting through the awkward tension. It is the closest I have been to her since the hallway yesterday.

"It's Chantilly cake. Layered. With berries," I huff. "Figured you might want to try it. Not sure if you have those in Pennsylvania. It's kind of hard to find."

"It looks delicious." But she isn't looking at the cake. She's looking at me.

"Have some."

She doesn't budge. I can feel the heat coming off of her.

"How was the meeting?"

I groan. "Lame."

Velda leans forward to look at some of the new mock-ups I've yet to sew for the pitch. I glimpse almost the whole of her back, nearly down to the cute dimples above her ass, through the cut-out in the dress. I want to run my fingertip along the faint horizontal line across her lightly tanned skin from a bikini string.

If she were *mine*, now is when I would attack, showering her with soft kisses and light touches, running my tongue along the waves of her spine up to the back of her neck, where her hair is elegantly pinned up. I would wrap my hand softly around her throat and pull her to me, whispering into her ear how badly I *need* to fuck her.

"I like this one," she says, ripping me from the momentary fantasy. "I would buy this."

She points to the coral-and-turquoise floral print long-sleeved rash guard. The thought of her in it sends another pulse of blood to my dick. I picture the fabric melding to the shape of her mouth-watering body. I picture laying her down on the couch while wearing it, sliding the crotch of it to the side, and slipping my tongue inside of her.

"Yeah, I like that one, too," I muster, clearing my throat. "But Clarence is going to hate it."

I abhor the print, he will say. *I don't see the point in women's rash guards. Stick to boards. It's your only strong suit.*

I feel my blood pressure rise at the thought of his comments, and my fingers tighten into a balled-up fist in my lap.

"Did you have fun on the date?"

I don't know why the fuck I asked. I don't actually want to know... unless it was *terrible*.

"Mmm. It was... fine."

Her lackluster response fills me with warmth and a bit of strange joy.

Not great. Not stellar. Not even *good*.

Just... *fine*.

"We went axe throwing."

"In that?" I glance at her sexy dress and heels that add several inches to her.

She chuckles and covers her face, a little embarrassed. "Yes."

"Sounds... fun," I lie.

"He did not like that I was better at it than he was." Her eyes meet mine, sparkling in the pendant lights above.

My gaze lowers to her puffy lower lip. There's a hint of redness to it. I remember the reapplication of her chapstick moments ago, and it dawns on me that they kissed. The mental image of her lips on his sends a woof of fire barreling through my insides.

You told her to find someone younger and she did. Breathe, Ansel, I tell myself.

"It's starting to sweat. You should try it." I clear my throat and nod at the dessert on the table.

She stands and bends over, giving me the most perfect view of her ass. She decides to forgo the fork and dips her finger deep into the side of it. She turns and places the cake on her tongue, eyes locked on me. Something glimmers in them. Confidence and assertion, like yesterday in the hall.

But there's something more, too. Something like a hint of seduction.

She savors the bite of cake and smiles, sucking the remnants of it off of her fingertip with the most stunningly-wicked smirk I have ever seen her make.

I am stunned, unable to move except to subtly shift my fist into my lap in an attempt to cover my newly amassing hard-on.

Her hands slide to her skirt, grabbing the fabric and hiking it up a few inches. She kneels to one side of me with a knee.

And then places the other. For a moment, I don't breathe as she straddles me. I am a lantern fly in a spiderweb. I close my eyes. Her lace panties brush against the knuckles of my hand, and my cock pulses with life beneath my palm.

"Velda... *don't*," I beg, breathing in her scent. Today, she smells faintly of cherry blossoms, sweet and delicate. It makes it hard to open my eyes. I want to smell it for eternity.

She leans forward, and I feel my nose brush the straps of her dress and drag across her skin. I feel her feather-soft fingers slide through my hair, exciting my scalp.

"Ansel."

That's all she says.

Nothing follows.

But the way my name sounds in her mouth now is sexier than the way she moans it in my wildest fantasies.

"*Please.*" Her nose brushes mine as she whispers it.

"Velda…"

It hurts me to say the word 'no' again. Physically *pains* me. I can't seem to get it across the threshold of my lips.

"*Ansel.*"

This time, the word is right in my ear, followed by the brush of her lips along the outer shell of it. I feel her crotch settle harder against the knuckles of my hand. Despite my stoic response, I can even feel the slickness of her slit through the scratch of the lace.

I swallow hard. With a single, adept twist of my hand, my fingers could be inside of her, probing for that little spot that will make her shudder in my arms like she's dying.

But my hands stay palm-down, covering my erection, keeping a safe barrier between us.

I feel like my fucking heart is going to beat straight out of my chest. The irony of bringing her to Rhode Island to *aid* this organ is not lost on me in the intensity of this moment.

I can feel my breath reflect back in my face from the closeness of her sternum as she begins to grind, slow and intentional, rotating her pelvis harder against my knuckles in the delightfully familiar circles I have seen her make countless times against the toy in the past few weeks.

...During our private little secret times.

I feel a finger trace the lines of my tattoos down my neck and through the open neckline of my silk button-down shirt. My skin ripples with goosebumps, and I stifle a soft moan in my throat.

I feel her tremble, arms sliding to the tops of my shoulders, forehead pressing against my own.

I still can't open my eyes. It takes every bit of concentration within me to keep my hands in place, to keep my lap from driving upward, bucking against her for some delicious friction. I would be too tempted to see if I could get her off without anything other than the grind.

But this, what she is *doing*, what I'm *allowing*... it is *beyond* playing with fire.

I am burning alive with the need to be inside her. The need to slip my tongue into her virgin-tight pussy and lap up every drop of her.

I feel a fallen tendril of her hair brush my cheeks as her body trembles against me.

"*Velda, this has got to stop.*" I feel my upper lip brush her lower one as I say it.

"*Kiss me again,*" she begs, her whispered words tearing me apart.

"*I can't.*"

I feel my resolve weakening with every rotation of her hips against my pelvis.

"*Why?*" I feel her chin press to the top of my head, arms drawing my face to her until my mouth is against her throat, one thrumming with an excited pulse. Her pelvis tips forward, driving sensually against me again, and it takes every bit of self-control to still myself.

I am tempted to cup my hands up, to grind them against her clit, but I flatten them as much as my straining cock will allow instead, trying my best to fight the temptation to make her cum against me.

"Fine."

The single word stuns me.

I feel her body bend backward. She feels like she is about to fall off my lap, and the intense shift in weight forces me to look.

She bends back with all the feminine grace of a ballet dance and tightens the grip of her muscular thighs. I can see her soaked panties peeking from beneath the rumpled bottom of her dress, now little more than a belt of loose, black fabric around her tapered waist.

She pulls herself back up to me with a slow-motion sit-up and grinds harder against my hand with a wad of Chantilly cake between her thumb and index finger.

"Then, at least eat some cake."

I stare at her, stern and serious, held erotically hostage by the golden-haired Goddess before me.

Finally, I part my lips slowly, waiting for her to feed it to me. My waved white flag of surrender.

Instead, she pulls the right strap of her dress down over her pale shoulder, exposing her bare breast to me for the first time intentionally. Her nipple is the same perfect shade of light pink as her cheeks, hard as a diamond.

She locks eyes with me as she smears the finger's worth of Chantilly icing down it, covering its rosy coloring with opaque white cream and engaging in another slow rotation of her hips so that her pussy rubs my knuckles again.

"*Fuck.*" A pained groan escapes my lips. It's the last sound I make before I lunge forward, betrayed by my abdomen, my spine, and my weak, crumbling will. I drag my tongue over her areola to indulge in the heavenly bit of icing. My lips lock around her nipple, and I feel my teeth drag across its pebbled surface, biting it gently and eyeing her with a promissory threat to clamp down harder if and when I choose.

She moans, loud and mournful, soft voice echoing across the expanse of the living room.

The sound of it damn near makes me cum.

My hands slip out from between us and roam up into her once-tidy up-do, pulling back with both, arching her back at a severe angle that gives me all the access I crave to lean forward and lick the gorgeous little sugar-coated bud again.

Her pelvis slips down against me, and in an instant, I can feel the warmth of her through my shorts. She moans again as I suck her nipple harder, following it with a soft, languid swirl of the tongue.

Fuck.

I'm going to Hell. I might as well enjoy it.

311

When I pull my face back, her once light pink areola is an agitated raspberry color, starkly contrasted by the fair triangles of pristine skin where her breasts have never seen sunlight.

Velda thrusts herself forward to kiss me, and I pull her back by the hair and shake my head. I drive my pelvis up against hers once slowly. I feel her body tremble with a soft wave of pleasure at the sensation.

"*I want,*" she pants, "*you to take me. Slow... and gentle. I want you to be my first, Ansel.*"

There is a long silence between us as she lifts herself a few inches and slides back down hard into my lap.

Her eyes are slit, intoxicated from the flood of chemicals rushing into her body.

She reaches down and slips her hand inside the waistband of my shorts. With one hand, I halt her search for my cock. With the other, I pull her closer to me, just out of reach of my lips, and hold her there.

"*No,*" I whisper.

Her hands go slack, and her shoulders soften. It is the last word that she wanted to *hear* and the last word that I wanted to *say*.

"Go to bed." I stare at her lips, the Devil on my shoulder urging me to take a parting taste before she leaves. Instead, I slide my hands to her waist to pry her off my lap. I tug her wrist out of my waistband before her delicate fingers find purchase on my rigidity.

Before something is done, that can never be undone.

The sting of the rejection in her eyes makes me feel hollow, and at this moment, I absolutely *hate* myself for it.

Reluctantly, she stands, one creamy breast still freed from the confines of her black dress. Her once-tight up-do is disheveled. She drags the wrinkled fabric back down over her hips and does something that I don't expect...

She smiles.

There is a wildness behind it, a smug satisfaction. It makes me want to bend her over the arm of this couch, shred her panties, and fuck that wet pussy of hers until she sees stars.

"*Gut novid*, Ansel," she mumbles before biting her lower lip. "You know where to find me if you change your mind."

The comment is a bullet. A direct hit.

I *do* know where to find her.

I know *exactly* which bed I could crawl into right now to fuck her into oblivion, to make her scream my name, and make every needy orifice on that taut body all *mine*.

But I don't move.

Instead, I sit in front of a marred Chantilly cake and a pile of rumpled spandex. I watch her spiked heels disappear up the stairwell as I wait for my heart to stop pounding like something out of a goddamned Edgar Allen Poe story.

***

An hour later, I have disposed of the remains of the Chantilly cake and taken one of the longest showers of my entire fucking life. I *refuse* to masturbate to the thought of Velda tonight. I am too close to caving in, and it's obviously not easing any of the temptation.

I towel off, throw on a fresh pair of boxer briefs, and slide into bed. Frustrated, I scroll through my phone, debating whether to start another long conversation with a woman on my myriad of dating apps just to distract my mind and maybe get laid by someone more appropriate in the near future. Someone who isn't a barely eighteen-year-old employee.

The doctor told me to get more sleep, and I feel like I'm getting less. I opt instead for something to wind me down. Something bland and not an ounce of sexy to ease my mind.

I pluck a book off my nightstand, a memoir about an Australian surfer who lost his arm in a shark attack and went on to win competition medals again a decade later.

My eyes scan the page I'm on, but I find myself re-reading the same thing twenty times before I give up and take a seat on the bench at the foot of the bed. I cradle my head in my hands, feeling my damp hair drip down my forearms.

I want to scream.

I hate myself for the way I feel, hate myself for not showing more restraint with someone in my employ, someone so young, so impressionable.

People are going to think I'm *grooming her* or something.

Oh. Fucking hell, am I *grooming her?!*

No. I tell myself that I brought her here with the best of intentions. She was so sweet and sheltered. I wanted her to expand her horizons.

And moreso, I brought her for my *health.* However, even though my last blood pressure reading was down a little, I feel like this shit is ripping me apart internally.

I wish I had more friends or a fucking parent to call, someone who could guide me in the right direction. A dad to tell me I'm either being foolish as Hell or to follow my idiot heart.

Dad.

Jesus.

I check my watch. It's after midnight. Officially the anniversary of my Father's death.

Great. Fucking add that *to the pile.*

A soft knock sounds on the door, and I look at the ceiling for answers, knowing no one has ever gotten actual verbal guidance from there. Still, I am hopeful that whoever is up there will tell me what to do.

The knock comes again, slightly heavier this time, in case I missed it before.

I don't bother covering myself. This is about the same amount of clothes she's seen me surf in. "Yes, Velda?"

The door swings open slowly. Velda is there, bundled in a fluffy robe, wet hair framing her glowing face.

"What?" It comes out more curt than I intended, but goddammit, I'm pissed.

Even though I can't fucking have it, what I want is right here in front of me.

So close that I can taste it.

And it tastes like Chantilly cake...

She studies me, trying to decipher how angry I really am and how much is for show. Surely, by now, she knows I'm part bluster, huffing and puffing like my big bad fairy tale namesake.

She picks at something on the door frame and shyly mumbles, "I was just wondering..."

"What, Velda? Please... spit it out. It's late."

"Um, I was just wondering..." She swallows hard, and I watch the lump descend to the slight gap at the top of her robe. *"Can I play with my toy?"*

It is her way of asking if I will operate the vibrator for her.

"No."

She stares, contemplating a rebuttal. I head her off at the pass.

"Good girls get to play with toys. Bad girls go to bed."

"I can be a good girl."

Fucking hell...

Hearing her say it makes me want to faint.

I shake my head. "What you did tonight..."

She steps forward, closer to me, and kneels down, an act that has my dick at full mast again the instant her knees touch the white carpet.

Fuuuuck.

316

"Then…" her voice softens, tone quieter, "can I give you a blowjob?"

A laugh erupts from my lips, and I cover them with my hand.

I didn't even know she'd ever heard that word before.

My little meek Amish beauty, my Sarah, Plain and Tall… *sexually corrupted.*

"I don't think you know what you're talking about, Velda. Where did you hear that from?"

"Please, Ansel?" She does a slow shuffle on her knees until she is poised between mine. My dick is so engorged at the sight of it that it is sending out agonizing pangs of pain.

"You want to suck my cock?" As I ask it, I don't even recognize my own voice. I don't know who I *am* in this moment.

She nods eagerly, fingers beginning to claw at the soft butter-blend material of my underwear.

"Strip."

Inside, I am screaming at myself, but a light of something shimmers in her eyes when I say it.

A spark of… joy.

She stands and, with trembling hands, removes her robe, baring her naked body, save for the black thong with the pouch sewn for her toy.

She is perfect. Lean and fair, with breasts aching to be given the adoration they so deserve.

I shake my head.

"No. *All* of it."

Eyes locked on me, she slides the black panties down her legs, and I drink the whole of her in, a being more stunning in person than she ever was in the far reaches of my perverted mind. I study the light triangle of hair between her thighs, the only part of her that I've not seen until now throughout the various adventures in our weeks of compounding *dirty little secrets*.

"Spin," I say, trying to hold everything inside. Trying to hold back how much a body like hers could bring a weakened man like me to my fucking knees.

She follows the order, and I commit her to memory, from the gentle curves of her calves to her round spank-able ass, to the graceful slope of her back.

"You really want to do this?"

She nods and kneels naked before me again in a pose of worship that makes my breath hitch the instant she does it.

"I don't know if I will be any good. But I want to try."

I rattle at the thought of mine being the first cock inside that beautiful little mouth.

"Okay." The simple word undoes me. I nod to the aching lump in my boxer briefs.

I'm not going to help her with this part.

I am going to give her every opportunity possible to chicken out. But I should have known she wouldn't.

She tugs my underwear down. My cock is so rigid and engorged that it nearly hits her in the face when she gets the elastic over it. She takes a moment to really take it in, to see what, until now, might have only been a strange myth in her mind. It dawns on me at this moment, due to lacking Amish sexual education, that it might be the first one she's ever really seen.

I wish it were not so aggressive-looking for her first time sucking cock. It's the hardest it has ever been in my life, an angry shade of pink up the thick shaft and a violent purple at the head.

She drags the underwear the rest of the way down my thighs, off my calves and feet. I lean back a little and place my elbows on the mattress for the best vantage point of it all.

With almost no hesitation, her fingers slip around it. She looks up at me.

"I'm nervous." Her voice sounds so innocent. So genuinely sweet.

I offer a smile, suddenly reminded that she is such a delicate thing.

"You're doing great."

She licks the tip, and I feel my jaw tighten. A stunning current of excitement rocks me as I feel her hot, wet mouth slowly envelop the head.

A moan escapes me, and my eyes threaten to close at how good it feels, but I war with them to stay open, needing to burn every moment of this into my memory forever.

Her lips are curled over her teeth, and her mouth is tight, warm, and enthusiastic as she glides up and down my shaft with a slow speed that is driving me fucking wild.

"*Mmmm, good girl,*" I growl, slipping my hand gently into her damp blonde hair, fighting every urge within me to pull her down on it until I bottom out at the back of her throat.

Instead, I let her set the pace and hold my hand to her lovingly as if my arm were just an extension of her.

She is running the show.

She slides back to the top and bobs back down, taking as much of me in her as possible with each downward stroke. She finds a pace she likes and increases suction with every slide up.

"*Fuuuuuuuck*," I groan, feeling lightheaded.

Two more minutes of blissfully existing inside of her tight mouth, and I am *there*, on the crest, my dam ready to burst.

"*Fuck, Velda, I'm gonna cum*," it is half a warning, half a Holy revelation, a buildup to a release harder than anything I have ever felt.

I expect her to pull back, to shy away from what is incoming, but she bobs down harder, taking me into the back of her throat and caressing my thighs as my body launches into a spasm.

My growl echoes off the walls of this room, followed by quiet, chastising voices in my head, crowing that I can never go back now, that I have hit a point of no return in this journey.

I feel Velda swallow hard, taking every last drop of what I have to give. My clenched fingers unfurl from the snarled mess I've made of the back of her hair. She lingers on my cock, lovingly cradling it in the warm cocoon of her mouth before finally pulling away from my lap with a smile.

I pant hard, back collapsed against the corner of the mattress.

She wipes her lips, eyes never leaving mine.

"Come here," I order, in between huge lungfuls of air.

She stands, bared fully before me. My hands grasp the smooth skin of her hips, and I pull her toward me, guiding her down onto my lap, my spent cock between our bodies.

My hands rise to the sides of her face and pull her to me. I kiss her softly, with passion, with gratitude, with care. She kisses back with warmth, with sparking excitement.

I tell my brain that this is a one-off, a single-time deal where all transgressions can be forgiven if I just pray hard enough.

But as my mouth moves south, lips and tongue delighted by the sensitive buds on her chest, I know I would be a fucking *fool* to believe that I won't let it happen again. I know as my hands slide over her hips and onto her ass cheeks in tandem with a gruff squeeze to both that I'm an *idiot* to even think that could ever be the truth. And I know, as I lift her into the air and twist to sprawl her on my thousand-dollar imported sheets, that I want more of her.

She looks up at me from propped elbows, perfect tits on display, and asks, "Are you going to get the toy?"

I smile, the spider to the fly, the *wolf* to the red-caped girl.

"I was going to do you one better."

Her eyes are blue beads, glassy and focused, ready for whatever I'm proposing. She swallows hard again.

"Spread your legs."

She smiles, my *Sarah, Plain and Tall*.

I part her thighs slowly with my hands and kneel on the seat at the base of the bed, exposing her virgin pussy between my glistening fingers like a blossoming pink tulip. She holds her breath as I touch her most intimate parts, mouth open, despite the fact that there is no air crossing its threshold.

"I'm going to return the favor." My head lowers between her knees, eyes locked like a jaguar about to pounce. "Unless you'd *rather* have the toy."

Her face is bright red now. She smacks her lips closed and shakes her head emphatically. I swipe a thumb lovingly up through her wetness to her clit. She bites her lip.

I lean in and slide my face between her thighs, replacing my thumb with my eager tongue, lapping up every drop of her as her guttural cries and gasps fill the room with a pure, symphonic overture of pleasure.

I lick a stripe up and suck her clit, the spot that has given her so much intense satisfaction these last few weeks.

I bury my face against her, teasing and licking, swept up in a vortex of time morphing the length of every second.

Her noises intensify until she is screaming out, twisting and bucking against my quick tongue with a body-tensing climax that has sweat streaming down the back of her thighs. Her perched feet on my shoulders are like new tattoos among the old, ones I'd keep on my body with the same permanence if I could.

My tongue slows, doing a final pass up through her glistening lips, now an angered pink from the presence of my facial hair. The tip of it probes, sweeping against her hymen and up around the thatch of saliva-slick hair to the fuchsia clit beneath.

I commit it to memory, this perfect illustration of female anatomy forever secretly marked by my touch as its first-ever tongue. I want to remember how it looks because *this... can't ever happen again.*

The moment I slip out from beneath her trembling thighs, they are replaced by a new weight, the weight of weakness, heavy from all the guilt it brings.

Velda lays in silence for a moment, catching her breath as I softly nibble her thighs from the bench, touching my teeth to her pliable flesh with gentle mock bites.

Finally, she forces herself to sit up, and I see the wet streamers of tears beside her glistening eyes, ones that go straight into the hairline at her temples instead of down her smiling cheeks.

I lean up and kiss her, pulling her head to mine with hands dewy from her sweat and arousal.

I can taste myself on her tongue, faint like her mouth has its own memory. I only hope that in the years to come, the ghost of me is always there.

41

Velda

It has been eleven days since I came to Ansel's room. Eleven days since experiencing two new firsts. In that time, he has kept things strictly platonic. Even with my toy.

I never breathed a word about it to Helena, even though we have spent many of the days together since, shopping, studying, and even doing yoga in her huge backyard full of flowers. We even did a photo shoot on the beach with some of Ansel's new prototypes and Helena behind the camera.

During those eleven days, I remembered my *Mamm's* favorite Proverb:

Idle hands are the Devil's workshop.

So, in between meal preparations, I busied myself with studying the materials for my G.E.D. and my driver's test. I also poured myself into sewing, teaching myself how to make more intricate items of apparel from patterns and making a closet full of beautiful clothes, though my parents wouldn't approve of any of the patterns. They believe that wearing anything flashy feeds into one's own vanity, which is, perhaps, one of the most frowned-upon sins in my community. Even our dolls are not allowed to have faces for this reason. It is why we all have to dress similarly when we are there, and part of the reason we don't allow our pictures to be taken.

In my community, we aren't allowed to wear purple. It is the color of the Jezebel, the harlot. But, since I have been here, awakened to so many pleasures of the flesh, the color has been calling to me, and most of my closet bears clothes in various shades of it.

When in Rome...

I know what Ansel and I have done is supposedly wrong.

In the eyes of the *Lord*.

In the eyes of the *church*.

In the eyes of my *community*.

Maybe I have strayed too far.

Maybe I am but a wayward member of the flock, in need of a shepherd to bring me back to righteousness.

But the things that I have done don't... *feel* wrong. My veil of shame has lifted since I have been here, since experiencing so many of these things.

A few nights after Ansel kissed me... well, after doing *many* things with me, I started to... *touch myself*... in bed. I pretend that my finger is his tongue.

I was shocked to find out that I could bring myself to an orgasm with just my hand! After a few nights, I realized I didn't even need the toy. Maybe I *never* needed it.

Maybe I had this skill all along and simply never knew about it. I don't know if *everyone* is capable of this feat, but when I discovered it, I felt...

Powerful.

I feel like I am forever changed by this secret knowledge of my body and how it works and responds.

I wonder, if I hadn't left Pennsylvania to come here... would I have ever discovered this power, this gift that makes me feel divine, this thing that allows me to control my own pleasure?

I ease my foot off the pedal and let the Bernina's whirring slow to a halt. I raise the presser foot and pull the garment up and out, slicing the string off on the built-in blade.

These people sure thought of everything!

I tug the dress over my head, feeling the soft purple jersey fabric brush my skin. I close my eyes, imagining it as Ansel's hands instead, caressing my body like he did eleven nights ago.

For the first time, I fear that I may have gone too far, experienced too much to settle for a life back on the farm with someone like Amos Miller. This chance to experience things has backfired horribly, and yet, at the exact same time, I feel like it has given me wings to fly, wings that had once been painfully clipped.

The people that I have met are not perfect, but I do not believe in my heart that *Gott* has damned all of these Englishers simply because they do not live like us. I do not believe that their ability to express their personalities through clothing and makeup makes them any less worthy of *Gott's* love. I do not believe that because they brush their teeth with electric toothbrushes, drive cars, or engage in sexual acts for pleasure, they are somehow less in *Gott's* eyes.

Ansel has taken me in, given me everything I've ever needed to *thrive*, and encouraged me to do more with my life. He awakened my body *and* my mind.

I adjust the fabric, amazed at how I look in it wearing the push-up bra Helena gave me. I eye myself in the mirrored wall of the room, studying the curves of my hips, my thighs, and the exposed tops of my breasts.

I know when I go back, I will have to give this all up. Every inch of fabric. Every book and trinket. I know that I will not be permitted such trappings once I am baptized, once all of these sins of my youth are washed clean, and I take my vows to the Ordnung.

But as this dress, in this shade of promiscuous purple, settles over my skin, and I see myself -- *really see myself* -- for the first time, I wonder if I will ever want to leave.

42

Velda

"Okay, you see that set coming in?" Ansel points to a group of three waves, each the same distance apart.

"Yes." I smile, straddling a long foam-covered surfboard. My body is hugged by the rubbery pink outfit I'm zipped into, which he calls a spring suit. He sewed it for his pitch in New Orleans and said that I inspired it because I'm 'bright... like the color.' He said if they approve it, he is going to name the design 'The Velda' on the website. He gave it to me as a present this morning, along with the longboard I'm on and the stretchy leash tethering my ankle to it so it can't float away if I fall off.

"You wanna give it another shot?" Ansel asks, wading in the saltwater beside me. Ever since I learned how to swim, he's been taking me out into the ocean as often as he can.

Last week, I asked if he would teach me how to surf, and I don't know if I have ever seen him smile quite so big.

"I'm going to fall off again."

"Yep." He nods. His curls are drenched. He looks so handsome when he's wet. "You will fall off a thousand times. But if I know Velda Yoder, she will get up one thousand and one."

I look back at the incoming set of waves.

"One more try. If you fall off, I'll treat you to ice cream." He shrugs. "See? It's a win-win."

He knows I have grown to love the ice cream place just down the beach. I vowed to myself weeks ago to try all twenty-eight of their flavors. So far, I've gotten sixteen.

I look at the waves again and finally nod to Ansel.

"I knew you had it in you." He swims backward a few feet away from my board. "Okay, you know what to do. Just remember the pop-up I taught you on the beach."

I nod again and study the wave. I spin on the board, feeling the full weight of my body press my ribs down into the foam. The swell comes, and I feel it lift me. I paddle with all of my might, feeling the burn in my shoulders and forearms. I feel the wave rush up, feel the fear twist in my belly like I am going to be thrown at the shore by an unseen hand.

At the top, I try to pop up like Ansel showed me, but the wave rocks me, and I only get my knee on the board before I teeter over the side and splash into the water.

It is hard to describe the sound of the ocean's heartbeat when you are fully submerged, but it's there, pounding softly all around you as you float through a mass of bubbles and feel the tickle of seaweed. It beats with a force unlike anything on land I have ever known. It feels like it is the earth's womb and that every time I claw my way to the surface and gasp my first breath of air, I am born all over again.

I wipe the stray hair from my eyes. My braid has to look like an absolute mess. My feet finally find purchase in the rocks and sand below, and I feel my tethered leg yank me with every wave as the board bobbles toward the shore.

Ansel is there, a small speck in the water where I was only moments ago, like an ant in a lake. His hands are raised in celebration, and I can barely hear his cheers through the wind.

I fell, but still, he's genuinely happy for me...

Happy that I didn't let fear stop me.

***

"What are you getting today?" Ansel asks, staring up at the board in front of us as the last remnants of water from his hair drip down his tattooed chest like warm rain. He looks so good right now that I want to lick every bead of it off of him until I reach his mouth.

I imagine him kissing me back, the way he did that night...

"Velda?" He says my name softly, and it snaps me out of my trance.

"Oh, um, chocolate chip cherry vanilla, please," I say to the young girl working at the ice cream stand. It's a small building about the size of my bedroom at Ansel's house. It sits on a curved road lined with tall grass, prickly beach roses, and knee-high rocks. Block Island Sound sits behind it, peppered with surfers all sitting in a row on their boards, trying to patiently bide their time until they can get a wave. On the sand, between the ice cream shop and the water, families sit on beach towels and large blankets, some in chairs, some beneath pop-up tents like the ones in New Smyrna. A group of kids bounce a white ball back and forth to each other over a net. Others are soaking up the sun with drinks in their hand.

"Here you are. One vanilla bean and one chocolate chip cherry vanilla." The girl hands two single-scoop cones over to us, and my stomach groans with anticipation.

"Thank you," I barely manage to say before I attack the frozen treat. Ansel pays her, stuffs some cash in the tip jar, returns his wallet to his pocket, and then places his hand on my lower back, guiding me down the beach road as we enjoy our treats.

"Thank you for this," I say, holding up my ice cream. The arms of my wetsuit flop against my thighs as it is unzipped down to my hips. My holographic bikini top keeps catching the light and lighting up bright dots all over Ansel's chest. He says it looks like a disco ball. I don't know what that is, but seeing the white spots on him makes me giggle nonetheless.

"Of course. I'm proud of you. Gotta celebrate the little things. Two months ago, you'd never been in a real pool before. Now you're learning to surf. With your persistence, I believe there is nothing in this world you can't do."

I blush at the compliment. He makes me feel amazing when he says things like that.

"Tom says tomorrow you take your test to get your learner's permit."

I am too lost in this moment to respond, watching his tongue slip across the creamy mound of his ice cream as he studies the surfers. The pointed tip of it digs a soft groove into the dessert. I am plunged back into the memory of the night he laid me down on his bed and devoured me in a similar fashion.

"Velda?"

"Yes?"

"I asked if tomorrow you're taking the test to get your permit."

"Oh. Sorry. Yes, I am."

"When do you take the G.E.D.?"

I lick a renegade drip of melting ice cream off my cone. "Giovanni has it scheduled for the Tuesday just after you get back from New Orleans."

"Oh, that's fantastic. If you pass, we'll celebrate. Maybe throw a party or something. You look like the kind of woman who would enjoy a rager." He grins at me, and I melt faster than the frozen cream in my hand.

"What's a *rager*?"

He laughs. "It was just a joke. It's like a wild party." He crunches into his cone, swallows, and then points the remainder of it in my direction. "Speaking of wild parties, I'm excited to take you to *Nawlins*. It's a cool place. It's like a celebration all the time down there. Tons of jazz music, flowing booze, good food, and all kinds of weird stuff. People throw beads at each other and wear masks. People dance in the street."

"Do I get to go?"

He scoffs. "Of course, you're going. Don't be silly. I need you."

I know he is only joking, but those three words fill me with a warmth that rivals the sun.

"I am excited to see… *Nawlins*."

He laughs. "Wow, see? You're already saying it like the locals. They may never be able to tell you're Amish."

I chuckle.

"I think you'll love it. Although, it's probably like Sodom and Gomorrah compared to where you're from." He dusts the crumbs from the waffle cone off his empty hands.

"Let's head back to the house. I gotta get cleaned up and head to work for a bit. I've got a meeting with the ad exec to talk about billboards they wanna do for our kids' grommet line."

"Okay. I will start making dough. I'm making a big chicken pot pie tonight."

He looks at me like he wants to say something, and his lips start to speak. Then he stops, deciding against it.

"What?"

He shakes his head and smiles. "Nothing."

334

"What?" I insist.

"Don't worry about it." He pulls his sunglasses down over his eyes, nudges me with his shoulder, and starts back down the road. "Come on. I'll race you back."

43

Ansel

"Alright, you're going to take a left up here." I point to the intersection up ahead, finally feeling a little more comfortable about Velda being behind the wheel. Twenty minutes ago, we were off to a rocky start when she backed into the trash can and then crept two miles per hour down the road the house is on. Slowly but surely, her tension has eased, and her speed has normalized.

She slows to a full stop and takes the left beautifully.

"Great job. You're going to stay on this road for about a mile now."

"Okay," she says, giving the Rivian a little gas and glancing at her speedometer to make sure she's adhering to the limit.

"This is the first time a woman has driven me anywhere since I was a kid." I laugh. "Not half bad. I could get used to this."

It's a joke. Inside, I'm still slightly terrified, but she doesn't need to know that.

Velda smiles, never taking her eyes off the road. This is a completely different Velda than the meek girl at the vegetable stand two months ago.

It looks good on her.

The *freedom*.

Independence.

Confidence.

I can't get over how lovely she looks today, with the sun hitting her perfectly through the throngs of trees. Her face is glowing, and her smile is easy. I pry my eyes away to stare out the window, enjoying the view of the local foliage and short rock walls, water glistening around the docks behind it all.

A short while later, I verbally navigate her into the parking lot of one of my favorite seafood joints, *Two Ten*, and I breathe a sigh of relief that we got here without her taking a side mirror off.

"Success!" I high-five her, and the biggest grin spreads across her youthful face.

"That was fun!" She rubs the upholstery between us and then looks back at me. "Can I drive us home?"

The way she calls it home sends a wave of warmth crashing through me. Until recently, it has only ever felt like a *house*, a dwelling to safely store my boards, surf, and sleep. But ever since she's been in Rhode Island, that felt like it changed. So slowly that I didn't even notice.

"Well, Little Red, you just fell right into the big bad Wolf's trap. That was my devious plan all along: to have a sober, designated driver so that I can drink to excess." I jest, chuckling as we get out of the car. I can tell she doesn't fully understand what a designated driver is and, therefore, doesn't get the joke, but it doesn't matter.

It wasn't that funny anyway.

I place a hand on the small of her back and lead her in the restaurant, a quaint little place right on the bay with dynamite food. I wanted to take her out, to show her a little of what makes Rhode Island special. Her learner's permit seemed like the perfect milestone to treat her to something nice to celebrate. When I asked her if she liked seafood the other night, she told me that she'd only ever had trout and bass. At that moment, I devised a plan to fix that so she could try a little of everything and expand her palette.

The hostess seats us on the deck with a perfect view of all of the yachts anchored in the placid waters just beyond.

I order a Mary Jane's Mojito CBD-infused cocktail for me and a soda for her, along with a tower of raw oysters, two rolls of sushi, the seafood *cavatappi a la vodka* (whatever that is,) a bowl of New England clam chowder, one of their famous lobster rolls, baked sea scallops, a shrimp cocktail, and a bowl of lobster bisque.

Fuck it.

YOLO.

The waitress's eyes bulge at the order, and she makes a joke about how they should have seated us at a bigger table to accommodate all of the plates. I inform her that we will surely be taking some to go, but that I want my lovely date to be able to try a little of everything.

Velda beams, smiling broadly, shoulders back poised in a posture that exudes a quiet grace. She stares out at the water, telling me stories about when her sister learned to drive the buggy for the first time back in Pennsylvania. I tell her about the first car I ever wrecked, and we laugh as she sips her soda. She tells me about how she read books growing up about the ocean and how the reality of it all far exceeds everything she imagined.

The food arrives, almost all at once, a feast fit for six people, at least. Velda enthusiastically tries everything, something I absolutely love about her.

I mean… well… I mean *admire*.

She has become quite fearless over the last two months, never saying 'no' to a new experience, always eager to test her limits.

We laugh and trade more stories. I show her how to add horseradish, hot sauce, and lemon to a raw oyster, anticipating a hilariously violent reaction to the slippery texture and typically-acquired taste.

I slurp mine down, and she follows suit, eyes widening excitedly as she does. She immediately asks if she can have another, and I'm floored. Most people have to learn to love them. Same goes for the sushi, but she inhaled half of each roll with glee.

"Save room for these. These are, like, the Rhode Island slash New England-y specialties." I nudge the plate with the lobster roll toward her and follow it with the small crock of clam chowder, which I inform her is pronounced "chow-duh" around these parts. I jokingly assure her that the pronunciation is *vital*.

You know... *when in Rome.*

She giggles and tries both, moaning at the lobster roll in a way that makes my dick hard the instant I hear it, rising like Lazarus from the dead at the noise. Hearing that purr of pleasure takes me back to that night that I dined on *her*.

She likes the chowder, but feasts like she's famished on the lobster roll. I compliment her on her new purple dress. She tells me that she made it, and I am certainly not surprised as she has made most of her wardrobe despite having the disposable income to buy just about whatever she wants. The dress is long and clings in all the right places, showcasing her sun-tanned shoulders and elegant neck. Her hair is draped over one strap of it in a complicated-looking fishtail braid.

I have a second cocktail, and she another lemon-lime soda. I tell her about some movies she should make a point to see. We talk about religion and the rigidness of her community. She tells me more about her massive family, her sister's recent wedding, and her family's financial woes.

She apologetically admits to me that she has been sending all of her paychecks back to Pennsylvania to help with the family farm, and my heart feels heavy in that moment, thinking about how her place in this world is still there --

not *here* -- a fact I have recently found myself forgetting, time and time again.

She admits that she has written them a letter every week since she's been here and shakily says that she hasn't once received a response.

She tells me that she misses some of them and fears others. And she finally peels her eyes from the feast to stare into mine while she tells me she's having the best time.

She confesses that she feels conflicted, that she doesn't exactly want to go back, and that the longer she stays, the more she feels she's betraying the values they have tried so hard to ingrain. She tells me that she's worried, that the more she experiences here, the harder it will be to ever feel truly happy in the life of simplicity and sacrifice she's been groomed to lead.

And though my face never once betrays me, my stomach wrenches, and my chest feels like it weighs a thousand pounds more with every word about her future life elsewhere.

This was always meant to be temporary.

We had always maintained that from the start.

But as the weeks have gone on, I have lost sight of that, slowly grown to cherish the warmth and excitement she infuses into every day. Her infectious desire to experiment and learn has reinvigorated my excitement in even the smallest things.

When she is gone, my life will return to being centered around keeping a thriving brand at the cutting edge of an ever-changing market and soothing shareholders.

Gone will be the days I break bread -- *fresh, warm homemade bread* -- with anyone at my kitchen island.

Gone will be the wild-flavored ice creams and long talks about theology and great films she has yet to see as we splash around in the pool beneath a blanket of stars.

Gone will be... everything about her.

Every simplistic joy, every exciting revelation, every meal made with love, every custom outfit she comes downstairs in.

Everything...

Gone.

44

Velda

"We gotta swing in for a second so I can drop off some of these prints of you for my course real quick." Helena points to the back seat where her pink portfolio lays flat, nestled beneath between paper bags covered in words like Prada, Coach, and Gucci. One even contains a skimpy little black pajama set that she bought for me. Something that she insisted that 'I had to have' because 'man or not, every girl deserves to feel hella sexy.'

She parallel parks in an open spot on the side of the road, and I am in awe of her skill. I wonder how long it would take me to learn something like that.

"Wanna come in? It might be a minute?" Helena nods over at the red brick building across the street, one with curved arches on the top half and an old sign saying something about it being an institute of design.

"They have a couple cool little galleries you can check out while you wait. I have a photo displayed in one of them."

"Yes, okay." I follow her inside.

"Feel free to hang out in there. I'll come get you when I'm done." She points to the *Student Exhibitions Gallery* just inside the lobby. "I'll only be a few."

I nod and meander through the gallery, awed by the paintings and photos on the walls. Sculptures randomly populate the concrete floor with overhead lights beaming down on them.

It only takes me a moment to recognize which image is Helena's because it is of *me*. In it, I am lying on my side on a flattened chaise lounge in her yard, propped on my elbow with a botanical garden full of brilliant flowers all around me. I am in a bikini, smelling the plucked coneflower I later used as a bookmark in the paperback in the grass below me.

The tag below says "*BLOSSOMING*," with Helena's name beneath it.

I didn't even know she took it, and yet it thrills me to see. For the first time, while I am looking at it, I feel beautiful. I feel like the photo has captured a *real* part of my spirit and who I am, a part not modestly hidden by chaste dresses eight inches from the floor.

If *Mamm* ever saw this, I would be on the verge of being shunned by the community. It represents everything that we Amish claim to hate. Vanity. Immodesty. Conceit.

But the image makes me proud. I feel like that singular moment of time is immortalized by the quiet click of Helena's shutter.

I move on to the other art. The impressionistic paintings, the lifelike realism... I feel inspired, being surrounded by it all.

I turn the corner and instantly find myself enamored by a mannequin with a sequined frock on it, dazzling in its wide array of colors.

Next to it is another mannequin in a different outfit... and next to it, another still. One with a bejeweled leather outfit, another wearing a flowing red gown with a strap of fabric twisted into the flowery design.

Beside the last one sits a waist-high wooden box with tri-fold pamphlets on it and a sign that says 'TAKE ONE.' I pick one up and flip through it.

It's a brochure for the school's fashion design program, complete with photos of more wild clothing: Strange shirts and jackets, vibrant skirts, and bizarre feathered ensembles.

I didn't know that they offered schooling for this sort of thing. Even though this is not something that would ever be allowed back at home, where everyone dresses similarly to avoid the perils of ego and pride, I can't seem to pry my eyes away from it. I fail to see the harm in certain shades or fun patterns. I fail to see the unholiness in glued-on jewels, fringe, lace trim, and buttons.

It doesn't add up.

I can't make it make sense.

All my life, I have lived as one of many. A unit. Women in the same clothes, with the same dolls, the same black buggies, the same drab house colors, the same wooden furniture.

How can it be wrong to enjoy how my figure looks in a bra?

How can it be so sinful to wear grape or plum or burgundy or amethyst or violet over any other paled color?

How can having a smile on a child's doll lead them from *Gott*?

I stuff the brochure in the back pocket of my shorts. I don't know why I take it. I could never go here. My family would never allow it. Nothing good could ever come of it.

Still, my body wants to scream when I try to put it back down on the platform.

Something in me is intoxicated by the fantasy of designing something worthy of being displayed on a mannequin beneath a spotlight.

"Yo, Encino Woman, ready to rock and roll?" Helena's voice asks from behind my ear, making me nearly jump right out of my skin.

45

Ansel

"Velda," I crow, wrenching this goddamn noose of a tie out from around my neck.

There is no answer. A feeling is in the air. A heaviness. Stifling and bitter.

Something is not right. I can just… feel it.

"Velda?" I holler it out the back door in case she's doing sun salutations in the neighbor girl's backyard again or swimming laps in the pool. I scan the beach, but it's empty. So is their yard, save for the Polish landscaper, who waves from the bed of Black-Eyed Susans he's mulching. I wave back and wander further. There's no one in the gazebo or pickleball court, and the pool is still as glass.

"Velda?" I yell it, this time back into the house as I do a lap around the lower level, brows furrowed in confusion.

I make my way upstairs quietly. There is no roar of the Bernina, no usual slice of scissors through fabric, and no running shower. It now occurs to me that she might be sleeping.

But that idea is squashed a moment later as I hear a delicate sob and two sniffles, all emanating from Velda's cracked bedroom door.

I peek in, watching her body shudder in near silence. She sits on the floor by the bed, tears streaming down her face. There is something clutched in her hands, a rumpled piece of paper that she's squeezing hard.

Her room is immaculate, save for a set of lacy nightclothes next to a pink Victoria's Secret bag and a brochure for the R.I.S.D. school atop the pile of paperbacks on her nightstand.

"*Velda*," I say quietly this time, with compassion. I take a seat on the bed and run my fingers over her soft blonde hair.

She looks up at me and sobs harder, burying her face in her cupped hands.

"I'm so… sorry. Dinner isn't… ready."

"I don't care about that." I toss my suit jacket on the bed and slide down, taking a seat next to her on the floor.

I cradle her face in my hands and gently wipe a few errant strands of hair from her soaked cheeks. "What's wrong, Velda? What's going on?"

"I don't… want to… talk about it," she manages between sobs.

I wrap an arm around her and tug her to my chest. I wish I knew what to do. I wish I knew what was going on, how to take her pain away. I hate seeing her this distraught. I don't want to pry. I know that if she wants me to know about the contents of the paper, she will tell me in her own time.

"I'm sorry." She tries to compose herself, wiping her face on her arms.

Though I hate seeing it because of the anguish she feels, she looks so beautiful in this moment, vulnerable and innocent, blue eyes welled with tears.

I take a deep breath and look out the window at the storm clouds rolling in, bringing with it darkness, destruction, cleansing, and renewal, all in strangely equal measure. The forecast called for high shore-bound winds before the rain, perfect for large, ideal surf swells. But my desire to ride the waves tonight evaporated the moment I saw Velda in pain.

"Come on." I rise and hold out a hand for her.

"What?" She looks at me, confused.

"Come," I say again and wave my hand. Finally, she stands, and I hoist her over my shoulder with ease, always forgetting just how light she is.

She groans and sniffles, head hanging against the middle of my spine, the back of her thighs in my arm, perfect little ass beside my face.

"What are you doing?"

I walk her over to her dresser, turn away, and lower slowly into a squat.

"Grab your pajamas."

"What?"

"Girl, I can't hold this position all day," I joke. "Grab your jammies."

I hear a wooden drawer roar open and the clumsy shuffle of her upside-down arms as they sift through her scant belongings. I see the crumpled paper fall to the carpet by my feet. It looks like a handwritten letter of some sort in pencil, made out to her.

Suddenly, I know what it is that has her so distraught. It has to be some kind of bad news from Pennsylvania. Maybe someone was injured in the fields, or a baby was stillborn. My mind races with a variety of possibilities in the span of three seconds.

"Got 'em." She mumbles into my spine, and I feel her chin rest there, arms slack, hands full of clothing.

Without another word, I carry her downstairs and into my bedroom, where I set her gently on the bed. I push a button on the remote for the home's only flat-screen T.V., and a streaming service bolts brightly to life on the screen, one offering dozens of hit-and-miss movies in genre carousels. I put the remote in her hand and bend down to the level of her face.

"Put your pajamas on. Get yourself comfy. Start a movie. I'll be back in a bit with dinner."

Her eyes grow large, brows creased with concern. "No! I need to cook for you, Ansel. It's my job."

"As your boss, I have just given you a direct order."

I smile, hoping she understands that I'm fucking with her.

"Pick a movie. I'd recommend a good comedy, but there's also drama if you need a good, hard, cathartic cry. I'll be back in… half an hour.

Your cute little butt had *better* be in that bed." I point to the far half of the bed, near the window.

She wipes her eyes and tries to fight the smile forming on her face.

***

I am back in twenty-five minutes with a Cobb salad, a small bowl of fresh fruit, a cellophane-wrapped whoopie pie -- *goddamn, those things are addictive* -- and a glass of her favorite soda, all on a nautical-themed serving tray.

"Dinner in bed," I say as I set it over her lap. She hides her smiling face behind her hands for a moment and then thanks me. I retrieve my dinner -- *a double of scotch, neat, and a bowl of grapes.* I change into a pair of gray sweatpants and a hideous *Point Break* T-shirt that I got at last year's *TwinFin* 'Secret Santa' party, and I take a seat atop the covers next to her.

A ridiculous scene from *Dumb and Dumber* plays, and I know she has chosen wisely. She giggles like a chipmunk as she eats, and I tell her about how this movie -- *and most of the other Farrelly Brothers movies, in fact* -- were all filmed right here in Rhode Island.

The hours roll on, and during the second movie, we snuggle in deeper, listening to the sound of the powerful storm rage outside, watching the room light up with brilliant bursts of branched lightning, feeling the whole house shake beneath us with deep bass-like rumbles of thunder.

In the middle of the third comedy, Velda turns the T.V. off and rolls over to look at me, half her beautiful face buried in the spare set of pillows I haven't once slept on in the years I've lived here.

"I should go to bed and let you get some sleep."

The moment she utters it, my head shakes, and my mouth reacts before my brain can argue with it. "No. Stay."

She stares at me. It could be four seconds or four hours. I haven't a clue.

"Thank you for doing this," she finally purrs, gripping the down pillow like she's hugging it.

"It's nothing. Shitty Cobb salad, free streaming movies, and a couple cans of soda. You're a really cheap date."

She snickers, and a double strike of lightning illuminates her smile. The moon plays hide-and-seek with a thick bunching of cumulus clouds, and the light waxes and wanes in slow, throbbing pulses.

"Do you want to talk about it, the letter?"

A sadness befalls her porcelain features, and her eyes lower to the wrinkled visage of Keanu on my chest.

"I have to go back."

The words slice like a razor-sharp knife, cutting me out of nowhere. I am just frozen, horrified at the gravity of those five little words.

"*Mamm* and *Fater* finally wrote. They said that they are afraid for my soul, being here among

352

the Englishers. They are demanding I come back to Pennsylvania."

"Do you *want* to go?"

She shakes her head and winces. A tear falls.

I wipe it from her cheek. "Then, just... tell them you don't want to go. Tell them you're not ready yet." I suggest it quietly, less like an order and more like something that should be followed with a 'please?' at the end.

Her eyes look at me with a seriousness that chills me, even through the moody darkness.

"They are going to put me in the *bann* if I do not return. My mother swears it."

"The *bann*?"

"That means I will be shunned by the community."

"For how long? A few months? A year? You could stay here..."

"For *good*, Ansel. The *bann* is for good. It means, I will not ever be welcome back. I will not be welcome to see my family again."

I want to tell her, 'Let them ban you. Come live here,' but I know saying that is wildly over-simplistic and reductive.

I feel the heaviness of what she is saying. This is her *entire life* at stake, the only thing she has ever known, her entire -- *huge* -- family.

Asking her to give that up to come live here would be fucking ludicrous.

This has *always* been part of the deal. This was *always* meant to be temporary.

But the thought of her leaving feels like it is slowly crushing the air from my lungs like an impossibly-large barbell has fallen across my chest.

"*I don't want you to leave,*" I finally whisper.

The low rumble of the raging storm in the distance gives this moment the dramatic feel it warrants.

My heart hollows at the thought of this sweet, beautiful woman soon vacating my life for good. No seeing her smiling face over potato pancakes in the morning. No watching her wobble to her feet on the crest of her first wave. No more hearing her slurp down oysters or listening to the gentle hum of the sewing machine as I respond to work emails; these fulfilling sounds of life in an otherwise silent house. No more vibrancy and light. No more moaning in hot tubs while a toy whirs against her. No more ice creams at the beach.

No more Velda at all.

Ever.

I brought her here to help fix my heart, and now it feels like it's shattering like glass, grinding into fine dust in the space between our bodies.

As if she can sense my ache, she places a hand on my cheek and strokes my jaw with her thumb. She touches my hair, traces the lines of my tattooed arm folded over Swayzee's too-serious mug.

Rain patters on the window, softly at first, harder moments later, until it builds into a raging downpour, smacking the glass with ferocity.

She leans forward, slow and deliberate, and kisses me.

I want to fall apart.

I want to crumble into pieces.

I want to have her hold me like a child and tell me that she's changed her mind, that she wants to stay for good and make a life here in Rhode Island.

I kiss her back in what feels like slow motion, feeling the spark as our lips brush, followed by the sweet tangle of our tongues.

The delicate hand on my face slides up into the hair behind my ears, beside my temple, and I close my eyes, trying to lock this feeling into my memory forever. Trying to store every taste, every sensation, every speck of her in a vault in my head. A vault that I can open every night here in this empty bed once she's gone.

Gone.

The word makes me feel *sick.*

Her body snuggles in closer to mine, tongue diving deeper into my mouth, soft and sensual. I lean in, tenderly caressing her flawless face, one full of youthful vitality and passion. Her arm slips beneath mine and tugs me closer.

I oblige.

Her hand slips beneath the untied waistband of my sweatpants, slides down along the curve of my ass, and squeezes, her lips never leaving mine.

I kiss her with a savage ache deep inside me that has longed for her since the day I met her. I lean in, feeling the tug of my shirt as she tries to yank it off. The moment I pry away to let her pull it over my head, I feel lost. *Adrift.* It isn't until my lips find hers again that I am finally found, clinging to driftwood on dry land from my lonesome shipwreck.

I would pay any amount of money to make her change her mind and stay so that we might bask in this feeling for the years to come.

As if there was some gap in time, moments of transition missing from my memory, I am on top of her, at home between her open thighs.

Moon-speckled hair frames her face, and her eyes glisten up at me, black circles in the darkness, sparkling with pure white reflections.

"Don't... go."

It's all that I can whisper, all I can mutter to stop this agonizing pain in its tracks.

But it's *cruel*.

It's downright cruel to say aloud as if she has some kind of choice. It is such a terrible weight to make her hold while she's already drowning. But it's two words I would never be able to forgive myself for holding in.

She doesn't say a word, no doubt anchored down by the burden of this impossible situation disguised as some kind of *choice*. She pulls me against her body, groping and clutching, enveloping me with an intimate affection so pure that I am not worthy of it, but I greedily let it fuel me anyway.

She squirms beneath me, hot with need, pulling me tighter, bringing me nearly as close as two people can ever be. Her toes claw at my sweatpants in an effort to remove them.

I laugh into her shoulder, hands beginning to roam beneath the hem of her camisole, thumbs caressing the soft skin of her stomach. She drags kisses down my chin and neck as my hands seek out her breasts beneath the ribbed fabric.

She writhes against my hard-on and I bunch her shirt up just beneath her shoulders, dragging my tongue and teeth along her hardened nipple. She moans, and I bite. Softly at first, then harder as her pelvis bucks.

I shed her top, and she pries at my bottoms again, finally getting the material over my bare ass.

"*Ansel, please,*" she pants into my neck and nuzzles my ear.

The two words wind me up like a toy that's about to break.

There is another gap in time where all I see is darkness. All I hear is the storm, loud and utterly apocalyptic, infused with soft moans and whimpers. All I feel is the dance of her heart through my own chest. All I taste is Heaven.

In moments, our bottoms are around our ankles, frantic feet wriggling them free until we are stark naked beneath the comforter.

Adam and Eve in the picturesque garden.

Zeus and Hera in the fluffy clouds.

Ansel and Velda in the raging chaos of the storm.

Up until now, everything we've done has all felt naughty or dirty, like something taboo I knew we shouldn't be doing. Wrong, but still so deliciously sexy.

But now, at this moment, with my skin pressed against hers, it feels *right*.

"Are you sure you want to do this?" I swipe a strand of hair from her dewy cheek lovingly with my thumb.

"Yes." She nods. "Just, please… go slow." She swallows hard. "I'm scared."

The words melt me. She feels so small beneath me, so frail. I feel undeserving of such trust, such innocence.

"I'll go slow. I promise."

I wriggle myself down the bed to the perfection between her thighs. I take my time there, licking and kissing and massaging her pussy until it is dripping with her desire. I linger there, through her groans of pleasure, until her legs are trembling, lips crying out in a howl that rivals the violence of the wind outside.

When I feel the sweat dripping down her shaking thighs and the agonizing pulse of my engorged dick, I rise and kiss her deeply, my ecstatic smile pressed to hers. As she strains to catch her breath, I retrieve a foil square from my bedside drawer, tear it open, and roll the latex sheath down my throbbing cock.

I return, nestling carefully back between her shaking legs, gently parting her thighs as wide as they will comfortably go, poising my head against her soaked entrance.

"I'm going to go slow."

I kiss her lips softly. They're pliable and pillowy, and I can't get enough of how fucking good they feel.

I kiss the side of her neck, her chin, her throat. I feel her body relax beneath me.

"It's probably going to hurt the first time, and I am so sorry for that."

She nods, fingers nervously wriggling against each other.

"If it starts to hurt too bad, just push against my hips with your hands, and I will stop, and we can wait."

"Okay." Her voice is so small and afraid.

"I'm in no hurry. We've got all night."

Those words relax her. She takes a deep breath and leans up to kiss me. I kiss her back and nibble her lower lip softly as she runs a hand up my bare back.

I rise onto my hands, back arching, and I press my tip gently inside of her. She squirms a little, nervous, and I pause patiently at the wall of her hymen, holding still, buzzing with eager excitement.

"Are you okay?"

She nods, and I kiss her lips again, sliding my cock in a few millimeters more as I do. She winces a little, and I pause again, prying my mouth from hers to glimpse the sweet anguish etched into her features as the wall of her hymen stretches against me.

She chews her lip.

"Breathe," I say, kissing both nipples softly as if we have the rest of eternity for this task.

She takes another deep breath, and as she does, I press in further.

Her palms dig into my sides, pushing me away reflexively from the pain and pressure.

"Relax your hands when you're ready. I won't go any further until then. Promise."

She nods again, breathing hard, hands still rigid against the bones of my hips. I drag my tongue softly across her skin, drawing damp lines along her collarbones, then blowing gently to cool them.

A minute later, her hands relax, retracting from my hips. I stare at her, the thunder outside a soundtrack to this otherwise silent moment of trust in another human.

She takes another deep, calculated breath, and I slide in further, feeling the gentle sensation of her hymen giving away. Such a quiet, simple thing for such a monumental event in our lives.

Once it breaks, I slip in further, hearing her hiss, knowing the pain I'm causing and being unfathomably grateful for it.

"*Fuck*," I whisper as my cock plunges into her fully for the first time. So warm, so tight. I hold there, feeling the tension in her body, seeing the tight scrunch of her closed eyes.

This feeling is euphoric, transformative.

"You feel so fucking good, Velda," I whisper as I shower her neck and ear with affection.

"Are you okay?"

She nods and pulls my shoulder toward her face, latching her teeth gently into the muscle there and moaning.

I draw out slowly, feeling her jaw ratchet down, feeling her grunt rumble through my deltoid, and I slide back in. She gasps and groans, pressing her forehead into my pecs, clawing my back with her nails as I slide in again.

She feels like Heaven. She is warmth and love, and all life's beautiful things rolled into one perfect being. And for this moment, I am one with her.

I pause as her body takes a moment to relax. I stay still as a statue, holding her as she mewls into my chest. When she finally lays back, I nudge her head to the side and whisper in her ear how fucking beautiful she looks, how fucking divine she feels around my cock.

I never want this moment to end, this moment of carnal pleasure and utter anguish, of bliss and torment and love and pain.

She nods again, ready to continue, and I draw back, sliding into her again slowly. She grits her teeth from the sting of torn flesh, and I kiss her and murmur how perfect she is and how next time will not hurt quite like this.

I speak as if there will ever *be* a next time. As if she won't soon be out of my life. I speak as if I haven't squandered precious time and as if a tomorrow exists for us. As if I will ever have the pleasure of feeling this exquisite again.

46

Velda

I awaken this morning in Ansel's arms. I study his tattoos as he sleeps. A bundle of blooming lilies whose stems morph into the outline of a crashing ocean wave.

Tears escape me as I think about returning home, leaving all of this strange new world behind.

Leaving *him* behind.

Ansel's eyes finally peel open, and they are the most dazzling array of colors that I have ever seen them be. He smiles, tenderly kisses me with a 'good morning,' and asks me how I'm feeling as his fingertips graze my bare skin.

I tell him that I'm sore, that I regret none of it, that I will never forget last night as long as I live.

He brings me ibuprofen and a glass of water and strokes my hair as I drink them down. I study his nude body until he snuggles back into bed with me.

"I've been thinking," he says seriously, hands clasped behind his head, burrowing into the fluff of his pillow. "You said you're scheduled for your G.E.D. test on Tuesday, right?"

My smile fades. "Ansel."

He knows I must leave. My family demands it.

"Hear me out. You've been studying hard for that. Stay until then."

"I can't. They want me to come home now."

"What's a couple more days? It's not even a week. Velda, think about it. You're this close. If you take the test and you pass, no one can *ever* take that certification away from you. Even if you go back to the farm—"

"If?"

"I meant *when*. When you go back to the farm, it'll always be yours. And if you ever decided you wanted to do something with it one day, you can."

"That piece of paper, it means nothing where I'm going, Ansel. It was foolish to even try for it."

"There's nothing foolish about growing, Velda. And learning. Everything you learned, that is with you now."

"Ansel, it's not even something I could *tell* people about. They will look down on me for it. They do things a very specific way."

"But *you* will know, Velda." His voice is a little louder now, filled with passion, pleading for me to understand. "*You* will know you have it. You will know the world outside can be yours, should you ever need it."

He stares out at the gray morning sky, windows dappled with the remnants of last night's rain.

Then, he looks back at me. "Come with me to New Orleans today. We'll eat, we'll dance, we'll…"

The thick air hangs heavy between us for a moment.

"…Do whatever you want to do. We come back, you take your test, we throw you a graduation-slash-going-away party, and then I will fly you back home."

I ponder his proposal for a moment before a grin creeps onto my face. I suppose a few more days won't hurt when considering all of my offenses.

"Pretty please?" His hand entwines with mine, and he starts to pull me closer to him.

"Okay," I finally say.

The moment it leaves my mouth, he rejoices, pulling me in the rest of the way, kissing me passionately in celebration.

He pulls away to check his watch. "We should get up and ready. Flight's in two hours. We should hit the road soon."

But I don't listen. I shake my head in defiance and slip my hand below the covers, wrapping my fingers around the hard girth between his legs.

"Oh, my beautiful little Morning Glory," he says in between nibbles of my earlobe.

I slip a leg over his thighs and climb on top of him, eager to find out if it's true… if it *doesn't* hurt as much the next time.

He laughs and holds me still, tilting his head to look at me like I'm the most beautiful painting he's ever seen.

He doesn't say a word. He just chews his bottom lip and fights a smile.

I rise to my knees and press my palms into his tattooed chest. His strong hands lift me at the waist, thumbs digging into my belly as he guides me over him, poising me at the top and supporting me until I choose to take it into me on my own.

When I do, even slow, it stings something fierce. I hiss as I lower, scrunching my eyes tight, fists curled into tight balls.

He holds still for a moment, holding my hips against his own until I relax. They roam up to my breasts, and I lean forward. Slowly, carefully, his hips raise, and he slides up into me again, filling me with a pressure that makes my head light in a delightful way despite the tenderness between my legs.

We slowly find a rhythm, him and I, one where my clenched thighs tremble in perfect unison with his languid upward strokes. He presses my chest back, his hands silently ordering my torso to arch toward his knees. I feel a pressure now, below my navel. Something delightful and new, a feeling growing powerfully in me like a pressure cooker.

Then he adds a finger, rubbing my clit in gentle circles as we rock like anchored boats in turbulent water.

As seconds morph into minutes, time has stopped cold in its tracks for the rest of the world. The hands of clocks have fused into place, allowing me to savor every moment that our bodies are one.

We sweat, moving together like two pieces of a flawless, singular machine. My legs shake with violence and this *thing,* this *powerful* sensation brewing deep within my pelvis smashes over me like a wave, thrusting me down into darkness like a riptide.

"*That's a good girl,*" he whispers as he leans up. He kisses me, never missing a beat with the slow grinding rhythm of his body as it continues to meld with mine.

"*You are so fucking beautiful when you cum, Velda,*" he says adoringly.

He clutches me tight, embracing my dampened torso with strong, flexed arms, screwing one hand gently up into the hair on the back of my head. He runs the tip of his nose and tongue up my throat, up the side of my neck. It gives me chills. My eyes close as he drives himself deeper, reaching something in me at such a perfect angle that my body unravels upon itself again. The fullness and the friction, it all edges me headfirst into another crashing tide. My head falls back, and I scream so loud that my throat hurts, my cry ringing out through a world in which no one else exists but the two of us.

47

Ansel

Walking down Bourbon Street with Velda is strange. There is an oppressive melancholic air over us in such a lively city, drowning out squeals of joy and celebration with an almost overwhelming heaviness. The juxtaposition feels dizzying, but Velda seems fascinated by her vibrant new surroundings nonetheless.

New Orleans. A historic city with a neon soul. The pulse of the American South, one throbbing in rhythmic time with the zydeco music oozing from every bar on this cobblestone strip of pot-hole-laden asphalt. A place where weirdness is revered. A city where the fetid stench of rain-diluted vomit and urine is narrowly trumped by the scent of sugary cocktails, flowing hops, and savory crawfish *etouffee* in a square of town that is equal parts remoulade, clarinet, and vagrancy.

Velda might as well be at a theme park, tickled by the flicker of every gaslight, every feather boa, every quirky outfit, every karaoke sour note, every spinning street performer, every speck of glitz and glitter. Her eyes bounce from the gaggle of half-naked women in pink wigs and faux veils to the man playing a neck-braced harmonica, hands *whapping* his dirty jeans, soles stapled with crushed cans to convert them into homemade tap shoes.

She nearly cries at the homeless men in cardboard condos, some with Pitt bull companions with Sad-Sam eyes, some using grimy underwear as a makeshift sleep mask, some begging blatantly for weed instead of money so they can blaze away the memories of their hardships.

Every single one we've passed, she's given some of her hard-earned cash to. And never once has it failed to make me smile at her humanity. Smiles that always fade as I remember that soon she will be gone.

She slurps down a virgin strawberry daiquiri from a Styrofoam cup and pets one of the horses waiting to drag around a carriage full of sweaty tourists for a private tour of the historical landmarks. I offer to pay for a ride, and she declines, says the horse and carriage remind her too much of Pennsylvania. Swallowing the painful lump in her throat, she returns her eyes to the city, electric and rowdy, one celebrating partial nudity and gluttonous excess. It is the absolute antithesis of where she hails from. She studies every inch, committing the sparkle of the French Quarter to memory.

We dance in the street outside of a honky-tonk. I let her pick out any shimmery mask she wants at one of the many narrow shops painted in sugar skull pastels. She chooses a feathery black one with silk ribbons and rounded flourishes around the entire border. She whispers in my ear that she wants to wear it -- *and only it* -- later for me at the hotel. My dick hardens at the mere mention of it, and I make a joke about how, in that case, she can have one of every mask in the store.

At dinner, we order one of damn-near everything so she can sample the Cajun delights. Before the waitress leaves, Velda pleads for oysters, a dozen raw, and I don't dare deprive her, despite the fact that we just ordered enough food for a table of five again.

After she eats, she politely asks for several boxes, which seems ridiculous considering all of the great food in walking distance. We package the leftovers and hit the streets, dodging errant beads hurled from the balconies above.

Velda gives a plastic container of leftovers to every homeless person we pass on our trek back to the *Bon Temps* hotel until she has nothing left but a satisfied smile beneath her mask like some sexy Amish superhero.

At the hotel, we fuck in the shower, with her pressed against the wall, legs shaking, draped over the crooks of my arms. She clutches my neck like I am going to float away and I am lost inside her warmth, body and soul, while hot water licks every curve of our united form. Her moans echo off the tile and glass, and they make me feel more animal than human as our pace quickens. I burrow deeper into her depths until the noise stops and the violent tremors of her petite body take their place. I hold her still in my arms, feeling her heart thunder through us, galloping Clydesdale hooves beating down into the earth. She pulses around me like her body never wants to let go. Finally, she does. She slinks to the tiled floor, grout digging perfect lines into her knees. She takes me deep in her throat, sucking and bobbing until I cum inside of her mouth, my favorite sight to see as I die my small death and slip into a momentary void of darkness.

An hour later, she is in my bed, fast asleep against my tattooed shoulder, snoring gently in her own private garden of blooming lilies. My heart constricts for a moment as I watch her, and though I don't talk to God much these days, I say a silent prayer, begging that He never let me fade from her sweetest dreams in the years to come.

I brush over all of the key points of tomorrow's nerve-wracking proposal on my laptop, and my eyes drift away. I glance over at her queen bed across the suite. Untouched.

With any luck, it will stay that way.

Because just for this weekend, I want to pretend.

I want to pretend that this is what the rest of our life looks like, her nuzzled against me as she sleeps. I want to imagine that, in some other world, we have a future, one where I show her the unique hearts of cities all over the world. I want to pretend this is us in a villa in Rome, celebrating our five-year anniversary. In a flat in London, on holiday. At a beach house in Sydney, a castle in Dublin, or five-star accommodations in Egypt.

Hell, I want to pretend that this is us at a Super-8 in bum-fuck Kentucky.

In this make-believe fantasy, where we *are* doesn't matter... as long as she is there, sleeping among lilies that will never wither beneath her weight as she slumbers.

I would take her anywhere.

I would give her the world.

In another life, this trip could have only been a *taste*.

My heart feels heavy as she adjusts, pressing her flattened palm over my heart, one that is breaking at the thought of her vanishing from my life.

In three days, I will have to say goodbye.

Forever.

In three days, she will go home to a place with no connection to the outside world, one in existence by design. Soon, she will pledge herself to her patriarchal community, vowing to adhere to every strange and suffocating rule they deem Holy. She will bear a buggy full of children from her perfect tapered hips, all for some boring fuck with half a beard who will *never* feel for her the way that *I* do in this quiet moment.

In three days, she will be landlocked, farm-bound... *gone*.

As she sleeps, I am tempted to tell her that I love her. To tell her that I don't know how or when it happened, but the love is *here,* and it's *heavy,* and I don't know what the fuck to do with it when she's gone.

I am tempted to brush the hair from her face and tell her that I will never fucking be the same again without her. That nothing will ever come close to the way I feel when I am with her.

She is my Sarah, Plain and Tall. My Girl with the Pearl Earring.

My *Velda*.

I want to bare my soul and force her to share the burden of all of these complicated emotions, but that wouldn't be fair to her. I love her too much to make her carry the weight of all this.

As I gaze down at her, a tear escapes my eye. It falls, landing softly on her face and rolling down her cheek, almost as if she is crying with me.

In the beginning, when we met, I wanted so desperately to claim her body, to selfishly ruin her for others so that she could never forget me.

But life's cruel joke is on *me*.

Because the tables turned and I became the one claimed in the end.

It takes two more hours to get to sleep because of the mounting anxiety I feel over the finality of our time together.

My only consolation is that when I finally drift away, I dream of her.

I dream of the beautiful life we lead together in an alternate universe, one in which Velda agrees to stay.

And though it is only a dream, it is sweet. It fills my heart with just enough bliss to rise another day, one where the end is looming even closer than the one before.

48

Ansel

"I can't believe I'm about to say this, Ansel," Clarence hesitates, choosing his words wisely. "I think... for once, you've come up with something really solid. The patterns are fun. I like the ferns and the plants. The color schemes are bold, but they seem to gel well with the other lines. I can tell you put a lot of time into this."

Alan chimes in, pursing his lips and pointing to the screen with his pen. "I don't know who you got to model these, but she's got a good look. Maybe she could be our subject for some of the print work."

Larry stifles a laugh, one loud enough to turn heads. He is well aware the model on the screen is Velda.

Alan continues, unwilling to inquire as to what Cummings finds so humorous. "She does. You should get her hooked up with Lamar. She'd be great for the billboards."

The comment sends a wave of stinging pain through me. I force a fake smile. *It isn't possible.* There isn't enough *time*. Their words are yet another reminder that she is leaving. This band-aid is being torn off slowly, and I only have myself to blame. I asked her to stay, begged for more time, never knowing it would be this hard.

I look up at the image on the white projector screen, one where Velda is frozen in a yoga pose on her longboard in the sand, body gracefully arched beneath a deep amber sky. The rash guard clings to every curve and bevel of her body's delicate framework like a second skin, one that opaquely shields the world from the absolute perfection beneath.

The board members shuffle off, breaking eagerly for their catered po boy lunch, but I can't take my eyes off the screen.

"Great work, Wolf." Clarence pats me on the back as the room empties. "Hans would've been proud."

As I finally receive the scraps of genuine praise I've been vying for, the only thing on my mind right now is the tick of the clock, the wasted seconds I'm spending away from the woman behind him in the tree pose with a face that fills me with a potent mix of adoration and ache.

49

Velda

New Orleans is truly a sight to behold from the *Bon Temps* penthouse balcony. So many inching cars, so many liberated people making their way down the main thoroughfare. From here, I cannot hear their laughter, but I can see their heads fall back, bellies shaking, bodies doubling over, hands smacking knees.

So many of them are smiling.

I don't think I've ever seen so many people this happy before. Where I come from, people rarely smile. Children are whipped into a quiet subservience before they even learn to walk. Women are so overwhelmed by so many tasks that they rarely have the energy for laughter.

Men are so serious, always digging, tilling, building, harvesting, hammering.

And then there are people like Saloma, who are nearly incapable of it because of the private horrors they've endured at the hands of those they are supposed to love and trust, at the hands of wayward family and delinquent church elders. They are taught that not forgiving those perpetrating such atrocities is somehow a greater sin than the one committed upon them.

At home, there is distrust in Saloma's eyes, as well as exhaustion and distance in those of the rest of my family. But here, everyone's faces are alight with joy, bodies flouncing in celebration and drunken abandon.

The faint whisper of a band playing in the streets cuts through the purr of traffic, and I am present again, soaking in the sight of it all. Everyone is dressed so differently, many in brilliant colors, adorned with flamboyant accessories, some in short wigs, high heels, glittering sequins, or sheathed in scant body stockings. Some wear top hats, some dresses, some costumes, some in bright rainbow tank tops.

I cannot imagine a more opposite sight from where I was raised, all *Gott*-fearing people in plain clothes, quiet and reverent, all staunch believers that their way is the only *correct* one. They spend their days discussing scripture and taking solace in a hard day's work. They are almost a faceless mass, unencumbered by nearly all trappings of vanity.

Soon, I must return to that.

I must hide my hair beneath a *kapp* and cover my body with a pastel dress to blend in. I'll have to learn how to derive joy from the mundane, learn to balance children with chores, submitting to my wifely duties above it all.

I'll have to forget this place and Rhode Island with its lobster rolls and rolling waves and strange horseshoe crabs.

I'll have to forget Florida. And the boardwalk and the surfers in bikinis. I'll have to forget the feel of the beach house hot tub and the way my body warmed at the mere sound of the words '*good girl.*'

I must do my best to forget the way that Ansel has made me feel over these weeks. How he pushed me to continue my education, how he gave me confidence behind the wheel of a car, how he took time every day to teach me how to swim, how he let me try everything on every menu so I could have a varied taste of this strange and beautiful new world.

But mostly, I will have to forget how hard I have fallen for him despite never meaning to.

The suite door slides open behind me, startling me from this daunting spiral of thoughts that feel far too large and cumbersome to overcome.

Ansel's hands slide onto the balcony on either side of me, and his body presses against the back of mine.

"How did the meeting go?" I rest my face on my crossed arms, still staring out over the city below.

There is no answer, and I am grateful for the silence.

I don't really want to talk right now.

Not with the deafening threat of permanent distance sounding like an alarm all around us.

His flattened palm slides the bottom of my hair up to the top of my head, exposing a bare spot of skin on the back of my neck. He covers it in kisses and soft bites, shooting sparks down through my whole body. I moan at how good it feels, this spot that we only just discovered last night that drives me wild. It makes me wonder just how many more of my body's reactions will remain a mystery to us both when I leave.

There are no words, only fingers hooking beneath the hem of my skirt and sliding slowly up the backs of my thighs. I feel my face flush at the feel of it, at the promise of the intimately pleasurable sensations coming next.

I feel the straps of my dress tug down my arms, and I straighten them, bending them back to allow him to free them both with ease. My fingers fumble the button and zipper at his waist, clawing with desperation while they are already in the area.

I feel my bra unclasp and tug away with ease, feel it patter against the glossy tops of my high-heeled shoes, ones I wear because I love how they make my legs look in a dress. I feel the padded cups replaced by the firm grip of two warm hands, thumbs and index fingers manipulating my nipples in a way that instantly dampens the area between my thighs.

His warm hands vanish, and as they slip away to grip my hips, I am very aware that people could possibly see us, see my nudity even all the way up here on the top balcony of the high rise.

He nudges me forward until my breasts are barely grazing the cold balcony rail. I hiss at the sensation, but I don't retract because it feels pleasant against my hot skin.

I feel fingers hook around the hip strings of my panties, and I feel them slide down my legs, disappearing somewhere behind him. The bunched dress around my waist soon follows it into the unknown void.

He nudges my legs, telling me through the stunning silence that he wants them spread wider, and I happily follow the order, open and eager to feel him press inside me again.

I expect the zip of a fly and the ruffle of fabric, but instead, I hear the quiet creak of knees lowering, feel a shower of kisses down my back, my butt, my thighs. I gasp as I am filled, instead, with the sweet plunge of his outstretched tongue.

I mewl softly as he makes a meal out of me on the balcony for all the world to witness the building of my orgasm. He slides in front of me, wedging between my taut legs and the rail. The perilous drop behind him couldn't be further from his mind.

He slides a finger inside of me and then another, hooking them toward him with an incredible pressure that makes me cry out in a breathless howl, knuckles white as fallen snow as my hands try their best to crush the steel in them.

Once the arch in my back flattens and the violent tremors slow, he slips them back out, sucking every bit of me off them with his eyes staring up into mine.

As I catch my breath and descend back to earth, I hear the removal of starched slacks, the dull elastic snap of removed underwear, and the hitch of my own breath as he enters me from behind, filling me up in a way that makes me want to moan as loud as I can. His fingers clench my hips as he rocks his pelvis into me in slow, loving strokes.

I pry my eyes open and stare out at the city, one swaying before me like I am a bird in the ocean, riding the waves as he takes me against the railing, wearing nothing but a melancholic smile. As we make love, the French Quarter blurs before me, morphed and twisted by the water in my stinging eyes, forming at the thought of all of this bliss someday becoming nothing but a distant, perfect memory.

50

Velda

The last few days have been a blur. The flight
back to Rhode Island was almost silent. Leaving
New Orleans pained us both. Since I have been
back, I must have re-packed my duffel bag
eighteen times, each time trying to determine what
I wanted to bring back. At first, the answer was...
everything. Every new book, every outfit, every
bra, every cool-looking seashell, every Mardi
Gras mask, sarong, and bikini...

And then, this morning, it finally dawned on
me that I won't be able to bring almost *any* of it
home. Where I am going, all of these things are
either useless, frowned upon, or forbidden.

There are no pools, no place to wear slinky
sundresses, no appropriate place to wear spiked
heels...

I can't take almost any of it.

I finally settle on the pair of sandals Ansel
bought me in Florida, two books that I think I can
sufficiently hide -- one with the R.I.S.D. pamphlet
as a bookmark, a stinging reminder of a career
that could've been -- and the piece of paper in my

trembling hands, one that says I passed my G.E.D. exam and have a real high-school level education.

Even though I can never tell anyone about it, this piece of paper makes me beam. I worked hard for this, studied every day, had Helena quiz me countless times, took practice tests, and listened hard whenever Giovanni tutored me.

I am grateful that Ansel urged me to finish it, even if I can't use it. It gave me a glimpse of who I am and what I'm ultimately capable of.

G.E.D.

Those three little letters make me feel like I secretly have the whole world in my palm.

I tuck it away in my bag, knowing that even if I have to put it in a baggie and bury it in the yard, I will keep this thing forever.

As a reminder of it all.

I do one final pass around my room, choking back the emotion roiling through a stomach that feels like it's revolting against me.

Ansel is silent as I pass him on the porch, sitting on the polished steps in a suit, picking apart a tiny flower petal-by-petal with a furrowed brow.

Tom leans through the open driver door from the passenger seat as Ansel's Rivian idles in the driveway.

"Ansel says you're driving us to the airport, for old time's sake."

I chuckle, but it disappears quickly as soon as I remember that the 'us' he is referring to are just Tomas and I.

Ansel isn't coming.

This morning, after we made love one last time, I wept in his arms and he confessed that he couldn't bear to see me get on the plane, that he wouldn't be able to be as strong as I *needed* him to be if he had to watch me board.

I smile at Tom and turn back. Ansel stands with a look on his face that says he is crushed beneath the weight of it all. I can't speak as he looks at me. I know if I do, I will just become a mess of tears, and that won't help either of us.

He wipes a strand of hair from the side of my face, eyes like glass, rimmed the same shade of pink as the inside of a conch shell. He smiles, and the tears hold there on his dark lashes, threatening to fall.

He touches the tips of my fingers with his as my hand dangles loosely by my side.

"This is the part where I beg you again, my parting plea…"

He blinks hard, and the tear escapes, refracting bright sunlight on its way down into the dirt.

"Please… stay."

I wipe the damp trail from his cheek and shake my head. I slip my arms underneath his and pull him as close to my body as he can be with clothes on.

He sniffles, and I pull away. He kisses me one last time, like the world is about to end.

Like we will never see each other again.

It feels like our hearts are breaking in unison, with no glue in sight to put it all back together.

"Can I just ask one favor?" He sniffles again, barely able to meet my gaze.

I nod.

"Don't forget me," he whispers into my ear.

"*Never.*"

It is the easiest promise I could ever keep.

I couldn't forget him, even if I wanted to.

The single word is all I can mutter through this throat, stuffed tight, bottling a wail of pain that will surely be released against my will days from now when the grief of this loss fully hits.

51

Velda

Tom brought me to the airport and handed me a fat, rectangular envelope before I boarded. He said that Ansel wanted to give me my final check in cash, plus a bonus to make sure that I had all I needed when I got back to Pennsylvania.

I cried the entire flight, blubbered so hard that the woman bringing me Sprites even consoled me, petting my head and assuring me that whatever was making me sad, things had a way of working themselves out for the best.

But I don't know if I believe that.

Ansel paid a limo to pick me up at the airport in Reading, and I spent the drive back to the farm composing myself and wiping away the last remnants of makeup Helena gave me from my face.

When I stepped back onto the farm, *Mamm* wouldn't even look at me. I have no doubt that it was *Fater* who actually wrote the letter summoning me home. Deep down, I think *Mamm* would've been fine if I were in the *bann*.

It has been a not-so-warm welcome home this week.

While Rebecca and Lavina wanted to hear all about my travels, *Mamm* was cold and called me shameful for living among the Englishers and had no interest in hearing about my "*sinful*" weeks beyond the Berks County line.

My back once again aches from the many chores that are considered my duty, chores that *Mamm* and *Fater* made sure I knew were the burden of others during the weeks that I was 'frolicking among the heathens.'

They assured me that now that I am back, it is time to 'put childish things aside' and be baptized. They growled about how it is time to make my commitment to the Ordnung and to the rest of my plain community. They insist, yet again, that it is time to take a husband and settle down before I am an old maid of twenty, childless and unloved.

I adjust my *kapp*, smooth the flat front of my pinned dress, and carry two buckets of water down into the bathtub in the basement for our family's weekly bath.

I pour water into the basin, recalling when I could shower every day beneath a faucet that felt like warm summer rain. My thoughts drift to the shower in New Orleans, where Ansel picked me up off the floor, pushed me against the tile wall, and stole my breath as our two bodies melded into one.

It has been happening nonstop since the day I came back.

These memories of Ansel are everywhere, even though he was never really *here*. Every meal we eat as a family, I remember making for him, too, hearing him rave about the taste. Every sip of water I drink, I will it to turn into sweet, carbonated soda like some divine miracle. Everything reminds me of my summer with Ansel. Every flat gray rock is a raw oyster. Every chirping bird sings the tune of a Bourbon Street musician.

I walk back up through the house, glancing at Levi as he sits at the table, shoving bread into his mouth with filthy fingers, covered in a layer of fine, umber soil. His clothes are drab and dirty, his once-white shirt now the color of watered-down tea beneath his black suspenders.

The look he gives me chills me to the bone. His eyes never leave my body, and I wrack my brain to think of what I can possibly do to turn his unwanted attention elsewhere.

But it is the hint of a smile he flashes at my breasts when I breeze by that tells me my days of being safe are numbered.

Beneath his oppressive leer, I wonder why I ever left New England. The choice seems so simple, really, to an outsider, but the permanence and cold nature of the *bann* is a mighty deterrent.

Everyone I have ever known in my entire life, up until nine weeks ago, would have shunned me from there on out.

No more braiding Rebecca's long hair, no watching Saloma's belly grow with her firstborn child, no quilting and singing with Lavina, no Atlee or Abram to beat at checkers, no more of *Fater's* grace at the dinner table…

All of it gone in a flash.

Though he never said the words, I truly believe that Ansel loved me.

I could see it in the way he looked at me.

I could sense it in the way that he held me.

I felt it in the way he kissed me, there toward the end, like his world was about to fall apart, like he would never be the same again.

I know this because I felt the same.

52

Velda

I stare at the heaped mound of soil in the earth at the edge of the woods. Beneath it lies the remains of a horse named "Bucky" who perished in a barn fire on my uncle's property while I was away. My *Fater*, Menno, told me the story on the porch a few nights after I returned, sparing no morbid details about the raging inferno. He claims it started when my cousin, Marissa, stole away to the barn with the boy she is smitten with. According to my *Fater*, she and Daniel disappeared there to kiss and perhaps do other 'ungodly' things.

If *Fater* knew what *I'd* been doing while this was happening -- *the things I was on my knees begging for in that penthouse suite in Louisiana* -- while Marissa's oil lamp was igniting a bale of hay… *Fater* would never look at me again.

Not in the eyes.

Not ever.

He claimed that Marissa panicked, afraid of the repercussions she'd reap for her sinful ways. She and Daniel fled the barn, one that butts up against the back of my family's farm, leaving poor Bucky to burn alive.

Mamm smelled the smoke first and heard Bucky's cries, but by the time she understood what it was from, it was too late.

Marissa and Daniel fled on foot, and the further they got from the barn, the more they feared the repercussions.

My *Fater* said when they found Marissa deep in the woods, crying in Daniel's arms, her own *Fater* beat her for hours with a belt, hitting her harder every time she made a peep.

During my time in New England, everyone I spoke to said something to the effect of "It must be nice to live in such a pacifistic community," but that idyllic misconception is far from the truth. *To spare the rod is to spoil the child.* Punishments here are intense and frequent as if the beatings are meant to break your spirit rather than teach you a real lesson.

It wasn't until I left Pennsylvania that I realized all families aren't *quite* like this. Helena always told me stories about her *Fater*, a man who *encouraged* her, supported her hobbies, and loved her despite the fact that she changed her mind often about her major.

I imagine that if Helena had done something similar, if she had caused a fire that did massive damage to her parent's home, sure, they would have been *angry*, but they also would have been *relieved* that she was alright. They would have scolded her and then hugged her tight instead of beaten her into numbed silence.

Wind rustles through the tall grass and massive trees. The heaped mound before me is the only thing totally still.

After Marissa's beatings ceased, *Fater* said that my uncle sat outside in a chair for hours and watched her dig a massive hole right here. She wasn't permitted to cry as her hands blistered and bled, or else the beatings would re-commence. Once the pit was deep enough, he made her, Daniel, and her siblings drag Bucky's remains inside of it. Then, he made them cover the creature in dirt so that it might fertilize the field and return to the earth.

The clack of hammers and the faint yell of male voices echo through the whispering farmland behind me as all of the men from the community remove the charred shell of the old structure and raise a new one in its place.

I look up to see my *Mamm* glaring at me from across the way, a steely scowl smeared across her face. She beckons me back with the brash wave of her hand, and I know she is angry that I've taken so long to return to her from the site of the work bee.

A full minute later, I am in front of her, holding out my tray, feeling her slam glasses of lemonade and water onto it in anger. Her cheeks pulse as she grinds what is left of her teeth. I can tell by her expression that I am on her last nerve with all of my constant pauses to ponder or daydream in the two weeks that I've been back.

"Take these," she orders in Pennsylvania Dutch and waves me back in the direction of the barn so she doesn't have to look at me. She wipes her hands on her apron and returns to the other women preparing the potluck for the men. Eventually, when they get to a point where the walls are up, they will all flock to the row of picnic benches in search of sustenance. In the meantime, it is my duty to keep them hydrated during the entirety of the day's frolic.

The clattering noise hurts my ears as I arrive at the barn, watching the menfolk inside mill around, carrying out various tasks to create something beautiful.

I, too, felt that power, that warm sense of accomplishment in creating something from nothing, every time I sat in front of that Bernina to sew.

"*Gut* morning, Velda."

I know the voice before I even twist to look at him. Its Amos. The Miller boy. The man I may as well have been promised to.

He smiles at me with dingy teeth and takes a glass of lemonade from my tray, gulping half of it down without a breath.

"*Gut* morning, Amos." I am cordial and even force a smile. He will most likely be my husband in a few month's time, after all.

"I saw you over there looking at the burial site." He motions over his shoulder to the resting place of the tawny quarterhorse, one I used to steal away and feed green apples to when he was just a pony.

"Yes. It is a shame."

He ticks his head to the side and settles his eyes to the dirt there. "*Gott* had to punish her somehow. They were not married. She should have avoided such lustful desires. If she had, we wouldn't be raising this barn right now."

"What about *him*?" I ask.

"What do you mean?"

"I mean… what about Daniel? Why was *he* not the one punished? Did *he* not commit the same act in *Gott's* eyes?"

"You surely must be kidding." Amos laughs as if it is the dumbest thing he's ever heard.

Then, he speaks again louder, in the direction of the frolic before us.

"*And so, she tricked him with all of her sweet talk and her flattery. He followed like an ox to the slaughter, like a fool on the way to be killed with arrows.*"

Amos grows more serious. He turns to me as if his words are more of a warning than the biblical regurgitation of Proverbs 7, as if he is aware of every allegedly 'sinful act' I committed while I was away. Forever tainted.

"*He was no more than a bird rushing into a trap without knowing it would cost his life. Don't even think about that kind of woman or let yourself be misled. Such a woman has caused the downfall and destruction of a lot of men.*"

He chugs the last of his lemonade and sets it back on my tray, twisting the base around in a ring of its own humid sweat before releasing it.

"Marissa's house is a one-way street down to the world of the dead. Daniel was *weak*. Weak enough to allow himself to be lured. And now Bucky feeds the worms, and her *Fater* suffers because of her."

He strides away from me, offended that I even had the nerve to imply that Daniel had any kind of culpability in the matter. Like it is preposterous that men have the same amount of self-control as women.

I am disgusted by his words and beliefs, and it makes me ill to think that the other men before me are groomed to feel similarly, preaching that woman is the cause of all lustful indiscretions, that it is her duty to stay chaste and not expose skin or stand on ladders in dresses above a man unless she expects to be attacked. I am disgusted that they act like men are simply animals with instincts impossible to control.

Ansel showed *weeks* of restraint, even when I showed none. Every time I begged, I could see him wrestle with temptation, so many times victorious over his desires. He didn't even have the threat of eternal *damnation* looming and, yet, he was able to exercise control, to think about things in the moment. He didn't attack like a wild animal the first time he saw my bare legs.

He thought things through, considered consequences carefully.

And then, when the time was *right*, it didn't feel like a sin. It felt like *passion*.

It felt like love.

It is the moment that Amos walks away from me -- this man who views me as something far less than he -- that I realize I cannot stay here.

As much as it breaks my heart to leave all that I have ever known behind, this simply *cannot* be my future.

53

Ansel

It's been a little over two weeks since she's been gone, but the ghost of Velda still lingers. Around the house. Along the beach. And in my bed. It haunts me with memories of small victories, of warm glances, of her touch. I still carry around the crushing weight of all that might have been.

The thought of scrolling through dating apps to 'get back on the horse again' fucking nauseates me. The names of my old booty calls strike bolts of dread into the pit of my stomach when I glance through old texts. I don't want them. I don't want empty fucking sex.

I want *her*.

I want *Velda*.

For seventeen days, I have wandered blankly around like some mourning widower doomed to wear a trench in the floor from all the brooding and pacing.

It's not that I'm not *happy for her*.

I am.

After all, she is still alive and gets to live the way she was destined to live, the path she ultimately chose.

I can't fathom what it must feel like to have to choose between leaving all of this or being shunned by your entire family. They're everything she has ever known until, what, *ten, eleven weeks ago*? I'd be fucking narcissistic to think that what I had to offer in that amount of time was worth throwing the rest of her life in Pennsylvania away for.

But still, the utter *lack of her* is something that, no matter how hard I tried in those final days, I simply couldn't prepare myself for.

Usually, when you break up with somebody, you don't *want* to see them anymore. Or they don't want to see *you*.

And when neither of those is the case, at least you can usually Facetime from afar or talk on the phone until you drift apart, until time heals the chasm that love tore through your heart.

But without a phone, without electricity, with all their stringent-fucking-rules, we can't even do *that*.

One day she was in my home, a home filled with the scent of fresh pot pies, humming with the whir of the Bernina, echoing with the chlorinated splash of arms perfecting the breaststroke, resonating with her soft moans…

Lately, I have taken to burying myself in work, staying longer each day to dive headfirst into the production and promotion of the newly approved women's line for *TwinFin*, even though every pattern, every scrap of fabric reminds me of her.

But today…

Today, I left early for some much-needed surf therapy.

I walk out the door, past the canvas print of Velda I bought from the neighbor girl's gallery showing and hung prominently in the living room as a daily reminder of her stunning beauty so that I may never forget her face as memories fade and the cruelty of time ticks on.

Blossoming.

It is the perfect name for the image and what she'd done every single day of our time together.

In the workshop, I select a board, and I slide my legs into my wetsuit, feeling my nerve endings spring to life as they rub against the gritty sand still inside. I zip up and let out a heavy exhale, hoping that the waves will help mend the brokenness within me like it did all those years before, the year my father went upstairs to take a shower and came down in a bag.

***

The waves are wild today, tall swells, peeling messily out here near the point break. The riptide is strong, and there is a small part of me that wishes it would swallow me whole and wash me away, never to be seen again.

I bob through the sloppy sets atop my board and look back at the shore to the multi-million-dollar home that was, until recently, vibrant inside.

I look at the pool, placid and tranquil as if Velda had never even been in it, as if I had dreamed the whole season.

I look next door at the spot where she and Helena used to tan on lounge chairs. Helena is not out there, but her gardener is, pruning a wall of blue hydrangeas.

The water is rising, making its way back to high tide, which makes now a subpar time to surf due to the large rocks along the break being hidden by shallow water and foam, forcing me to navigate through it from pure memory.

A good-looking set comes in, and I paddle fast toward shore, shoving forceful handfuls of water behind me to keep up. At the crest, I pop up, just as I have a million times before, and I drop down into the greenroom, head inches away from skimming the curl. I steady myself and carve up the barrel. It's the rush of adrenaline I seek, a moment of excitement followed by a tranquil journey to the shore.

In a split second, everything changes as the fin of my seven-foot-five gun clips hard against something below the surface. My miscalculation halts the board instantaneously, and I take a header, shooting face-first into the rocks below.

I feel the crack of unforgiving stone against my temple. The leash attached to my ankle whips me forward into the face of yet another boulder. As my body is thrashed against it, everything blinks to black.

54

"Velda, you should ride the buggy back. It is not safe for you to walk so far." Saloma frowns at me as she locks the door of our family's Farmer's Market behind us.

"Please don't worry."

She thinks I am going to see another movie at the cinema. She thinks that the moment she leaves, I will turn left and walk over to the theater.

Rebecca pets our horse, and I wish she would pay attention to me for just a moment. I wish she would realize that this is the last time I will ever see her, the last time I will ever be allowed around her.

Because I won't be turning left.

I will be turning *right* and making my way down to the train station.

In my dresser at home, I have left a handwritten letter for every single person in my family, even *Mamm* and Levi.

The letters are my confession. A confession that I want a life that I cannot lead in Berks County, a confession that I want more for myself.

There is another admission, too. One that will be far more difficult for them to understand. I tell them that I have fallen for an Englisher, surely their worst fears realized.

It took me three days of stealing away and rushing chores to write them all.

In each, I tell them about some of my experiences beyond the Pennsylvania border, about my G.E.D. and learner's permit. I tell them I learned to swim and detailed the rush I got from the first small wave I ever caught. I tell them I danced on Bourbon Street with a thirteen-piece band that felt like it played just for me.

I tell them I attended a party on a pier in New Smyrna and stayed at a palace adorned with glass sea turtles. I tell them about the sewing machine and the seafood. I tell them about Helena and how kind she is when she is in service of those less fortunate.

I tell them about Ansel, how he treated me with kindness, adored my cooking, and broadened my horizons, making me realize how capable I really am.

And I admit the saddest thing of all, for *them*, I'm sure…

That in eighteen years on this earth, when I was there, I finally knew what it was like to be *home*.

55

Ansel

"Mr. Wolf?" Tom's voice is in my ear, and I feel a bony hand squeeze my arm through wrinkles of fabric.

My head pounds, and I feel nauseous. My eyes peel open to a room, pale blue with a framed photo of *The Elms* mansion on the wall in a thin, gold frame. To my right is an I.V. with monitors *blipping* and tubes running in various directions.

To my left sits Thomas in a powder-blue pleather chair with a rip down the back, bleeding cotton out of the gash. There is a genuine look of worry in his eyes, wrinkles pointing down to a hook nose far too big for his slender face.

"Oh, thank *God*." He gasps a sigh of relief and sits back, running the thin fingers of both hands through his coal-black hair. "Jesus, Ansel…"

For a second, I don't know where I am, but moments later, it comes to me, smacking me in the back of the skull like a wave I didn't even know was coming.

I'm in the fucking hospital.

The same one I watched my mother wither away in. The same one she checked into and didn't return from the better half of a decade ago.

403

I look at Thomas and will my lips to move, to ask what happened. They won't budge, but Tom speaks as if he understood the unasked question with some sort of mystical clairvoyance.

"*You had an accident.*" I feel him pat my arm again. He is talking to me as if I am far away, or a child, or like I have brain damage.

Jesus Christ, do I have brain damage?!

"You were surfing. You had an accident. The neighbor's gardener saw you go down. He pulled you out of the water. He gave you C.P.R. An ambulance came, and now you're here."

He cracks a smile, and for a second, I feel like maybe the damage isn't too bad. Otherwise, he wouldn't have grinned.

"They said you had me down as the emergency contact in your phone." He points to a pile of my things on a tiny table in the corner. My cell, my sandals, and my beach towel are there, all still sandy.

He smiles as he laughs, but in it, I can see a modicum of pity in the expression. Like it says:

Poor Ansel...

Ansel, whose closest person in the world is his coffee-runner.

Ansel, who nearly just died alone.

Ansel, who no one would have noticed was missing, if not for the neighbor's landscaper. Washed out to sea like debris...

Tom waltzes out into the hall and waves at someone. As he returns, I realize who it is.

Doctor Wetzel was one of my mother's doctors. His frame is tall and imposing, white hair brushed boyishly across his age-spotted forehead.

"Well, hello there, Mr. Wolf. Long time no see." He presses his lips together and taps my chart on the bed near my covered feet. "Glad to see you're awake. How are you feeling?"

"I…" I clear my throat. It feels like I swallowed sandpaper. "I have a headache. And… I feel dizzy."

"Well, Mr. Wolf, you're lucky that's *all* you feel."

One second, I'm riding a wave. The next second, I'm looking at the doctor who called my mother's time of death. I feel a sense of panic wash over me from this loss of time, this blip in my existence, the realization that I could have been out for days… or weeks.

"How long have I been here?" My mind races, thinking about T.V. shows where people wake up from comas two years after the incident as if mere seconds have passed. I grab at my facial hair, trying to gauge the time I've been in here by how long it's grown.

"About two hours."

I nearly choke on my own breath.

Thank-fucking-God.

"You took quite a spill, it seems, while you were surfing. You were concussed when the E.M.T.s brought you in."

I touch the spot near my temple and feel the bandage there.

405

"As you can tell, you sustained a few very mild injuries. You've got the cut, some swelling, a couple of bruised ribs, but your lungs sound clear, which is good. You're lucky to be alive."

I shall be dumped where the weed decays and the rest is rust and stardust.

Vladimir Nabokov said that.

I recall the quote in this moment, where I am alive in a hospital gown instead of at the bottom of Block Island Sound, becoming food for the scavenging sea Robins.

...Where the weed decays.

"We want to keep you tonight to run some tests and make sure there's no trauma to the brain or broken bones we don't know about."

I nod and wince, laying back in my bed. I feel like four hooligans kicked the shit out of me *Clockwork Orange*-style.

But I'm *alive*.

Suddenly, Velda is at the forefront of my battered mind. I wish she were here with her hand on my arm instead of Tom, telling me that everything will be fine.

And then -- it's *stupid*, I *know* -- but suddenly, I wish there *was* an injury to my brain.

I know that's fucking *horrible* to say, but it feels like that might be better than how I am feeling.

Just a *little* damage.

Just enough trauma to scrub the memory of her from my mind.

406

Just enough to forget the way she looked at the ocean.

Just enough to forget the way she tastes.

Just enough of a dent in my cranium to shake loose the image of her standing at an altar with a man with a bowl cut and suspenders or bearing children that have his pasty skin and her angelic, cerulean eyes.

I wish there was just barely enough to ease the fucking *ache* of knowing that...

I will never see her again.

56

Ansel

As darkness descends over the picturesque New England coast, I can't take my eyes off the moon-splashed waves smashing against the rocks.

Rocks that nearly claimed my life.

While I was in the hospital, Dr. Wetzel and the nurses kept giving me updates. Ones that started with…

"Good news, Ansel…"

Good news, nothing is broken.

Good news, your scans all look great.

Good news, the split in your forehead is in a good spot. Right against the hairline. Probably won't ever even see the scar.

It was all just white noise after a while.

Sure. Great. Awesome. My thick hair for the win.

Yeah, cool, my bones are all where they are fucking supposed to be.

What about the *bad* news?

Bad news, Ansel, no one would have known you were fucking gone until Monday when Tom couldn't get ahold of you for your morning Dunkin run.

Bad news, Ansel, *you're gonna die alone.*

Bad news, Ansel… she's *not coming.* She's *never* coming.

Cold wind whips, and, far away, lightning lights up the sky at the furthest edge of the Block Island Sound, dancing through the clouds like a flickering lamp behind a wall of gray cotton.

There is a rumble of thunder, like an angry God's first of many warnings, and I can feel the change in the humidity on my skin.

Rain is on its way.

It reminds me of the night…

That night.

The night where my body and hers were one, taking our time, gentle and slow, as water pattered on the panes. The night where her sparkling eyes were fully present, her delicate body communicating more to mine than her words possibly could.

I doubt I will ever hear the rain again without thinking of how much I love her, without remembering how deeply ingrained in my heart she became. And how, all the while, I never even knew it was happening.

The thunder crackles harder and I decide to head inside so I don't have to change a rain-soaked bandage later. I decide to take the long way around to grab the mail from the curb. I make my way around the side yard, past the gazebo and the pool, all of which feel like empty, lifeless real estate. I breeze past the drooping willows, moving in the stormy air like giant long-haired hippies, swaying arm-in-arm.

As I make my way around the corner of the house, I see the candy-apple glow of taillights as a parked vehicle idles in front of my low stone wall.

Who the fuck is this?

I see a body leaning in through the passenger window, ruffling through something white and handing it to the person behind the wheel. There is a brief commotion, and then the driver peels away and takes off down the road, leaving someone behind.

I take a few more steps through the darkness, rehearsing my words carefully so I can find out what the fuck this person is doing here.

That's when I see the short-sleeved dress, mint green and conservatively draped to the person's ankles.

Velda stops at the edge of the driveway, frozen like an animal in the road at the sight of me. The moment I recognize her, I stop in place, sandals rooting firmly into the fresh-cut grass like I'm a tree that just grew fifty year's-worth in a flash.

She smiles, and my heart thunders. Seeing her feels like a surreal dream, and I am afraid it is, that this is some strange delusion, like I have fallen asleep at the beach and this lucid moment will be torn from me when I awaken and break my heart all over again.

But the feel of the *air*, the *sounds* all around, the smell of seaweed and salt, this is not like any dream I've ever had.

This is *real*.

I want to say so many things to her that they all jam into a wadded lump of concrete in my throat, and I can't mutter a single word.

She steps toward me with that meek smile I so adore. She starts to speak, stops, and adjusts the duffel on her shoulder in the silence widening the gap between us. She takes another step, and then another. Thunder rumbles again, threatening to open up the sky in a cleansing deluge at any moment.

"Ansel..." she finally says. And though it is only one word, it is two syllables straight from the only mouth that could bring any mortal to his knees.

"You came back." My words are quiet with shock, with a blissful disbelief at it all. "*How?*"

She smiles shyly, and it warms me.

My Sarah, Plain and Tall.

My innocent Girl in the Pearl Earring.

"I took the train."

"You're... *here.*" I feel like my knees will collapse if I take a step toward her.

She nods. "I *am*."

"Do your parents...? Are they okay with...?" I can't finish a thought.

She shakes her head, and her smile fades.

"I left."

Her eyes meet mine again, the soft amber light of my porch glinting in them.

"For good."

My heart hammers at the news of this, at what it all might *hopefully* mean if I am understanding her right.

"I heard a rumor that there might be a job opening here." Her eyes are playful. "I heard you were in need of a cook."

"The rumors are true."

I force my useless fucking legs to take a step toward her and another still.

"My last one up and left a couple weeks ago."

"I'm sorry to hear that." She smirks and looks down at her bag.

"I…"

I'm choked up, eyes filling with tears as my face morphs into various expressions in an effort to keep from crying. There is a hand around my throat, squeezing painfully, but the words finally come.

"I was… *really* in love with her, too."

I blink, and the tears fall in unison, one from each burning eye. I cross my arms in front of my chest.

"What was she like?" she asks softly, stepping closer, crossing her own to mimic my body language.

"You probably would have liked her. She was amazing. Stunningly gorgeous."

As I continue, she steps closer.

"Sweet… Driven… *Adventurous*. She could sew and surf… and, man, she made a *mean* whoopie pie."

She chuckles at that and stops in front of me, close enough to reach out and touch.

"What happened? You know, between you two?"

"Well," I sniffle, mortified by the presence of my tears, "you know... sometimes... when you love something, you have to set it free."

"*Hmmm.*" She nods at the grass. "And *then* what?"

She looks up at me, eyes glimmering, and I don't know if I have *ever* loved her more than I do at this moment.

"And if it comes back to you... then, it was meant to be."

The moment the grin graces her lips, I lean in and kiss her with everything in me. I cup her perfect face in my hands as she kisses back, and I feel her own warm tears coat the line where our lips meet.

"You've got the job," I say against her lips with a smile.

I scoop her up, wrap her legs around my waist, and carry her inside. She laughs, wrenching off her bag and tossing it to the floor of the kitchen. I set her on the island. With her legs still wrapped around me, I kiss her softly, pulling away for a moment to stare adoringly.

I still can't believe she came back.

She touches the bandage near my hairline, looking worried. "Oh no. What happened?"

I press my forehead to hers and snicker, "The ocean kicked my ass for being dumb enough to let you go."

She caresses the side of my face and touches my bottom lip lovingly with her thumb.

"I missed you, Ansel."

It makes me smile. I am too stunned to find the right words to respond, too overcome by the fact that she came back to tell her that I have missed every fucking thing about her.

So, I kiss her softly, showing her without uttering a single syllable how truly grateful I am for this moment with her, this second chance.

Showing her with the union of our lips, ones I thought I would never taste again, how much I love her.

I lift her again and carry her into the bedroom just as the rain unleashes, smacking down hard, streaking the glass in every window of the room -- *our* room.

I lay her down across the bed -- *our* bed -- and settle in next to her, anxious to feel her body in my arms, where it belongs.

I pull her to me until our bodies are touching, each propped on one elbow. She stares at my tattoos, tracing the exposed lines of the lilies on my neck with her finger, something I have missed feeling every single day since we parted.

"What?" she asks as if I look like I'm dying to say something.

And then I realize that I am. I'm aching to utter the words to her.

414

"Say it," she says, quietly prodding.

I wipe a renegade hunk of blonde hair from her eyes, one fallen from her tight braid. I feel blissful and happy as I open my mouth to speak.

"Welcome *home*, Velda."

About the Author

Odessa has a passion for writing stories that feel like an escape from the mundane. She is a recipient of the *Pencraft Award for Literary Excellence*. She is also an award-winning filmmaker, artist in multiple mediums, film industry grip, and cancer survivor. She spent over a decade working on high-budget films and television shows.

Though born in Wyoming and spending most of her adult life in the American South, she now lives on the beach in Connecticut with her boyfriend and their rambunctious jack russel *terror*. When she isn't writing or reading, she's partaking in a masochistic puzzle, tending her massive vegetable garden, fumbling through an escape room, or kayak fishing.

Odessa Alba is a romance pen name (an easy way to keep her genre fiction separate for readers) & has published award-winning extreme horror under her real name, Erica Summers, and also has an upcoming cozy mystery series under the pen name Trixie Fairdale.

Acknowledgments

First and foremost, I would like to thank my sister and business partner, **Heather Wohl**. You are so strong and beautiful. Without your encouragement, I would not be a fraction of what I am. I love you.

I would like to thank **Mary Byler**, a former Amish whose memoirs changed this entire story into something that feels far more genuine and real. The horrors that you endured in your life in your community will live rent-free in my head for life, and I just want to say that you are an inspiring human being for not only surviving but thriving after so much hardship. If you haven't read her book yet, you should. It is the most heart-wrenching read of possibly my entire life.

Dave Sikora, you are the love of my life. Thank you for always rooting for me and supporting every hair-brained shenanigan I come up with. You are always in my corner and always there with a "you *GOT* this" whenever I need it. I love you so much.

And **Lindsey Holt**, you are a voracious champion of our books, an adoring fan, and proof that not all heroes wear capes. Thank you for all that you do to unite our Rusty Ogre Publishing books with readers everywhere.

A Note From The Ogres

Even though this book was proofread thoroughly by professionals, beta readers, and ARC readers… mistakes happen. We want our readers to have the best experience possible. If you spot any spelling, grammatical, or formatting errors, please feel free to reach out to us at:

rustyogrepublishing@gmail.com

Reviews

If you could take the time to leave an honest review after you've read this book, we would greatly appreciate it. We respect your time and promise it doesn't *have* to be long and eloquent. Even a few words will do!

As a small publishing house, every review helps others determine if this book is right for them and greatly increases our chances of being discovered by someone else who might enjoy it.

More Rusty Ogre Romance

The Billionaire's Assistant

Odessa Alba

A NEW ENGLAND BILLIONAIRES BOOK

The Ugly Sweater
PARTY

A FORCED PROXIMITY ROMANCE NOVELLA

AURORA ALBA &
ODESSA ALBA

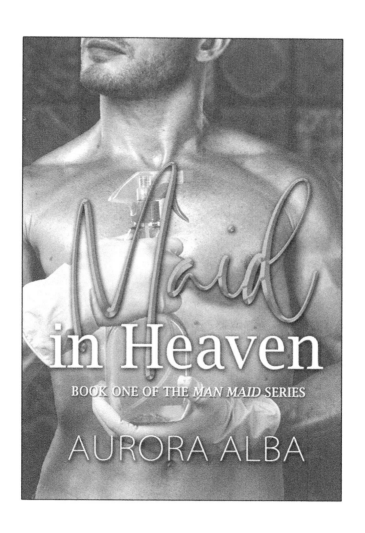

Maid
in Heaven

BOOK ONE OF THE *MAN MAID* SERIES

AURORA ALBA

Call of the Wild

A DESTORIAN ADVENTURE NOVELLA

Heather Wohl

Coming Soon

Tangled Heirs

Odessa Alba

A NEW ENGLAND BILLIONAIRES BOOK

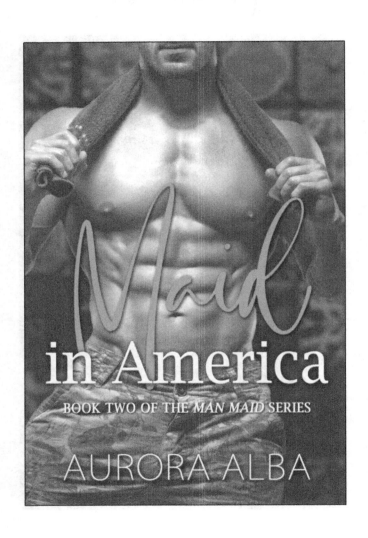

Maid
in America

BOOK TWO OF THE *MAN MAID* SERIES

AURORA ALBA

Made in the USA
Monee, IL
14 February 2025

12284333R00243